THE **RELATIONAL ENTERPRISE**

THE RELATIONAL ENTERPRISE

Moving Beyond CRM

to Maximize *All* Your

Business Relationships

Kenneth Carlton Cooper

AMACOM

American Management Association

New York • Atlanta • Brussels • Buenos Aires • Chicago • London • Mexico City
San Francisco • Shanghai • Tokyo • Toronto • Washington, D.C.

This publication is designed to provide accurate and authoritative information in regard to the subject matter covered. It is sold with the understanding that the publisher is not engaged in rendering legal, accounting, or other professional service. If legal advice or other expert assistance is required, the services of a competent professional person should be sought.

Library of Congress Cataloging-in-Publication Data

Cooper, Ken.
        The relational enterprise : moving beyond CRM to maximize all your business relationships / Kenneth Carlton Cooper.
        p.   cm.
        Includes bibliographical references and index.
        ISBN 0-8144-0669-6
        1. Customer relations—Marketing.   2. Relationship marketing.   I. Title.

HF5415.5.C665 2002
658.8'12—dc21   2001040182

Printing number

10   9   8   7   6   5   4   3   2

To Bob, Larry, and Dan

CONTENTS

Foreword by Craig Conway, President & CEO,
  PeopleSoft, Inc.   *xiii*
Preface   *xv*
Acknowledgments   *xix*
Introduction   *1*

PART ONE. RELATIONAL ENTERPRISE BUILDING BLOCKS   5

Chapter 1. The Expanding Definition of "Organization"   7

Expanding the Organization   8
Organizational Relationships   9
The Blurring of Relational Roles   13
Summary   15
Learning Points   15

Chapter 2. The Expanding Definition of "Employee"   17

De-Facto Reengineering   18
Redefining "Core Competence"   20
The Multiclass Workforce   24
Informal Employees   25
Summary   26
Learning Points   26

Chapter 3. The Expanding Definition of "Customer"   28

Windows Into the Relational Enterprise   28
Portals as Profit-Makers   31

Summary 36

Learning Points 37

Chapter 4. The Relational Structure 39

Hierarchical Structures 40

Reengineering and the Case Worker 46

The Emergence of Roles 49

Summary 52

Learning Points 52

PART TWO. RELATIONAL ENTERPRISE SERVICE PROCESSES 55

Chapter 5. The Relational Business Cycle 57

The Ramifications of Self-Service 57

The Business Cycle 60

Summary 67

Learning Points 68

Chapter 6. Maximizing Interaction Satisfaction 69

Measures of Interaction Satisfaction 71

Satisfaction Through a Roles-Base Structure 74

Summary 75

Learning Points 76

Chapter 7. A Second Generation Definition of 360-Degree View 78

A Bidirectional 360-Degree View 79

Lifetime Customer Profitability 80

360-Degree View and the Business Cycle 82

Summary 86

Learning Points 87

Chapter 8. Expanding the Definition of CRM 88

In-Use Definitions of CRM 89

Three Kinds of CRM 91

Consolidation Into RM   93
Summary   95
Learning Points   96

Chapter 9. The Expanding Range of Collaborative RM   98

Characteristics of an Effective Channel   100
The State of Bandwidth   105
Collaborative RM Channels   106
Summary   110
Learning Points   111

Chapter 10. Transitioning to a Customer Interaction
Center   113

Defining the Customer Interaction Center   115
Levels of Service   118
CIC Universals   121
The e-CIC   123
Summary   124
Learning Points   125

Chapter 11. Effective Relational Processes   126

Value-Added Processes   128
Systematizing Relational Processes   131
Who Owns the Process?   134
Summary   135
Learning Points   135

PART THREE. RELATIONAL ENTERPRISE SYSTEMS   137

Chapter 12. New Relational Data Types   139

New Data Types Are Required   141
People-Oriented Data Elements   142
Product-Oriented Data Elements   151

Summary   153
Learning Points   153

Chapter 13. Understanding Relational Systems   156

Relational Systems Architecture   157
Types of RM Applications   159
An Employee Example   165
Summary   168
Learning Points   169

Chapter 14. RM Analytics   172

The Analytics System   173
The Importance of Analytics   173
Analytics vs. Accounting Systems   175
From TCO to Transition Costing   176
Use of Balanced Scorecards   178
Employees Must Be Able to Use Analytics   180
Roles-Based Analytics   183
Summary   188
Learning Points   189

PART FOUR. RELATIONAL ENTERPRISE LEADERSHIP   191

Chapter 15. Benefits of Relational Systems   193

RM Justification Philosophies   194
RM Justfications   198
A Critical Error in Evaluating Benefits   202
Summary   203
Learning Points   204

Chapter 16. Evaluating Relational Systems   205

Look Beyond Features   206
Customization Is Not an Option   209

Tailoring Is Not Customization   211
Customization Philosophies   213
Customization Architectures   214
Summary   216
Learning Points   217

Chapter 17. Evaluating Relational System Vendors   221

Basic Reasons to Pick a Vendor   222
Vendor Solution Philosophies   224
The Future of CRM Systems   232
Summary   232
Learning Points   233

Chapter 18. Managing RM Change   235

Organizations Can't Evolve to Get There   236
Random Change Is Even Worse   237
The Change Track Record   237
Rules for Success   239
Summary   243
Learning Points   244

Chapter 19. Creating the Relational Enterprise   246

Review of Learning Points   246
It's a Matter of Scope   249
Types of Workers   250
Creating the Enterprise Relationship Process Owner   252
The Office of Enterprise Relationships   255
Transition Steps   257
Summary   262
Learning Points   262

Epilogue   265
Appendix: Relational Enterprise Resources   267
List of Abbreviations   285
Index   289
About the Author   297

FOREWORD

The era when a company determined its success solely within its four walls is over. Success today demands that an enterprise communicate and collaborate across the entire business landscape of customers, suppliers, and employees.

A new definition of competitive advantage has emerged. It is no longer enough to simply do what *you* do well—the actions and abilities of others are now key to your success. Relationships have become the next killer app.

Internet technologies provide the tools and infrastructure necessary to thrive in this new business environment, allowing enterprises to integrate customers, suppliers, and partners, as well as employees, into their business processes. Software applications allow companies to manage—and optimize—these relationships.

But technology alone is not enough. The enterprise itself must adapt.

The level of adaptation required is far from superficial, but strikes at the core of how a business is organized and run. Consider the distinction between front-office and back-office processes. Traditionally, front-office served the customer; back-office ran the company. In today's competitive environment, this siloed approach creates barriers to efficiencies and weakens a company. The front-office and the back-office have merged.

The internal boundary between front- and back-office was only the first to fall. The lines between an organization and its ecosystem of customers, suppliers, partners, and vendors of all types are quickly being erased.

Today's successful enterprises are adapting to this new landscape to form robust and dynamic relationships through which customers can get the information they want and need from any channel—the phone, the Web, or even wireless devices. Suppliers have access to core business processes like inventory and demand forecasting, and employees have real-time access to integrated information to do their job. Information is made available to individuals and organizations based on their roles, not their titles. The result is employees who are empowered, suppliers who can make informed decisions without delay, and customers who become partners.

Such seamless access to integrated information requires a technological leap. It also requires organizational change to enable—and capitalize on—collaboration among customers, suppliers, and employees.

In *The Relational Enterprise*, Ken Cooper masterfully describes the changing dynamics of today's business landscape. More important, he provides a succinct road map for making the necessary transition to a "relational enterprise." Too many business books simply identify a problem or trend. Ken not only describes the relational enterprise—he focuses on how to achieve it. The future organization is going to look very different from the one we work in today. *The Relational Enterprise* helps you understand why, and what to do about it.

PeopleSoft is delighted to provide examples of the technologies Ken discusses. We've made a considerable investment in delivering a secure, scalable, pure Internet product suite that crosses operational, collaborative, and analytical relationship management functions. This technology leadership is paving the way for our customers, who are setting a precedent for the way businesses will operate in the future.

Becoming a relational enterprise is not only achievable—it's a necessity.

Craig A. Conway
President, CEO
PeopleSoft, Inc.

This book is a practical blueprint for implementing a new organizational entity—the relational enterprise. Everyone agrees that we are working in an era of unprecedented change. Marketing and service agendas are clear. The Internet is a key tool in every organization's strategy. We can focus on loyalty, relationships, one-to-one marketing, personalization, customization, and self-service. In 2000, more than twenty new relationship technology categories were created.

Everyone is in agreement on *what* to do. There's just one topic no one is talking about. *How* is the organization going to get it done? How are managers going to integrate all these new initiatives, and what will the organization have to look like to accomplish them?

My colleagues at CooperComm and I have spent over twenty-five years consulting to improve customer-facing processes and satisfaction. We have been conducting research and training vendors and implementation partners worldwide on relationship management. Several truths have emerged:

1. The traditional hierarchical, departmental organization structure is obsolete. Fundamental terms of business—employees, customers, suppliers, etc.—need to be completely redefined.

2. Leading edge relational systems have finally reached the point where required service levels and processes can be provided to customers.

3. e-Business technologies are revitalizing some "passed fad" concepts such as open-book management, continuous process improvement, and reengineering. There's new life for several of these great ideas.

4. Organizations are now in a race to execute the transition to a relational enterprise. Competitors won't vote lagging vendors off the island, customers will.

5. The task that remains is to understand how to leverage all of this for an updated organizational structure. Analysts are talking about a new functional department within the organization, led by some sort of customer relationship czar. This doesn't go far enough. The relationship function is more strategic than that, and the changes to an organization must be far more extreme. How do you get there?

Chapters 1 through 4 of this book establish the conceptual foundation. They completely redefine traditional terms such as customer, employee, organization, and job.

Chapters 5 through 11 focus on the new realities of customer service. Ask anyone and they can immediately give you an example of poor service. These chapters provide the measuring stick for designing truly effective customer-facing systems.

Chapters 12 through 14 detail the IT agenda. Relational systems must leverage new concepts and implement required service practices—all with a focus on profit maximization.

Chapters 15 through 19 will benefit IT and management decision-makers. The CRM implementation track record is very poor. To be successful, there are many strategic and tactical decisions that have to be made in selecting partners and vendors, and in implementing an integrated system. There are also important issues in risk management and organizational health that must be addressed.

The Appendix provides a collection of resources for further learning. Some of the references are classics that must now be considered as back in their prime. Others are up-to-the-minute, Web-based resources that offer late breaking news.

All the chapters contain endnotes and references to trade literature, books, and analysts' opinions. There's an overwhelming amount of information available on relationship management, and it is surprisingly consistent in its content and conclusions. We have included as much of this research as possible, most of it very recent, so that you can see the depth and breadth of the agreement about relational enterprises. All quotations not specifically referenced in the endnotes come from personal communications and interviews.

Some of the computer screen shots used in the book have been cropped and/or enlarged to enhance readability of the relevant content.

The research firms are fond of saying that relationship management is useless without analytics. Well, analysis is useless without action. This book shows you what it takes to become a third–millennium relational enterprise. The prize? Profit maximization and a six-month lead on the bad guys . . . and a *very* interesting next few years.

Kenneth Carlton Cooper
June 2001

ACKNOWLEDGMENTS

I have been blessed by having great people in my own relational enterprise. Acknowledgment and thanks go to:

Rich Huttner for having faith and getting me kick-started.

Jim Everett and Jane Dixon of Endeavour Business Learning for dragging me into CRM in the first place.

Bob Stuckey, Larry Heidemann, and Dan Ryan as subject-matter experts. I had the good fortune of spending fourteen hours coming back from white-water rafting with a terrific financial, operational, and sales professional, respectively. This book is full of ideas that were refined on that trip.

Sue Landis at Anheuser-Busch, who keeps me focused on what customer satisfaction and effective training are all about.

Sam Gallucci and Jim Goldfinger for having initial faith in the idea.

PeopleSoft for the inclusion of their product screens and strategic content. Leveraging their long-standing expertise in HR systems, I've always thought their slogan should be, "Nobody knows relationships better than PeopleSoft."

All the great folks at PeopleSoft who have supported and assisted with this book: Craig Conway, Robb Eklund, and Laura King for their enthusiasm and cooperation; Brenda Bidne, Mark Biskeborn, Elizabeth Mutlu, Marie Hill, and especially Jessica Chereskin for all the screen shots and visuals; Kim Frances, Anne Campbell-Baker, and Gigi Remington for their help in getting permissions; Mike Cummings for being the point person for all of my consulting and training; Chris Wallace for being there when needed; Shelley Olson, Barb Sadtler, Kirk Anderson, and Jeri Shore for support in PSFT training; Cathy Rheiner for being the benchmark in sales management and effective selling of CRM; Ed Mora for feedback on what customers are really thinking; Gita Gupta and John Grozier for helping me with the technology; Harald Battista for showing what CRM sales enthusiasm truly is; Charles Grover and Dave Tonnison for letting me sit in the room while they developed leading edge CRM functionality and architectural concepts; Mark Sinfield for being Mr. Wizard; and all the sales, technical, and consulting partner students in my CRM sales courses, who provided me with essential training while I taught them.

META Group, *the* leading CRM analyst, whose work I've referenced throughout the book.

David Avakian of The Varsity Group, and cartoonists Darrin Bell and Theron Heir, whose permission to add their material has made the book even better.

My associates at CooperComm, including John Bujnak for research and competitive analysis, Dan Cooper for graphics and manuscript preparation, Karen Gentles for her research and customer focus, and Jeff Cooper for systems support.

Adrienne Hickey, my editor at AMACOM, who provided steady counsel through the ups and downs of content decisions and scheduling. Plus, she took the title I desperately wanted to keep and made it better. We may even get to meet some day and, if we do, there's a free lunch in there for somebody. Also Mike Sivilli for a smooth project and Niels Buessem for an amazingly sharp eye and a better-written book.

Sue Cooper, who as always was patient and supportive during a particularly challenging book project.

THE RELATIONAL ENTERPRISE

INTRODUCTION

What an exciting time to be in business. Just as the first Model T assembly line kicked off a revolution in the way goods were produced, the development of e-business technology and a changing customer culture have created the need for radically different business structures. Consequently, managers across entire organizations have a full agenda of change awaiting them.

The list of new topics is nearly overwhelming: one-to-one marketing, permission selling, e-business, e-commerce, customer relationship management, partner relationship management, enterprise/extraprise relationship management, customer interaction centers, B2E, B2B, B2C, and P2P—to name a few. As a result, today nearly every organization is involved in some sort of significant change. There is no shortage of professional advice, and the bulk of it is on target. No matter what the job title, nobody's plate is empty.

Then there are the old standby topics that haven't necessarily been successful in many organizations: continuous quality improvement, business process reengineering, enterprise resource planning, rightsizing, downsizing, outsourcing, core competence, customer satisfaction, and so on. Just check the bookshelves for a list of what the experts thought organizations should be implementing in the 1990s and beyond.

Old or new, there is a major problem. Everyone is talking about what organizations should be doing differently, but no one is talking about what kind of organization it's going to take to accomplish it. Many past programs were little more than fads, which became one of *Dilbert's* "dead woodchucks" due to the lack of corresponding organizational change.

This remains a problem. The traditional self-contained, departmentalized, hierarchical organization is still the standard. Its reporting structure dates back to the Roman army. Its mass production and specialization of labor processes are seventy-five to a hundred-plus years old. Ebenezer Scrooge, if he had learned how to use a PC, could step into most modern organizations and manage their operational and accounting systems. He'd be cost-conscious and great at downsizing workers. He would have a department, a boss, a title, a job description, and subordinates. He could point to himself on the organization chart, and have set lines of responsibility and authority. The only thing that might confuse him a bit is this e-business thing.

> *Simply put, today's organization is designed for the business of yesterday.*

The organization of the future is going to be a *relational enterprise*. This is a new organizational structure defined by the core organization plus all the related constituents that are involved in its business. Fundamental terms, such as employee, job, competitor, or partner, will take on brand new meanings. Alternative workforce capabilities, which allow immediate resizing, will be created. A totally new internal structure, supported by emerging relational systems, will be implemented. In all, the coming change will be dramatic and extreme.

Morphing to a relationship-driven organization requires simultaneous and equally dramatic changes in fundamental areas that are covered in the four parts of this book: structure, service processes, systems, and leadership. Think of these as four roof support posts of a building. Without any one post, the entire building is at risk. There are no partial solutions, no shortcuts. There is also no priority, no order of implementation. Nothing proceeds until all four posts are in place. Becoming a relational enterprise is an all-or-nothing transition that starts with basic organizational structure. Partial, single-point solutions (i.e., suboptimization) may truly be "antisynergism"—where the whole is *less* than the sum of its parts.

Also, some of the change agenda is not necessarily new. Many of what Scott Adams' *Dilbert* cartoon has called "dead woodchuck" ideas are still valuable. The difference may be in the extent to which they are leveraged, or in whether they are properly implemented at all. Unfortunately, many organizations failed to fully realize the benefits of yesterday's hot topics before moving on to one of today's "must-do" initiatives. So we will revisit faded concepts, such as reengineering and open-book management. Only this time we will see them in the modern light of workflow and analytics.

Getting the Most Out of This Book

This book shows you how to "set the posts" to become a relational organization. In our worldwide training and consulting, we have found that the best way to teach managers how to approach such a tremendous undertaking is to break up the tactics into short, targeted learning points. This way, the individual lessons are more readily mastered and applied. Specific activities are easier to segment and assign to individuals for simultaneous action. This also makes the book more convenient for busy professionals to read and reference, since content is chunked into small segments.

This book is designed to be read front-to-back, although it isn't necessary to do so. Jump ahead to any section that can provide immediate help. Just remember that the entire book should be read for you to learn how to set all four posts. Also, each chapter ends with a summary of learning points. You may want to review those before reading the chapter, thereby increasing retention by providing a pre-outline of each chapter's contents.

Above all, the value you get from this book will be from what you *do* as a result of reading it. If the agenda is change, then the most important challenge is how to make *all* of it happen. It begins with understanding organizational relationships.

PART ONE

RELATIONAL ENTERPRISE
BUILDING BLOCKS

The Expanding Definition of "Organization"

Some years ago my friend Bob the Accountant and I taught in the evening program of a local college. We sat one night comparing students and commiserating about classroom problems. We both agreed that the one major irritant was the student who raises a hand and asks, "Is this going to be on the test?" If the answer was "Yes," then classroom energy shot upward and everyone expectantly put pen to paper. Otherwise, it was as if we were saying, "Nope, I'm just a clueless idiot filling time with worthless information you don't ever have to worry about knowing."

To counter this, Bob introduced the class to his principle of "foot stompers." These were key concepts certain to be on the test in some form or another. At appropriate points during lectures, Bob would actually stomp his foot much like a trained horse counting off its age. "Let's take a look at methods of capitalization (stomp, stomp)," he'd say. Everyone got the message and class proceeded much more smoothly.

So let's begin with a look at the most basic entity in business, the organization (stomp, stomp). This is *the* critical chapter for you to fully understand and master. The remainder of this book supports the funda-

mental message here about the scope and reach of a modern organization in the new e-business economy. Nothing less than a complete
restructuring is going to be enough, and it's all because of the changed
nature of what "we" means.

There's an important observation to be made before learning
about relational organizations. This chapter is not some theoretical,
blue-sky technology projection. Nothing we are talking about in this
chapter is future tense. Everything you will see here is already being
done by some company somewhere, and we've included several examples. It's just a matter of taking these current trends to their logical
conclusions.

Think of it this way. The starting gun has just been fired and the
Oklahoma land rush for relationships has begun. There are no winners
yet. The ultimate champions will be those organizations that are fastest
and most effective in recognizing and leveraging the concepts we are
introducing. It begins with understanding the enlarged scope of an
e-business organization.

Expanding the Organization

A traditional organization can be defined as:

*A body of people who are consolidated, unified, systematized,
and structured for some specific purpose.*

This is very much an in/out definition. When people speak of "my
organization," they are referring to their employer or their department.
Other organizations are labeled with external terms, such as vendor,
supplier, partner, channel, distributor, advisor, competitor, and so on.

The boundaries of the relational enterprise are far more blurred.
Who "we" is takes on new meaning in this era of partnering and inter-
connected systems and processes. In-ness and out-ness are far less delin-
eated. Categorizations are less precise, because single individuals take
on multiple roles, and single roles apply to multiple individuals across a
variety of organizations.

The new definition of an organization is:

A grouping of people and employers who have a profitable relationship. They are distributed, independent, loosely structured, and are connected by their interactions with the core organization.

Expanding the view of an organization to an enterprise is not new. William Davidow and Michael Malone defined a virtual corporation back in 1992, and outsourcing became a common strategy in the 1990s.[2] The difference is that a relational enterprise takes this view far beyond the tactical level, opening the concept of "organization" to include a wide range of entities—most never before considered part of the core structure. The first step is to understand the list of potential relationships.

Organizational Relationships

Everything starts with the core organization. Consider this to be separate from its employees, an entity in its own right, much like a corporation is a distinct legal entity. The question is, "With whom must an organization build a relationship?" This is an excellent brainstorming exercise for a management team, and results will vary somewhat depending upon the organization. Let's examine the relationships one-by-one, starting with the "big four."

- **Employees.** This includes everyone who works for the organization and is on the payroll. The traditional employee role is to operate the organization and produce its goods and services.
- **Customers.** These are the people or entities that buy from an organization. Historically, the goal has been to find as many of these as possible through mass marketing, then sell each one as much as they will buy.
- **Partners.** These are important extensions of the organization (wholesalers, retailers, distributors, etc.), often acting as representatives in the marketplace. Partners need to share data bidirectionally with the organization at a very detailed level. Partners also need to be integrated in customer service and

production processes at all stages of the customer relationship. This collaboration is growing. A 2000 Forrester Research survey of fifty manufacturing companies found that 72 percent plan to engage in joint online efforts with their retailers, compared to the 42 percent that currently do.[3]

- **Suppliers.** Supply vendors are key collaborators in planning, production, and service cycles. High efficiencies that minimize costs require tight integration with an organization's systems and processes. The supply chain is becoming increasing automated and interdependent.

This is basic, and not very remarkable—certainly nothing that portends a dramatically expanded business structure. That's because the big four are only a portion of the relational enterprise. There are many more relationships that must be included:

- **Alternative Workforce.** These are individuals who "work for" the organization but are not on the formal payroll. This includes contingent workers, contractors, outsourcers, and vendors who bundle in complementary services into the core product offerings. When McDonnell-Douglas sold off its IT department to IBM's ISSC for over $400 million, thousands of employees no longer worked for McDonnell-Douglas but were back at their desks the next Monday morning. Even though they were ex-employees, McDonnell-Douglas still needed to have a relationship with them.

- **Retired Workforce and Dependents.** As the population ages and resizing efforts encourage early retirement, employers will see a significant growth in the number of retired workers and their dependents. The relationships can go far beyond involvement in the company pension or retiree benefit plans.

- **Supply Chain.** There is potential for additional relationships by moving up and down supply chains of an organization's customers, partners, and suppliers, then to their customers/suppliers, and so on. What results is a tree-like chart that branches out into multiple levels.

  For example, Anheuser-Busch sells beer to its family of

800 + wholesalers, who in turn sell to retailers. Anheuser-Busch's corporate university not only provides management and customer service training to its wholesalers, it also offers bartender and server training to restaurants and bars—its customer's customer. A-B also maintains a public hotline for any questions concerning its product or the delivery and retailing services in between the brewery and consumer—its customer's customer's customer, or what we could call its great-grandcustomer. The relational enterprise can find itself reaching four or five levels deep into a relationship chain.

- **Advisers.** There are numerous companies that provide specialized advice and are essential contributors to an organization's strategy and execution. These include firms providing services in the areas of financial auditing, public relations, advertising, legal, real estate, and consulting (can't forget that!).

- **Regulators.** There are myriad potential regulators, a list that can vary significantly from organization to organization. Some common ones include: Internal Revenue Service, Securities and Exchange Commission, Federal Trade Commission, Equal Opportunity Employment Commission, Civil Service Commission, and the Occupational Safety and Health Administration. Depending upon the industry, there might be specialized regulators such as the Department of Education, Interstate Commerce Commission, Nuclear Regulatory Commission, Food and Drug Administration, Public Service Commission, or local health and building inspectors. All you have to do is look in the government section of the White Pages; there is no shortage of possibilities.

    There are also private sector regulators such as ISO 9000 auditors, ISO 14000 auditors mandated by major automotive manufacturers, and state quality or national Baldrige award evaluators.

- **Stockholders.** Another thought-provoking option for potential customers are individuals or institutions who feel strongly enough about the company to invest in it. Depending upon what the corporate covenants allow an organization to do, there may be potential for a profit relationship in addition to the ownership status.

- **Competitors.** This is the most startling of all potential connections. Antitrust lawyers and price-fixing prosecutors at the Justice Department must be quivering. How can a company have a formal relationship with its competitors? This is actually becoming a standard option in an organization's marketing and sales plans.

Vendors have seen third-party sites spring up that evaluate their products alongside competitors. The reaction is, "Well, if somebody's going to compare us to competition, we ought to do it ourselves. That way we can at least control what's said about us and make it convenient to buy at the same time." This is why in August 2000, GM announced a retail car-selling site that would include vehicles from other automakers and provide links to competitive dealer sites.[4]

In the year 2000, a number of supply-chain joint ventures were announced. Twelve PC vendors—including Compaq, Gateway, Hewlett-Packard, and NEC—announced the creation of a company to "address supply-chain inefficiencies." Each founding member pledged $5 million to the venture. Marriott and Hyatt announced a partnership and selected GoCo-op as the e-commerce service provider. Five large home-builders announced HomebuildersXchange, a business-to-business supply chain exchange. Eleven large real estate companies created an exchange/incubator company.[5]

In April 2001, Borders Group chose Amazon.com to run its Web bookstore operations. The result is a cobranded site that will provide all of Amazon.com's online service with Borders' store information.[6]

It's fun to ask sales executives, "Who in your department carries the quota and calling responsibility for revenue from your biggest competitors?" and watch the facial tics start. What was unthinkable several years ago is now a commonplace business practice. Will we see archrivals such as Coke and Pepsi, Anheuser-Busch and Miller, or Siebel and Oracle start working together? When GM is willing to link to a Ford dealer's site, the day might not be too far off.

THE NEW ORGANIZATIONAL CHART

The new organizational chart is very different from the ubiquitous hierarchical tree chart showing who reports to whom inside the organization. The new chart looks like Figure 1-1, a network map of relationships. Our customers have dubbed this the "spider chart," and the name seems appropriate. Every organization should develop its version of this chart in order to understand the active relationships that can be leveraged for additional profits.

Figure 1-1. The relational enterprise.

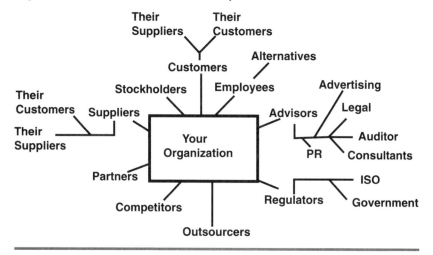

The value of such a chart is that it provides a clean, clear, visual summary of organizational relationships. There is just one problem. The categories don't map to people or organizations on a one-to-one basis.

The Blurring of Relational Roles

Organizational entities can have more than one function, just like we saw with competitors who were also sales partners. This blurring of roles occurs all throughout the spider chart.

Use the chart to address a key question, "Where are the profit opportunities?" The answer is, *everywhere!* Every single relationship has the potential to generate profit. The reason is that with an e-business economy and portal technology, every individual in the extended relational organization can be a customer. Conceptually, the spider chart really should look like Figure 1-2.

Figure 1-2. Everyone's a customer.

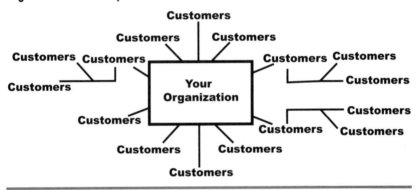

So everyone can be a customer. Here's another possibility—customers can be employees. How is this possible? When you give customers an incentive to sell for you, they become commissioned salespeople. I can receive a fifty-dollar discount on my next insurance premium because a relative bought a policy and gave my name as the reference. I can earn a discount on my home office phone bill by signing up for personal long distance with the same carrier. As your customer, I'm now on your sales plan.

This is one of the reasons traditional sales force automation (SFA) has been such a general failure. Certainly, salespeople are often very reluctant to enter volumes of required data. The bigger issue is that, in an e-business economy, the direct sales force is only a portion of the sales process—and perhaps not even the most important. Customers sell each other through references, word of mouth, and "I hate [your company]" Web sites. Independent third parties such as associations, industry analysts, trade publications, or consumer groups make recommendations. Competitors provide outside information about other companies. Lots of people and organizations are involved in selling.

Roles also blur within the organization. Other departments such as service, administration, billing, shipping, research and development, and support all have a significant influence on sales success. While they might not be commissioned, they are also salespeople if they interact with customers. And it doesn't matter how good the sales process is, product performance is still required in order to create satisfied customers and repeat sales. So customers can be salespeople. Partners can be salespeople. Anyone in the spider chart might contribute to the sales process. It's no wonder SFA has fallen short of expectations.

Summary

What confusion! The organization is no longer defined as what's within the bounds of its offices and factories. An organization is now defined by the breadth and depth of its relationships—a network that can go deep into customer, vendor, and partner supply chains.

Even the categories in the spider chart are not totally accurate because people and entities are taking on multiple roles. You have suppliers who are customers, customers on sales commission, competitors who are partners, administrators who are salespeople, and outsourcing vendors who customers think are employees. It is no wonder that traditional organizational structures and processes are totally inadequate to address current challenges.

An organizational spider chart is the new conceptual map. The blocks are functions that don't necessarily relate one-to-one with people or organizations. Understanding how to build a spider structure is best accomplished from the inside out, beginning with employees.

Learning Points

1. The relational organization, illustrated by the spider chart, is a foot-stomper for organizations that plan to survive and thrive in the transition to an e-business economy.

2. "We" is redefined for the organization. "We" is now anyone with whom the organization has a relationship.

3. Every relationship has profit potential.

4. The "big four" relationships are employees, customers, partners, and suppliers.

5. There are many secondary relationships that need to be included in the definition of a relational enterprise such as customer and supplier chains, competitors, and so on.

6. Functional roles are blurring. There is no longer a clear-cut distinction between such roles as customer, employee, competitor, and partner.

7. Everything in this book is going to leverage the spider chart definition of organizational structure.

NOTES

1. John Tierney, Lynda Wright, and Karen Springen, "The Search for Adam and Eve," *Newsweek*, January 11, 1988, p. 46.

2. William H. Davidow and Michael S. Malone, *The Virtual Corporation: Structuring and Revitalizing the Corporation for the 21st Century* (New York: HarperBusiness, 1992), p. 294.

3. Matt Hicks, "Wired Channel: Manufacturers Collaborate with Distributors Online," *eWeek*, March 5, 2001, pp. 47–53.

4. Bob Wallace, "GM and Its Dealers Propose Auto Web Site," *InformationWeek*, August 21, 2000, p. 38.

5. Dan Briody, "Corporate Giants Form Exchanges," *InfoWorld*, May 8, 2000, p. 30.

6. Christopher T. Heun, "Amazon, Borders Team for Superior Customer Service," *InformationWeek*, April 16, 2001, p. 30.

*"I can't wait to get laid off so I
can get a severance package and
my rehire bonus."*

CHAPTER 2

The Expanding Definition of ''Employee''

A "body of people" was mentioned in Chapter 1's definition of an organization. Most managers would consider this to mean "employees," those individuals who are paid wages or salary to work in an organization. The employer/employee relationship is easily identified formally, by answering this question: Who fills out the wage and benefits statement for tax authorities at year-end, and who receives it?

In a relational enterprise, the formal definition of employee is obsolete. The proper definition is simply, "Who works for you?"

People who are on the official payroll are only a portion of the people who actually work for and get paid (in one form or another) by a relational enterprise. There is an "alternative workforce" that may not be on the payroll, but acts in the traditional employee role. Setting up a unified strategy for leveraging an alternative workforce structure is a critical element of success for today's organizations. Unfortunately, many leaders are locked into an employee-only philosophy, where their only organizational improvement tool is a mass layoff.

De-Facto Reengineering

In the early 1990s, a major consumer goods firm in a viciously competitive industry determined that it needed to cut costs. Choosing the popular option, management decided to institute a "rightsizing" program that offered employees financial incentives to either retire early or to accept a buyout and quit the company. The goal was to reduce a headquarters staff of 10,000 by 10 percent. It was something right out of *Dilbert.* "I know, let's pay our best and most experienced people to leave us for our competitors."

Mass layoffs are anti-selection of the fittest. Perhaps a few employees coasting towards retirement are eliminated and normal attrition takes care of a few more. Unfortunately, the more successful people who are financially stable or who know they are quickly re-employable grab the money, say "thanks for all the fish," and take off. The office becomes a headhunter's feeding frenzy as competitors sift through the organizational wreckage looking for bargains and hidden diamonds. And the potential of a next round isn't lost on the keepers, who get their résumés updated and back in circulation.

Often, the expected savings of the layoffs are not attained because outside costs go up. The work still needs to get done, so former employees are hired as contractors. As one new "consultant" remarked, "I had to be laid off to finally get paid what I'm worth."

There are also significant costs to process the actual layoff. There is all the management and staff time spent in human resource activities and administration. Many companies fall under the federal Worker Adjustment and Retraining Notification Act, and can be penalized for not providing sufficient notification of the layoffs. There may be other complications, such as state laws on notification and severance pay, and health insurance extension rights under the federal Consolidated Omnibus Budget Reconciliation Act (COBRA) or special state regulations.[1]

Who tends to stay? Timid or less marketable employees hang on and hunker down. They reduce any risk taking to a minimum in order to keep a low profile. Success is measured as a rainout—no hits, no runs, and, most important, no errors. The game was never played. The willingness to stretch for improvements takes a permanent hit. Why risk failure and attract attention?

What makes layoff strategies even more destructive and expensive is that they are often cyclical. This organizational thrashing is extremely costly in terms of both people and finances. For example, in a layoff of 3,400 employees, Charles Schwab gave each former employee a generous severance pay, stock options, and insurance payment benefits on the way out. Then it provided a bonus of $7,500 for anyone who rejoined the company within eighteen months. This turns the old-fashioned golden handcuffs of employee retention into what business columnist David Nicklaus calls a "golden bungee cord" of employee rehiring.[2]

Certainly, these costs are old news to managers today. Yet organizations continue to utilize across-the-board layoffs as a primary restructuring method—what we call "de facto reengineering." Why? Because the amount and makeup of work in the organization is not stable.

Figure 2-1 shows the current situation. Nearly every organization has both predictable business cycles and uncontrollable outside influences. While the workforce stays stable, the amount (and type) of work to be done can vary dramatically and quickly—as in the Charles Schwab example. So there is rarely a match between the volume of work that needs to get done and the size of the internal workforce. What the organization must develop is a structure that lets it "accordion" its staffing in response to demands. The goal is to implement a structure that doesn't lose critical employees during the continuous resizing.

Figure 2-1. Traditional workforce.

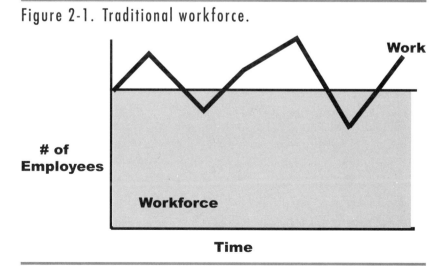

Redefining "Core Competence"

In *Competing for the Future*, Hamel and Prahalad defined core competence as "a bundle of skills and technologies that enables a company to provide a particular benefit to customers."[3] These competencies are described as organization-wide capabilities that can be leveraged as part of an overall strategy.

In a relational enterprise, core competence is defined based upon business functions. The task is to understand what functions in an organization are central to the core business, and what parts are generic, "cut on dotted line" candidates for alternative-employee, partnering, or outsourcing arrangements that allow flexibility, increase efficiencies, and lower costs.

The relational enterprise must be distributed, relatively uncoupled, flexible, and loosely structured. Work is done by a number of people, some of whom may actually be traditional employees. Core process competencies and people are identified and a conscious strategy of what's to be done inside the organization and what's to be done outside is being implemented. Now, how does that get done?

The key is in the definition of a "core competence" resource. This can be either a workgroup or an individual that is critical to the specific business of the organization and that provides competitive advantages. Core competence people should never be laid off and their work should never be outsourced; their efforts are value-added and fundamental to the core goods and services of the organization. This philosophy is illustrated in Figure 2-2.

The remainder of employees fall into a generic category, or what David Nicklaus calls part of a "just-in-time employment system, where firms can let people go quickly in bad times and hire them just as quickly during a boom."[4] Expand this concept of letting go/hiring to outsourcing and insourcing, and a new employment structure emerges.

Let's look at this from a departmental level. Assume the consumer goods company above was in the candy business. The question becomes, "Does this department need to have special candy bar selling knowledge, or is this a generic function?"

The generic functions are easy to identify: facilities and vehicle maintenance, security, lunchroom, mailroom, shipping, warehouse,

Figure 2-2. Core competence workforce.

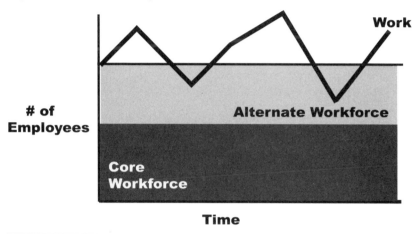

copy center, travel, auditing, and so on. These can all be outsourced to vendors that can spread the variability across multiple clients, and more readily adapt to the changing activity and service requirements.

Many of the core functions are equally clear: sales, marketing, distributor relations, advertising, plant operations, and so on. They require candy industry expertise and are critical to the success of the company.

THE QUESTION-MARK FUNCTIONS

Deciding about the remaining functions is not so obvious. What about the in-house lawyers? Do they have specialized knowledge that would be impossible to get from an outside firm? PC support? Are there proprietary programs that have to be supported, or is the software easy enough for an average technician to learn? Is accounting a core competence? How about IT programmers, human resources, billing, customer service, and public relations?

In my experience, most of the question-mark departments qualify for the generic workforce category. In the consumer goods firm above, we estimated that departments totaling only about 20 percent of the headquarters employees really needed to know how to sell candy. The other 80 percent were candidates for alternative employees. We have found this to be a good rule-of-thumb.

In most cases, the question-mark functions should all end up in the noncore workforce group. For example, Monsanto Chemical Company's legal department needed specialized knowledge about the complexities of making, storing, handling, transporting, and selling a wide range of bulk chemicals and products. Yet Monsanto still outsourced the department's work to an as-needed outside law firm rather than maintain a "just in case" legal staff. (They later brought the legal staff back in-house due to high costs and poor service—a typical thrashing cycle.)

In today's economy, vendors are eager to learn their clients' business—if they don't already specialize in that industry. Instead of having to complete an extremely difficult business process reengineering project, organizations can simply "cut on dotted line" and convert immediately to the vendor's superior processes.

This is why META Group predicts that by 2003, *40 percent of an organization's workers will not be formal payroll employees.*[5]

ALTERNATE STAFFING

These alternative workers will be members of what Vicere and Fulmer call "the shadow pyramid"—those outside the core activities.[6] The new organization will look like Figure 2-3, a structure mixing core functions and alternative employee relationships.

Don't confuse this with simply outsourcing a few functions. This is outsourcing on steroids, causing a wholesale change in the makeup of

Figure 2-3. Third-millennium organization.

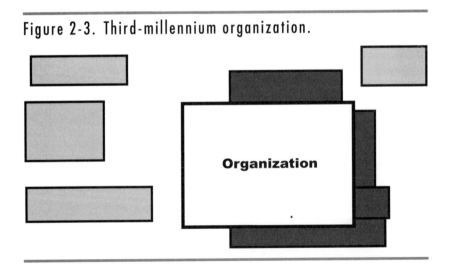

an organization and its full-time workforce. And it's not just outsourcing. The 40 percent will also consist of individual contractors, contingency/temporary help, vendors and partners expanding their services, and leased employees.

A new aspect of this service expansion is peer-to-peer (P2P) mass collaboration. For example, instead of having the support for its product come solely from its employees, a manufacturer could implement a P2P support system. This could consist of providing a place for employees, alternative workers, suppliers, partners, and even customers to provide each other with service information. One vendor of such systems estimates that clients can reduce customer turnover by 5 percent and generate a 30 to 40 percent increase of bottom line profits with this approach.[7]

Another form of alternative staffing is *employee leasing*, one of the fastest growing employment services and also one of the least understood. The leasing company hires an organization's employees and then leases them back for a monthly fee. The vendor takes care of all salary, benefits, and HR overhead, spreading the costs over its entire "inventory" of leased personnel. New employees can be hired through a team process, or solely at the discretion of the client. Additional services, such as recruiting, training, and organizational consulting, can also be included in the lease price. This can lower total cost of employee ownership for client organizations.

Dave Avakian, president of The Varsity Group, an employee leasing firm, highlights the thinking of organizations that lease employees: "The administrative burden of being an employer gets in the way of focusing on customer satisfaction and profitability. Employers want a comfort and stable HR infrastructure without the management headaches. They just don't know how to build it."

Employee leasing clients report that the primary benefits of moving from an employee model to an alternative workforce model are strategic rather than pure expense reduction. Managing the human resources function is a maze of rules and regulations, with complex interpersonal problems along the way. Human resources, although an essential overall function, is not truly dependent on the core business of the organization. It can readily be moved completely outside the organization for *all* employees.

The Multiclass Workforce

There are unavoidable ramifications with this hybrid mix of employees in the new alternative workforce. At this point in the discussion of core competence, the human resources people and many operational managers get upset at the thought that there will be a multiclass hierarchy of workers. Managers feel that this damages people's sense of belonging and unity. There is no more calling everyone in the organization an "associate" or a "regular employee."

I've been on both sides. After I left IBM in the mid-1970s to start my training business, I had the opportunity to come back into IBM as a management and sales consultant. IBM's first basic belief under the Watsons had long been, "Respect for the individual." Upon coming back as an outsider, I was surprised and dismayed at how differently I was treated. Evidently the belief was actually, "Respect for the IBM individual." I was no longer part of the team, and worse, had turned my back on it.

This class stratification is unavoidable. Among payroll employees, there will be the anointed keepers at the top. At the bottom will be those targeted for outsourcing, and in the middle will be those on the bubble, hoping that a compelling proposal for taking over their work doesn't come in. (As Billy Crystal's Fernando character used to say, "You know who you are.")

Beneath the payroll employee class there will be another hierarchy of off-payroll workers having varying levels of commitment to the organization, from those operating under a long-term outsourcing contract to contingent help scheduled day-to-day as needed. It is already common that they are all working side-by-side throughout the relational enterprise, and it will soon become even more prevalent.

EVERYONE REPRESENTS THE ORGANIZATION

Here's the challenge to organizations: As far as customers are concerned, *all these people are employees and represent the organization.* It won't help to tell the customer, "Hey, sorry for the poor service, but that was just a clueless temp who was in for the day. Don't blame us."

The first new relational enterprise skill to be mastered is integrating the various types of workers into an effective team. Partnering expert Jim Everett of Endeavour Business Learning recommends that organizations tailor their new-hire training programs for these alternative workers. The goal is to orient and acculturate alternative workers so that they behave like other members of the organization and work as teammates with employees.

A good example is Anheuser-Busch's training program for consultants. Before I was allowed to lead wholesaler management training sessions, I spent a week in a beer wholesale operation. I rode with salespeople, crawled coolers, pulled broken product out and cleaned shelves, helped set up displays, attended a 5:00 A.M. sales meeting, watched trucks being loaded, got yelled at by an angry retailer, sat in on cash check-in, and more. At the end of the week I was no expert, but I began to know what it meant to live up to A-B's motto, "Making friends is our business."

I also received special instruction on the standards for an A-B partner. A-B is fanatical about marketing, a world leader. They don't miss an opportunity to sell. After twenty-five years of work at A-B, my closet is full of branded clothing. I was taught that whenever I wear one of their shirts or carry a bag they gave me, I'm a walking billboard and reflect on A-B quality. When I see angry or rude travelers with a client logo on their chest or travel bags, it indicates that there was no acculturation process. These people were never taught the organization's standards.

Informal Employees

One last workforce complication is the trend to have all kinds of people in the spider chart take on the employee role. When organizations pay employees for referring job candidates who are eventually hired, they have turned the average worker into a recruiting manager. When marketing creates campaigns that reward customers for bringing in additional prospects, it has turned buyers into commissioned salespeople.

Many relational organizations have also gotten into the candy-striper business (remember the striped outfits hospital volunteers wear?). When an organization asks a local MBA class to help with a customer satisfaction survey in return for earning college credit, it has hired free researchers. When customers are encouraged to post and answer each other's support questions on a sponsored chat Web site, they are now acting as free service technicians. When one free online service states that signing up means that it will periodically download computational work and use your CPU in the background, it is obtaining free computer hardware capabilities. "Anyone who works for you" no longer means that someone has to get paid.

Summary

Simple outsourcing suddenly looks fairly tame. This new definition of employee means more than having a few outsourcing contracts in force, no matter how big those contracts are. There is a wide range of workforce alternatives that relational enterprises must use to make certain that their core competence human resources stay intact while minimizing the cost of their just-in-time alternative workforce. A hybrid workforce is more than an HR department tactic, it requires a core strategic effort to create a workforce that can respond to everchanging human resource requirements.

So this is what is happening inside the organization. The next step is to understand what is happening outside the organization in the extended relational enterprise.

Learning Points

1. Employees are a fixed resource. Workload varies cyclically and randomly. The only way to avoid the trauma and cost of layoffs and rehires is to develop and execute an alternative workforce strategy.

2. You should *never* lay off core competence employees. Everyone else is a candidate for the alternative workforce.

3. Alternative workforce solutions are a quick way to reengineer processes. If you delay in this area, you risk losing strategic focus, competitiveness, and substantial profits. Vendors work

in their own core competence areas and have superior expertise and economies of scale.

4. Know thyself. Every organization should review all workgroups to determine, "Is this a core competence that we need to do our business?" Groups that aren't core functions, and this could represent up to 80 percent of employees, are candidates for alternative workforce solutions.

5. A multiclass workforce is inevitable. New systems and processes are going to have to deal with them as separate entities, and leaders will have to adapt accordingly.

6. Alternative workers need special orientation and acculturation into the organization so that they can provide the same level of performance as formal payroll employees.

NOTES

1. Matt Hicks, "Lessons Learned in Layoffs," *eWeek*, March 12, 2001, p. 57.

2. David Nicklaus, "Despite Layoffs, the Days of Worker Empowerment Are Far From Being Over," *St. Louis Post-Dispatch*, March 28, 2001, p. C1.

3. Gary Hamel and C. K. Prahalad, *Competing for the Future: Breakthrough Strategies for Seizing Control of Your Industry and Creating the Markets of Tomorrow* (Boston: Harvard Business School Press, 1994), p. 199.

4. David Nicklaus, "Despite Layoffs, the Days of Worker Empowerment are Far From Over," *op. cit.*

5. META Group, META Group CRM Conference: Opening Remarks, February 21, 2000.

6. Albert A. Vicere and Robert M. Fulmer, *Crafting Competitiveness: Developing Leaders in the Shadow Pyramid* (Oxford: Capstone, 1996), p. 64.

7. Scott Campbell, "Support Systems Adopt P2P Model," *CRN*, February 2, 2001, p. 41.

CHAPTER 3

The Expanding Definition of ''Customer''

Think of an old-time general store, where customers could shop for food, hardware, clothes, and white goods just by walking from aisle to aisle. The proprietor recognized you when you came in and knew what you liked. As he greeted you he would highlight some of the new merchandise he knew you'd find interesting. He might even order in something special for you as a surprise, figuring you'd likely buy it. Profits were linked to his ability to build a relationship with you and to know your special wants and needs as well as you did.

Windows Into the Relational Enterprise

The Internet equivalent of a general store is the *portal*. A portal is application software that provides a browser-based view into a wide range of data, i.e., a one-stop shop for a dizzying array of applications, goods, and services. The information is well organized, the site attractively designed and easy to use, and the services can be readily found.

Service providers such as AOL and MSN and search sites such as Yahoo are all examples of the consumer portal philosophy. Need snow conditions for a skiing trip? Start at your portal. Need to book hotel and plane reservations for a trip? Start at your portal. Want to talk to friends, visit a digital video newsgroup, check the news, locate a company, or get a financial forecast? Start at the same portal.

Portals are becoming a big business. IDC has estimated that approximately 60 percent of corporations plan to have a corporate portal installed by 2001.[1] Merrill Lynch forecasts that the enterprise portal market will grow to $14 billion by 2002. META estimates that almost 85 percent of businesses will have some form of portal by 2003. Portals have been labeled "the technology of choice for delivering content and mission-critical application data to employees and customers" and are being considered a new tier in enterprise IT architecture.[2]

Figure 3-1 is a diagram showing how portals link to enterprise data. Portals present the complete range of applications and data to the various constituents in the spider chart. The portal technology upon which the figures in this chapter are based integrates over 200 individual

Figure 3-1. Enterprise portals.

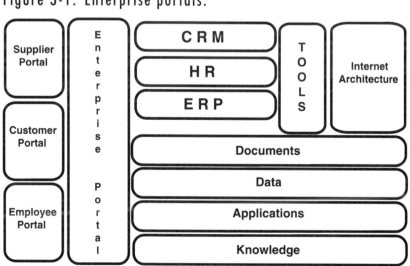

roles (more on this in Chapter 4) and has 7,500 transactions mapped between the ERP, CRM, and analytics systems in order to provide this integrated view. We'll be talking in later chapters about why all of these functions have to be integrated to meet service requirements and satisfaction goals.

Figure 3-2 is an example of a customer portal. The menu on the left side of the screen gives users access to a variety of information and functions, including session histories, orders status, billing, active contracts, open cases, field service schedules, catalogs, e-store, subscriptions, and communications areas. The portal also allows personalization of display options and profile self-maintenance.

A version of an employee portal is shown in Figure 3-3. Access to internal information is indexed on the left. Accounting information, such as personalized budget status and expense reports, is accessed on the right, and a variety of frequently updated company information is displayed in the center area. The portal provides complete access to standard functions, such as calendaring, scheduling meeting rooms, benefits updates, partners and customers, and much more—all available through hyperlinks or the search box in the upper left-hand corner.

Figure 3-2. Customer portal.

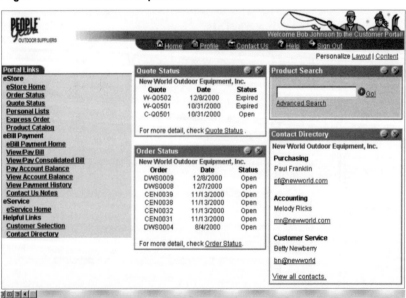

Figure 3-3. Employee portal.

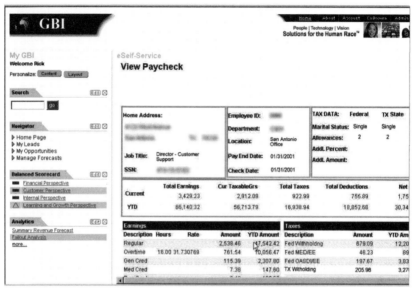

Partners can also access relevant information through an organization's portal. Figure 3-4 is an example of a supplier portal home page. Supply-chain functions, such as orders and inventory, are included, and pending to-do's are highlighted. Company news and events can be featured when available.

Once portal technology is available, a relational enterprise has the ability to provide everyone with whom it comes in contact a unified, convenient, easy-to-use view of the organization. This creates efficiencies in communications, and also raises satisfaction. But best of all, it provides a tremendous opportunity for additional profits all throughout the spider chart of potential constituents.

Portals as Profit-Makers·

There is significant potential profit in being someone's first stop on the Internet. When electronics retailers advertise complete personal computer systems either free or for less than $100, you wonder how they

Figure 3-4. Partner portal.

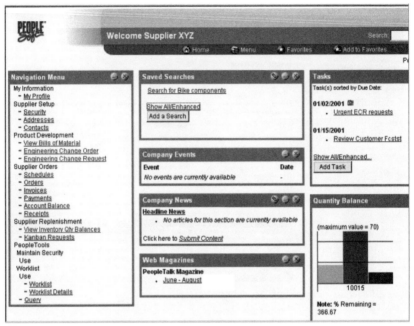

can possibly make money at this. (Volume?) They can do this because buyers are required to sign up for four years of access through a specified Internet service provider (ISP), where they are targeted with mandatory advertisements and service offerings. ISPs and participating vendors fully expect to earn their investment back from the advertising revenue and transaction commission value of the portal relationship with its captive customer. Fortunately, anyone can enter this game.

TURNING EMPLOYEES INTO CUSTOMERS

Relational enterprises are setting up similar programs through the use of business-to-employee (B2E) portals. The initial benefit is to facilitate communications between employees. For example, Bank of America (BOA) has announced plans for a "self-service work environment" portal for its 144,000 employees. It will offer access to BOA information, industry news, stock quotes, work tools, training, financial and travel services, and e-commerce. The portal will even allow personalization of content displayed.

This plan provides BOA with far more than just better intrabank communications. BOA has built partnerships with vendors that supply consumer products and services. For steering employees to these vendors through its employee portal, BOA can conceivably negotiate for a percentage of each transaction. Similarly, a major health-care and financial provider offers its 45,000 employees work/life assistance offerings through its portal, and is considering expanding into concierge and discount buying services.[3] Consumer features make portals potential profit centers, which are designed to help employers recover some portion of their payroll through e-commerce advertising and "finder's fee" commissions.

Revenue potential may be one reason why employers such as American Airlines, Delta Air Lines, Ford Motor, and United Airlines are willing to subsidize the purchase of home computers and Internet access for employees. Ford is offering its 370,000 worldwide employees a PC, printer, and unlimited Internet access for $5 per month over three years. Delta is making a similar offer to its 72,000 full- and part-time employees for $12 per month. Intel's offer to its 70,000+ workforce is free.[4] United even plans to extend access its MySkyNet portal program to 30,000 retirees by the end of 2001.[5] There is no way to justify including retirees as being for better internal communications. They don't work there any more! The only rationale is that the portal provides an opportunity to generate e-commerce revenue, so the more the merrier.

Folks, it appears that Amway, Mary Kay, and Shacklee have won. To anyone who has seen an Amway "chalk talk," this portal buying functionality sounds a lot like network marketing. Similar to sales directors building their downline, relational enterprises make money by connecting as many people as possible to a portal containing e-commerce offerings.

Portals mean that the old definition of a customer as "someone who buys an organization's core product" is obsolete. Organizations worldwide are battling each other for share of eyeball. With a portal, *anyone they touch* is a potential customer (of a sort) who can create profit. This means that every constituent of the spider chart shown in Chapter 1 is a potential customer, not just one of the boxes.

EXPANDING CUSTOMER PROFIT OPPORTUNITIES

Many managers are aghast at the concept of implementing a Web site with generic e-commerce offerings. They insist that their core business is steel, chemicals, restaurant furniture, or whatever, and that messing around with selling sundries over the Internet is a needless distraction. Worse, it dilutes the brand and confuses prospects and customers.

Publishing giant Pulitzer, Inc., feels differently. In March 2001, Pulitzer announced development of a new portal site for its *St. Louis Post-Dispatch* newspaper.[6] Pulitzer was shifting from delivering news on its site to becoming a Web portal for consumer information, one that would also offer content from twenty-four other information providers. The portal operation was being set up independently from the Post-Dispatch and was expected to be profitable sometime after 2001.

Forrester Research Analyst Charlene Li commented that newspaper publishers are moving beyond providing pure news sites because these are little more than the primary product.[7] This acknowledges the fact that most organizations will have to go beyond their core products and services to garner regular site visitors. A relational enterprise realizes that focusing solely on its core business is now a weakness that will ultimately have an impact on its entire revenue stream. Even core product/ service customers will be infrequent visitors if the vendor site offers no added value over core competitors' sites.

In *Enterprise One to One*, Peppers and Rogers point out that the old model was to sell one product to as many people as possible.[8] Mass production made it, and mass marketing got it bought. The new model is to develop a continuing relationship in order to sell as many products as possible to each individual customer.

This is why office supply vendors Staples and OfficeMax are now offering over 100 business training courses through their Web sites.[9] As an OfficeMax customer commented, "We already use the site. If you can consolidate the number of bills you have to write, that's a plus."

Training isn't the core business of office supplies retailers. Yet management in both companies recognized that there is value in the shopping relationships they have established with the small businesses that make up their customer set. Adding e-learning training offerings to their sites is an ideal way to provide additional value. The result is not only a new revenue source, but also a chance to reach beyond their traditional small-business market. The expanded customer base might now include new prospects, such as someone just seeking education, or departmental managers in larger organizations with tight budgets looking for a low-cost training option.

This is a typical commission arrangement. Staples is partnering with Personable.com, and OfficeMax is utilizing Arthur Andersen's Virtual Learning Network to host the online learning portion of Office Max.com. By using outside e-learning suppliers for fulfillment, the retailers are limiting their investment to making an enhancement to their existing Web sites.

Relational enterprises are realizing that there is a significant profit opportunity to offering a customer portal, but that it will require something beyond the organization's core services or products to attract frequent portal visits from general consumers. One way to make this easier is to leverage a captive audience.

TURNING PARTNERS INTO CUSTOMERS

It gets even more interesting when portal technology is applied to supply chain business-to-business (B2B) relationships. Certainly, the communication benefits are appreciated by both buyer and seller, but there is also an enormous revenue opportunity for the buyer—particularly when it is a significant part of a supplier's business. And you can forget the satisfaction issue, because suppliers may well have a gun to their heads if they want to make the sale to a major account.

Pretend you are a large automobile company or a dominant retailer with thousands of suppliers. This gives you an enormous captive alternative workforce and vendor chain market. You might say to one of your suppliers something like this: "We'd like to buy your floor mats, but in return you're going to have to do all your business buying through our portal. You need to book your travel through our site, and buy your phone services, Internet access, office supplies, furniture, fixtures, vehicles, etc., through us. It's better for you anyway because we have such an enormous buying power compared to you as a little standalone that our prices are probably lower than you can find anyway. And you can offer access to our portal's discounted prices to your employees as a benefit. Otherwise, we'll just have to get our floor mats from someone more willing to partner with our B2B portal. By the way, we'd also like you to make our portal available to your suppliers and customers. When can we get together to work out an announcement plan?"

For example, in 2000 GM announced plans to market its portal to the more than 200,000 employees of Delphi, one of its first-tier suppliers, and other suppliers through its employee to employee (E2E) marketing program. Companies such as Motorola, Kodak, and Exxon are working with an employee e-commerce site that offers discounts of up to 50 percent on products and services. In some cases, employees can make purchases and have the costs deducted directly from their paychecks. This is creating a brand new channel strategy.[10]

Similar to the revenue opportunities of a B2E portal, organizations want to recover some portion of the money they pay suppliers for goods and services. This is a demand that can put a supplier into a difficult position. What happens when several customers all insist that a supplier shop at their site? On a small scale, this happens to me as a consultant. When setting up site visits to several companies in a single week, all the clients usually want me to book the trip through their particular travel agency.

With multiple buyers using this approach, it is a first come–first serve situation. Whichever competitor initiates the portal relationship is most likely to lock in the supplier's purchases. As more vendors implement portal capabilities, the competition for share of eyeball will increase and the opportunities for even coercive site revenue will dwindle.

Summary

Portals are an enabling technology that makes defining a customer as "someone who buys your product" totally obsolete. A customer now fits the classic resort property criterion for qualified prospects: "Can they fog a mirror?" The new definition of a customer is "anyone alive you can get to buy something from you or your portal." This might mean a buyer of your core product—the traditional definition. But it now also includes anyone the organization touches, plus those touched by the touchee, i.e., everyone in the alternative workforce ranks along with individuals up and down the supply chain. Organizations can be paid for advertising access and earn a flow-through commission from each resulting portal transaction. The entire spider chart is now a potential customer.

This is starting to get very messy. Someone is going to have to establish and manage relationships with potentially hundreds of service providers who are linked to the portal: airlines, hotel chains, auto makers, banks, real estate firms, furniture warehouses, office supply retailers, beauty aids distributors, and so on. Just walk around a WalMart store to see what the list could contain.

Who's going to do all this? The IT department programming the Web site? Sales? Marketing? There's really no existing group in the traditional organization that is set up to do this. That's why Pulitzer created an independent department to run its new portal operation. What are the procedures to coordinate a sales-oriented portal? The need to manage these expanded customers sets creates catastrophic changes in the processes and systems of the traditional organization, which is where we're headed next.

Learning Points

1. Portals are the preferred method of making information available throughout a relational organization.

2. The goal now is to sell more stuff to each person rather than to find more buyers for one product. This requires going beyond core goods and services and leveraging consumer e-commerce partnerships.

3. Portal technology is an enabler for selling unlimited numbers of products, and earning advertising and commission revenue. Why else would people be willing to give away personal computers in return for guaranteed portal access?

4. It means that relationships are the most important sales commodity. Great places to start are captive audiences: customers (B2C), employees (B2E), and suppliers (B2B). Then organizations can expand up and down the contact chain of each.

5. To quote Granny Clampett and Snuffy Smith, "Time's a wastin'." The contest is for first-site access habits and share of eyeball. In a battle, being nice about it is an option. Companies are using all their leverage to lock in visitors.

NOTES

1. Brian Fonseca, "Yahoo Partners to Boost Its Technology," *InfoWorld*, January 15, 2001, p. 27.

2. Preston P. Forman, "Portals Fill Key Enterprise Info Need," *CRN*, February 26, 2001, pp. 81–2.

3. Norbert Turek, "Portal Helps Aetna Employees with Work and Life Issues," *InformationWeek*, December 18, 2000, p. 144.

4. Catherine Fredman, "The Completely PC Workforce," *Executive Edge From Gartner*, December 2000–January 2001, p. 1.

5. Rick Whiting, "Airlines Foster Communications With PCs," *InformationWeek*, May 22, 2000, p. 155.

6. Peter Shinkle, "Pulitzer, Inc., Announces New STLtoday.com Web Portal," *St. Louis Post-Dispatch*, March 14, 2001, pp. C1–C2.

7. Ibid.

8. Don Peppers and Martha Rogers, *Enterprise One to One: Tools for Competing in the Interactive Age* (New York: Doubleday, 1997), pp. 20–1.

9. Sandra Swanson, "Office Supply Vendors to Offer E-Learning," *InformationWeek*, August 21, 2000, p. 40.

10. Ephraim Schwartz, "The Selling of the Intranet: Comarketing Deals Drive Business-to-Employee Model," *InfoWorld*, May 8, 2000, pp. 1,12.

*"Hierarchical structure is at
the end of its life. Now it's
flexible roles."*

CHAPTER 4

The Relational Structure

I was speaking in Hamburg, Germany, to a group of data warehousing consultants from PriceWaterhouseCoopers (PWC). A colleague heard I was going to be there and e-mailed a joke involving Germans and consultants—something fairly hard to find. Now telling jokes to a second-language audience is always risky, and a German group is one of the toughest in the world. But I'm a sucker for a humorous opening, and here is how it went.

The German division of a firm challenged its American counterparts to a rowing competition. The first race was held and the Americans were barely to the halfway point as the German team crossed the line. The fine firm of PWC was retained to study the race and they identified the problem as one of organization. The Germans had eight people rowing and one person calling cadence, while the Americans had one person rowing and eight people counting the stroke.

The American management team made adjustments and prepared for the rematch. But they were surprised when they

did even worse, barely passing the quarter mark when the Ger-
mans finished. Again PWC was retained and found the cause.
The Americans had again used one rower, but had organized
the eight teammates into four rowing supervisors, three rowing
managers, and one rowing vice president. In addition, the
rower was given a performance incentive and the supervisors
offered a bonus if the Americans won the race.

After the second loss, the rower was fired for poor perform-
ance, the supervisors lost their bonus, and the managers were
promoted for identifying the problem.

Now this isn't a thigh-slapper, but it generated outright laughter
from my audience of consultants. In talking during the break, several
attendees observed that the American rower could have worked for some
of their clients. I told them that it was the same on our side of the ocean:
There are too many top executives who think they can reorganize their
organizations into efficiency and success. The problem is that the traditional hierarchy organizational construction set has reached the end of
its usefulness. Hierarchies don't fit new internal or customer processes,
and hierarchies don't properly utilize employees.

Hierarchical Structures

A reporting hierarchy is the primary structural tool for nearly every
organization in the world. Ask anyone at random, "Who is your boss?"
or "Who reports to you?" and there will be an answer. Human resource
experts have long promoted the need to have the official performance
review given by a single manager. Even 360-degree feedback systems
clearly label respondents into manager, peer, and direct-report categories.

Figure 4-1 shows a typical organizational hierarchy. These charts
are built with military precision—which is where the idea originated.
The foot soldier of ancient Rome and a modern infantryman would
both recognize this structure. In the U.S. armed forces, you can at any
time draw a continuous reporting line between the commander-in-chief
and the newest recruit stepping off the bus at boot camp.

That's the strength of a hierarchy. Everybody knows where they fit

Figure 4-1. Organizational hierarchy.

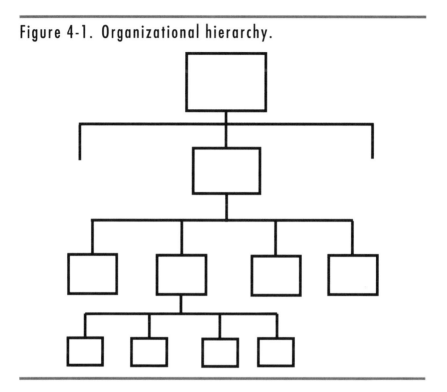

in, whom they report to, and who reports to them. Another strength is that work is readily divided up among departments. At the top of the chart, there are the major functions of production, sales, administration, and management. Sales department sub-structures can be assigned specific product lines, geographies, or market segments—and so on down the line until there is just enough work for a single individual to do. Then positions on the chart can be created, job descriptions written, and people matched to the tasks required. It's all very orderly, well defined, and manageable. Mr. Spock would consider this Vulcan heaven.

The hierarchy also makes expansion relatively easy to accomplish. Need more sales coverage? Just carve out an additional region from existing territories and clone the entire regional structure, as shown in Figure 4-2.

The only problem is that this is no longer a valid organizational chart. What's missing is a connector at the top, an additional level to maintain the required reporting relationship. This is why one major manufacturer has over 30 levels between the president and a front-line

Figure 4-2. Expanding the hierarchy.

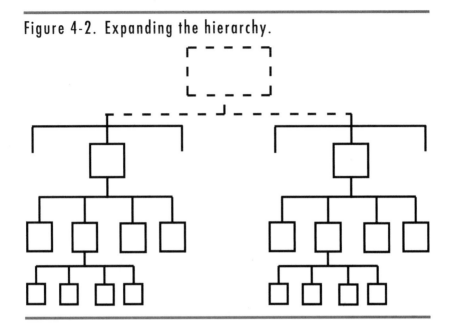

factory worker. One person in the middle of this chain reports up through five vice presidents. Organizations inexorably grow thicker as they expand outwards. With the common rule-of-thumb of five direct reports per supervisor or manager, a staff of 125 front-line workers requires thirty-one additional people filling three additional levels of management (twenty-five supervisors, five managers, and one vice president.)

FLOW OF INFORMATION

Another problem is communication. How does information flow in such an organization? As Figure 4-3 shows, information flows up and down the hierarchy. If information needs to get from Group A to Group B, it typically must flow up to a common link between the two groups—usually a high-level executive position.

For example, a retail goods firm was involved in a quality improvement program and wanted to help factory workers relate better with customers and feel more a part of the sales effort. So a process was set up for factory employees to submit a form whenever they were in a store and their company's products weren't available. The form went to the worker's supervisor, who sent it to the department head, who forwarded it to the plant manager. The plant manager then sent it to the vice

Figure 4-3. Communications flow.

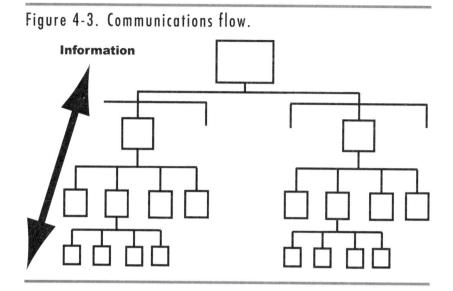

president of sales, who gave it to the regional sales manager, who sent it to the sales supervisor, who gave it to the salesperson to check out what was going on in the account. As you can imagine, what started out as a positive way for plant workers to get involved with sales ended up in an old fashioned butt-kicking for the salesman, with sales management wondering what was so wrong in the territory that plant people were complaining about it.

So the salesperson went out to visit the account, found out why there was no product on a particular date four weeks ago, filled out a form, and sent the answer back through the entire chain. He also filed away a bit of resentment at the stupid plant people and for his bad luck that there is a factory in his territory. The plant person was eventually told, "They were out-of-stock and a delivery didn't come in that day until after you were there." Who knows how much money was spent to find out that critical bit of market information. We estimated it could easily have cost $500 or more per report.

That's the problem with communicating across functional elements of an organization. Information goes up and down the structure, but has a difficult time going across it. As an aside, what should have been done in the example above was to teach the plant personnel to go up to the store manager and say, "I noticed that you're out of Birnbaum's Denatured Air. It's one of the main reasons I come in here, and I just wanted you to know that I really missed getting it this time." This creates a demand the salesperson can leverage, lets the retailer know that factory personnel frequent the store, and costs the system nothing in communications costs. Somebody e-mail Scott Adams.

FLOW OF WORK

How information flows in a hierarchy is in direct contrast to how work flows, which tends to progress horizontally from department to department along the front line, as shown in Figure 4-4. This means that multiple individuals from separate departments are involved in most processes. As a result, many different people affect the overall satisfaction generated with the process's customer, whether internal or external. So who is responsible for the results of the process when it crosses hierarchical lines?

There is an old saying: "When everyone is responsible for customer service, no one is responsible." Who "owns" customer satisfaction and can make it a certainty in a hierarchical reporting structure? Some employees may want to, but they reside in departments focusing on only one part of the process. This is often referred to as the "silo

Figure 4-4. Work flow.

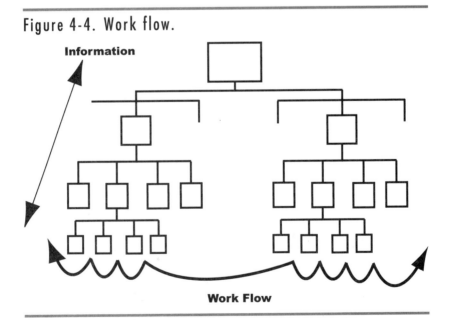

effect," the analogy being the image of a row of grain elevators that are touching but keep their contents totally separated.

Here's a great example. Several years ago my mother had outpatient eye surgery at a local hospital. Let's call it St. Louis Merciful Medical (SLMM.) The procedure went well, and her bill amounted to just over $5,000. About a month after the operation, Mom received a computerized bill from the hospital for $2.75. SLMM said she had been given a box of tissues in the patient kit and that it was not covered by Medicare or her supplemental insurance. Mom didn't remember ever receiving the box of tissues and, being a senior raised during the Depression, didn't want to pay for it if she didn't use it. I suggested she forget about the invoice, but Mom also didn't like having any debts. She decided to call the hospital.

Now one of the rules of customer service is: Never mess around with retired people. They have lots of time on their hands and are looking for entertainment.

Mom made it her life's work to get a credit for that $2.75. She called accounts payable and was told they couldn't do anything about it, that she should call accounting. Accounting said they couldn't issue a reversal, that she should check with nursing to see if she actually received the box and didn't realize it. A nursing floor supervisor said that she had no idea, that Mom should talk to her doctor about it. The doctor couldn't believe he was being asked about a lousy box of tissues and said to call the hospital. The patient advocate at the hospital said to call accounts payable. This process went on for weeks.

In the meantime, Mom started getting threatening computerized dunning notices about the overdue amount. The theme was, "If you don't pay up, we'll send this to a collection agency and ruin your credit." I told her that the chances were nil that a collection agency would chase after a fifty-cent commission, and that a bill of $2.75 in contention wasn't going to wreck her credit. Besides, she wasn't ever again going to be buying anything major anyway. The collection notices kept coming.

From the very beginning, it was clear that it was definitely going to cost the hospital more than $2.75 to send the bill, talk on the phone about it, receive the check, post the payment, reconcile it on the check registers, and archive the records of the transaction. This process can range from $50 to $200 per payment, depending upon the hospital. In fact, a single phone conversation costs the typical organization about five dollars in employee time and phone infrastructure costs, so SLMM had already lost money after the first call.

Mom, depression-era to the end, finally paid the bill in order to keep her credit clear. Yet it was pay and resent. Within a week, she steered her best friend who was having the same operation away from SLMM to another hospital. "They cheat you on your bill at SLMM," she said. As a professional cruciverbalist (crossword puzzle author) selling to New York magazines, Mom gave talks on puzzles to retiree groups all over the city. She always managed to work in the SLMM story. Right before Mom passed on, she could document over $50,000 in medical fees she had cost SLMM for their $2.75 box of tissues.

I've thought about sending this story to the president of the hospital, but I'm not certain he would truly get it. There was no one person in the entire system who could say, "Look, Mrs. Cooper, forget about the bill. I'm going to make sure the notices stop so that you don't have to call again." The result for the hospital? A net loss of about $2.75 vs. a potential loss of $50,000.

It's an ugly story, but a common one. The hierarchical structures in place in nearly every organization in the world guarantee this division of labor. You can't tell a salesperson that you need something serviced. You can't tell a service person that you want to buy something. You can't tell an accountant that you want something serviced. You have to abandon talking to a live person and take your chances with voice mail roulette hoping to reach someone with the knowledge and authority to take care of you.

Reengineering and the Case Worker

In *Reengineering the Corporation,* Hammer and Champy proposed a solution to this problem. They introduced change keywords such as fundamental, radical, and dramatic. The focus was on taking processes that crossed departments and consolidating them for efficiency and better service. They proposed a "case worker" (or case worker team) as the new personnel structure.[1] A case worker philosophy consists of making a single individual (or small group) responsible for completing a process from end-to-end. The authors observed that a case worker–based process is typically ten times faster than the sequential, multiperson process it replaces. This is accomplished by redesigning workflow to combine several jobs into one. The consolidated job is then a good fit for self-directed work teams.

The organization chart for a reengineered enterprise might look like the clump of self-contained circles shown in Figure 4-5. Work is now a collection of processes. The organization is very flat, and highly trained and motivated front-line employees are given the tools and authority to serve the process's customers.

For example, at its Austin, Texas higher-education inside sales office, Apple Computer had approximately 120 people grouped into four-

Figure 4-5. Process-oriented structure.

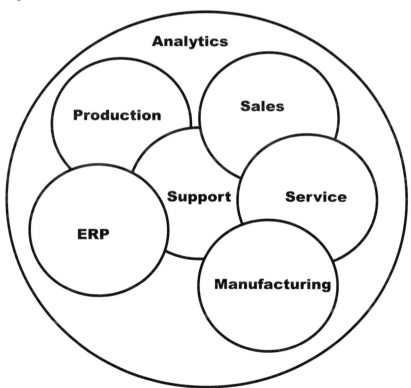

person self-directed sales teams. Each team consisted of two salespeople, one administrator, and one technical specialist. The groups were true case worker teams with all four teammates being equally responsible for a single sales territory. When customers called, there was always someone on the team who could help them no matter what the issue.

The entire group reported to a single manager—and he was a contractor. That's about as flat as an organization can get. He really didn't manage the teams as much as he acted as a sales resource in case they had problems or specific needs. For example, we were brought in because administrators had come to him and requested sales training so they could do a better job with customers.

Despite such success stories, reengineering in general, and case workers specifically, yielded mixed results in the workplace. Although a few organizations were able to generate significant benefits from reengineering, many attempts were failures. A key problem was people.

Hammer and Champy both admit needing to better address the human factors of such dramatic change.[2] Reengineering faced massive resistance from the middle management "black zone of death." There was employee burnout from overload. Many organizations missed the point of reengineering processes and used it as a way to position knee-jerk massive layoffs as forward thinking management strategy. Others had the right intent, approached it the right way, but just couldn't make it happen. To front-line workers, reengineering looked like assigning more work to fewer employees under the guise of improved customer service.

In large-scale reengineering projects, the failures were spectacular. Levi Strauss initiated a reengineering effort in 1992 that was to address nearly every major business process at the jeans maker.[3] The idea was to start with a "blank sheet of paper" and redesign the company from the ground up. Six years later, Levi Strauss dramatically scaled back the project, and admitted that it had been a mistake. The vice president of information services commented, "It was a wonderful exercise. But . . . I wouldn't do it again. The problem with a blank sheet of paper is that the world is not blank. Your company is not blank. You have facilities. You have customers. You have people. You have an environment in which you operate. You can't change everything. You have to recognize that."

According to a Cambridge Management Consulting director, "Very few large companies have managed to do big-picture, radical reengineering, and those tended to be companies that were under the gun and had very strong leadership." This is why a Computer Sciences Corporation survey of information technology executives found that "Implementing business process reengineering" dropped from No. 1 in importance in 1994 to No. 14 in 1997.[4]

A major contributor to reengineering's low success rate was the fact that it was technologically ahead of its time. Consolidating processes requires a similar consolidation in data and supporting systems. Real-time information across the entire process has to be available to each single case worker. At the time reengineering came to the forefront in 1993, the Internet was just emerging from academia and government, Web databases and high productivity programming tools didn't exist, data warehousing products were only used in high-end applications, and data was strewn across the entire enterprise. Decision support applications weren't available, and the concept of a balanced scorecard had been proposed only one year earlier.[5]

Consequently, while reengineering remains a tool in the process improvement kit, it is not a very popular one with executives who oversaw failed projects, with managers who watched their positions being threatened or eliminated, and with workers who had sole responsibility dumped on them for complex processes. The question, then, is whether or not current e-business technologies make a case worker structure viable.

The Emergence of Roles

Reengineering's goal is to consolidate a process so that it can be completed in its entirety by a single person or a small self-directed team. Experience has shown that executive leadership can't implement reengineering, middle management sabotages the effort, and front-line workers resist what they perceive as work overload. Most enterprise processes are too complex and varied for an individual or small group to handle them end-to-end.

A relational enterprise is built on a wholly different unit of measure—the *role*. The variety of roles is extensive, as the list of typical enterprise resource planning (ERP) system roles listed in Table 4-1 shows. Earlier chapters discussed how traditional organizational categories, i.e., employees, employers, customers, partners, or competitors, are blurring. Individual constituents throughout the spider chart are being required to fill multiple roles that vary from task to task and within tasks.

Ask workers in a relational enterprise what their position is, and you will get the diaper answer, "It depends." (This is the only answer you'll ever need to be a good consultant, or a winning politician.) You will hear something like:

> *I'm the team leader for sales expense accounting. I'm a member of the online expense process improvement team, and I'm an occasional subject matter contributor to our group's IT liaison.*
>
> *On my last phone call with a salesperson, I did three different jobs. I gave some sales manager–style coaching on expensing some proposal costs. I provided lawyer-like policy guidelines on spending legalities. And I was an administrator looking up the caller's year-to-date spending totals to budget. My job title varies moment to moment.*

This new structure, if you want to call it that, is based upon the idea that each interaction with internal and external customers requires employees to take on variety of roles. Because an individual's duties are constantly changing, appropriate data, systems, and resources have to be available to a wide range of enterprise constituents.

The new organizational chart, as was illustrated in Figure 4-5, is hardly a chart at all. It is an attempt to depict a role-based job description: "Whatever it takes to satisfy the internal/external customer on this interaction." Individuals or teams won't be responsible for an entire process. They could potentially be involved at any point in the process at any time in the process.

Whomever Mom called first at St. Louis Merciful Medical—whether it was management, billing, nursing, or the patient advocate—should have been able to get into the accounting system and wipe out that $2.75 bill before she created any more work for the organization. No matter what the actual job title of the person receiving that call, he or she was in the "customer service agent" role the minute Mom's call came through. Their unwillingness to help or the inability of their sys-

Table 4-1. Relational enterprise roles.

Accounts Payable Banking Specialist
Accounts Receivable Banking Specialist
Account Manager
Accounts Payable Manager
Accounts Payable Specialist
Accounts Receivable Specialist
Asset Management Application Administrator
Asset Manager
Benefits Administrator
Benefits Application Administrator
Billing Application Administrator
Billing Specialist
Bills and Routings Application Administrator
Broker
Broker/External Buyer
Budget Coordinator
Business Analyst
Cash Manager
Company Events Publisher
Company News Publisher
Compensation Administrator
Consulting Resource
Contract Administrator
Contract Billing Administrator
Contract Financial Administrator
Contracts App Administrator
Cost Engineer
Cost Management Application Administrator
Cost Manager
Credit Analyst
Credit Manager
Customer
Customer Portal Administrator
Customer Sales Representative
Customer Service Representative
Deal Manager
Deduction Management Application Administrator
Deductions Specialist
Design Engineer
Email/Calendar Pagelet Administrator
Employee
Engineer
Engineering Application Administrator
Enterprise Planner
Expense Manager
Expenses Application Administrator
External Applicant
Facilities Administrator
Faculty
Guest Account
General Ledger Accountant
General Pagelet Administrator

Global Application Administrator
Global Payroll Administrator
Global Payroll Application Administrator
HR Application Administrator
HR Specialist
Health and Safety Administrator
Inventory Agent
Inventory Application Administrator
Inventory Manager
Legal Administrator
MIS Administrator
Manager
Marketing
Mobil Order Management Administrator
News & Events Pagelet Administrator
Optionee
Order Management Application Administrator
Order Promising Application Administrator
Payables Application Administrator
Payroll Administrator
Payroll Application Administrator
Payroll Interface Application Administrator
Pension Administrator
Pension Application Administrator
People Tools
Practice Manager
Process Scheduler Administrator
Product Configurator Application Administrator
Production Management Application Administrator
Production Manager
Production Planning Application Administrator
Shipping Clerk
Staffing Coordinator
Stock Administrator
Stock Application Administrator
Strategic Analyst
Supplier-AR Specialist
Supplier-Account Manager
Supplier-Application Administrator
Supplier-Customer Service Representative
Supplier-Engineer
Supplier-Production Manager
System Administrator
Task Administrator
Time and Labor Administrator
Time and Labor Application Administrator
Training Administrator
Treasury Accountant
Treasury Application Administrator
Vendor
Web Publishing Administrator

tems to take her problem to resolution on the first call ultimately may have cost the hospital over $50,000 in marginal revenue.

Summary

In a September 2000 conference speech, Tom Peters advised:

The next ten years will see a revolution: 90 percent of white-collar jobs will be destroyed or altered beyond recognition.[6]

Peters is adamant that current organization structures and job descriptions are no longer adequate for the spider-chart linked, role-based, e-business, relational processes of today.

Relational management systems must be designed for roles, not job titles. Employees cannot be masters of one process, but instead must be facilitators of many. Rather than carrying the impossible burden of an entire end-to-end process, participants in a relational organization must get involved throughout all the stages of an interaction with an internal or external customer. This will require having systems that provide information on the full range of issues that affect those customers, and that can provide information throughout what we call the "customer cycle." This is a topic for the next chapter.

Learning Points

1. Reorganizing an enterprise is not an effective performance improvement strategy.

2. Hierarchical organizational structures are obsolete. They stifle horizontal communication, and the segmentation of work makes it impossible to ensure customer satisfaction because nobody "owns" the customer.

3. Reengineering looked promising because of its potential for dramatic gains in profitability and competitiveness. Unfortunately, the technology wasn't ready for it, and its massive scope and disruption of personnel were obstacles too difficult to overcome.

4. Reengineering's case worker concept appears to have value given today's technological capabilities, but the one person–one process philosophy isn't practical with complex processes.

5. Work is moving away from heads-down jobs with distinct duties and moving toward workers taking on a variety of roles depending upon the minute-by-minute needs of a customer during their interaction.

6. Systems and processes are going to have to support these new requirements.

NOTES

1. Michael Hammer and James Champy, *Reengineering the Corporation: A Manifesto for Business Revolution* (New York: HarperBusiness, 1993), pp. 51–3.

2. Hal Lancaster, " 'Reengineering's Authors Reconsider Reengineering," *Wall Street Journal,* January 17, 1995, p. B1.

3. Jeff Moad, "Coming Unzipped: There Are Lessons in How Levi Strauss's Top-to-Bottom BPR Effort Unraveled," *PC Week,* November 17, 1997, pp. 147–8.

4. Jeff Moad, "Keeping the Faith in BPR: Champy, Others Still Believe in Radical Reengineering," *PC Week*, November 17, 1997, p. 147.

5. Robert S. Kaplan and David P. Norton, "The Balanced Scorecard— Measures That Drive Performance," *Harvard Business Review,* January–February 1992, pp. 71–9.

6. Michael Vizard, "Two Views of the New Economy, Peters: Most Companies Will Fail," *InfoWorld,* September 25, 2000, p. 24.

PART TWO

RELATIONAL ENTERPRISE SERVICE PROCESSES

CHAPTER 5

The Relational Business Cycle

Imagine walking into the doctor's office and being told, "Here's a wooden stick and a flashlight. There's a mirror in the examination room. Take a look down your throat and decide what you have. I'll give you a chart where you can look up what to do about it." Sound far fetched? While there are no Internet-based physicians, health-related self-service sites make up a sizable portion of the Web. Who knows? Someday we may be shining a Webcam down our throats while a physician says, "Hmmm . . ." over the audio portion of our Internet link. Fortunately, there are lots of other situations that are more suitable for self-service.

The Ramifications of Self-Service

The customer demand for Web self-service should be causing major changes in organizational structure. Self-service is the only situation where organizations can pawn their work off onto customers and increase customer satisfaction. People love it on the Web. The first time customers download support documents in the middle of the night for a presentation that has to be ready first thing the next morning, they are ready to kiss you on the lips.

Everybody wants self-service across his or her entire relationship with organizations. Once people on the spider chart have gone to the trouble of serving themselves for one interaction with an organization, they will want to serve themselves on *everything* they have to do with that organization. They don't want to have to look up product information on the Web, call their salesperson for order status, and then call the service department to schedule installation. They want to be able to access product information (marketing), their order status (sales), build schedule (production), shipping date (fulfillment), installation time (service), and billing terms (administration) on their own. Think of it as a window that lets customers see into every cubicle in the office.

Self-service requires systems that allow any constituent in the spider chart to take on all of the roles in the organization. Leveraging what we learned in Chapter 4, this is the ultimate caseworker situation, but with a major twist. Work isn't consolidated for employees to handle end-to-end. With a self-service philosophy, customers are their own caseworkers. Web-based self-service requires processes and systems where no one from the organization handles the relationship end-to-end. Once customers have the ability to access and modify information about an entire process by themselves, every constituent in the spider chart can potentially do the same thing.

Figure 5-1 shows an example customer portal screen. In this illustration, customers can access all the information including:

- Accounts
- Trouble tickets
- Orders
- Contact relationships
- Historical interaction reports
- Interaction to-do's
- Performance reporting
- General business and industry news, weather, etc., based upon content and layout customization

Figure 5-1. Customer portal personalization.

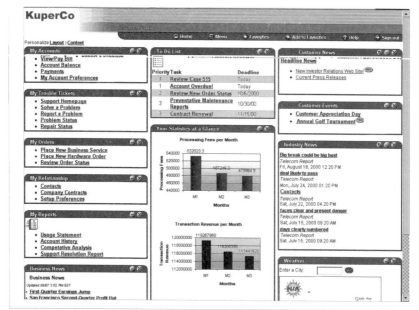

So this customer portal screen involves billing, accounts payable, support, service, e-commerce, contact management, time management, statistics, and general consumer news. The same behind-the-screen systems that provide this to customers can readily be made available to workers.

The problem in implementing a one-person-for-all-interactions philosophy is that organizations are stuck between two incompatible structures. Internally, there is a reporting hierarchy, division of work among departments, and process data spread all throughout the organization. Externally, the IT group is trying to build systems, such as the portal examples, that integrate information and workflow into a single view for the big four constituents in the spider chart (employees, customers, partners, and suppliers.)

Once externally-facing self-service systems are built, the traditional internal structure no longer makes sense. The systems architecture that allows a single customer to take on multiple roles and follow a transaction throughout its entire cycle should also enable employees to take on the same multiple roles. After getting past the security concerns of who should be allowed to do what, everyone in the spider chart can potentially interact in every process. It's a matter of understanding what roles must be implemented.

The Business Cycle

In a 1993 training video, Rath & Strong consultants John Guaspari and Edward Hay teach how to create a value-added process flow chart.[1] They recommend selecting an object, such as paperwork, and following that object through its entire life from origination through archival storage. This is similar to Hammer and Champy's IBM Credit example, where two vice presidents walked an application for financing through their system.[2] What results is a series of steps that can then be evaluated for whether they add value to the customer. In particular, moving the item from one department or one employee to another is non–value-added.

A special flowchart is used to visually document complex processes that cross departmental boundaries. Figure 5-2 shows how process steps can be charted separately by department and interactions among departments can be easily identified. Early customer-facing systems did little more than facilitate these interactions with notification rules so that nothing was inadvertently dropped in the transfer. The basic function of the process remained the same.

Figure 5-2. Traditional processes.

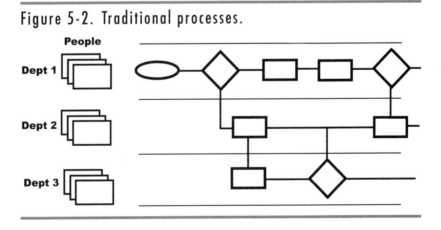

Figure 5-3. Reengineered processes.

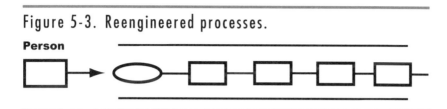

Reengineering would have that process changed into Figure 5-3, where there are fewer steps and all of them are done by a single person (or within a single team.) As we have seen, this isn't the best approach with today's systems and customers' demand for self-service. Why? Because there is a universal customer truth:

No customer process stays within one department.

The relational structure must allow an individual to take on multiple roles and interface with a variety of processes at different points in their cycles, as shown in Figure 5-4.

Actually, Figure 5-4 isn't accurate because it still shows processes as separate end-to-end islands. The correct way to analyze work is to

Figure 5-4. Roles-based processes.

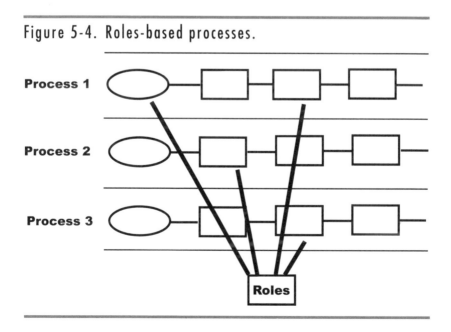

use the flow of a relationship. The stages of a process, the various places a roles-based interaction can take place, make up the "business cycle."

The relational business cycle shown in Figure 5-5 consists of seven stages. The market, sell, and service stages are outward facing—typically called front-office functions. Produce, fulfill, administer, and analyze are inward facing—typically called back-office functions.

Remember the concept of roles in reading the following descriptions of the phases. As Figure 5-4 shows, one worker can take on multiple roles and interact at multiple stages of the business cycle. Conversely, many different individuals (or roles) can interact at a single stage of the cycle. With roles, there is not a one-to-one relationship between people and stages as there is with the traditional "1 person = 1 job = 1 function" organizational structure.

The seven stages of the business cycle are defined below.

MARKET
This is the beginning of the cycle and focuses on demand creation and the initial sales effort. Organizational roles involved in the Market

Figure 5-5. The business cycle.

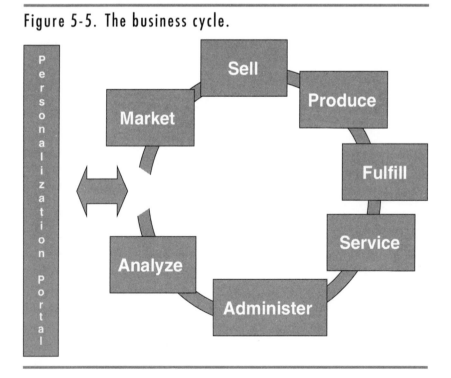

stage include: production planning, product/service marketing, inside sales, outside sales, and partners. Market stage functions cover:

- Creating marketing campaigns
- Converting leads generated by marketing into qualified prospects
- Coordinating sales efforts with partners
- Providing data for inventory, production, and personnel planning processes

SELL

The Sell stage focuses on demand fulfillment and revenue generation. Organizational roles involved in this stage include: financial forecasting, inside sales, outside sales, order management, inventory control, customer support, field service, billing, and partners. The customer role also requires self-service: configuration, e-store, order entry, payment, order tracking, and support. Sell stage functions cover:

- Use of sales data for forecasting and production planning
- Inside, outside, and partner sales-force automation
- Product configuration for salespeople and self-service prospects
- E-store site for shopping, ordering, and payment
- Ubiquitous access to inventory data to ensure order fulfillment
- Complete information on order status
- Support call center and self-service Web site
- Mobile field service
- Partner integration with all of the above Sell processes

PRODUCE

The Produce stage deals with the goods and services of the organization. This can include the roles of: demand planning, order management, supply chain planning, manufacturing, quality control, supplier, and partners. Self-service applications are: e-store, supplier, and reporting. Produce stage functions include:

- Accessing order and production status
- Accessing information on quality, understanding the drivers/ problems, and providing data for defect prevention programs

FULFILL

The Fulfill stage addresses the satisfactory delivery of products and services to customers. Roles for this stage include: outside sales, order management, supply chain planning, materials management, inventory management, billing, warehousing, shipping, and partners. Fulfill stage functions include:

- Processing orders and ensuring that specified products or services are delivered
- Making certain that inventory is on hand and that products and services can be provided when requested
- Making the order and delivery status information available in real-time
- Providing data to order promising functions for consignment inventories and off-site fulfillment. Self-service needs are: e-store, order promising, billing, and shipping and delivery tracking
- Billing accurately while meeting the terms and conditions of the purchase order

SERVICE

The Service stage makes certain that products and services meet both order specifications and the expectations of customers. Roles can include: outside sales, field service, support, inventory management, asset and configuration management, quality control, contracting, legal, and partners. Employee-facing roles can include: help desk, asset management, and benefits administration. There are self-service requirements: inventory, service, support, help desk, and benefits. Functions for the Service stage include:

- Providing support and help from both agents and through self-service

- Creating and resolving service cases and problem reports

- Keeping track of warranties, service entitlements, and service level agreements

- Scheduling installation and dispatching service

- Notifying and escalating service issues according to workflow policies and contractual service agreements

- Tracking order, billing, and service histories by customer and product

- Matching workload to manpower, and training service providers when needed

- Managing and making information available on multiple layers of new, used, and spare parts inventory from warehouse, sub-warehouse, truck, depot, and customer locations

- Providing input for the continual quality improvement of products and services

ADMINISTER

The Administer stage involves the widest range of organizational roles: support, service, help desk, procurement, contracting, personnel, accounting, finance, billing, accounts receivable, accounts payable, payroll, project management, treasury management, advisers, third-party regulators, and partners. Self-service functions include billing and procurement. In addition to the standard tasks of running an organization, functions in the Administer stage include:

- Storing and sharing data from all interaction channels, such as in-person, phone, fax, wireless device, mail, e-mail, dynamic chat, Web site messages, application integration, and electronic data interchange

- Updating and accessing billing and receivables information

- Updating and accessing contract and warranty information

- Updating, accessing, and integrating suppliers with warranty claims and payables information

- Entering trouble tickets for IT support
- Updating personnel records, benefits, and payroll status
- Supporting the new hire process

ANALYZE

Although customer transactions end with the Administer stage, the work of the organization is not complete until after the Analyze stage. Analysis closes the loop on customer transactions and feeds the next cycle beginning with marketing. Roles involved in the Analyze stage include nearly every role mentioned in the previous stages. Analysis must be done in the following areas:

- Balanced scorecard measures
- Marketing effectiveness
- Sales effectiveness
- Customer profitability
- Project management
- Support effectiveness
- Analytic forecasting accuracy
- Asset liability status
- Supplier performance
- Supply chain management
- Quality standards attainment

This description of business cycle roles is extensive, but not exactly scintillating fireside reading. Its purpose is to explain what Figure 5-4 tries to show graphically, that the business cycle requires the involvement of many roles across the entire organization. There is no way a single person or small team can perform all of the functions listed above for any one business cycle process. Yet this is the "holy grail" of organizational improvement.

The second point is to show that many different roles are involved at each stage. Truly, the business cycle does not stay within one department. Since no department can "own" the end-to-end cycle, then no one owns customer satisfaction. For one person to handle an entire stage of the cycle, that person must be able to perform in all the roles defined for that stage. This sounds almost impossible to accomplish, but can be done with integrated systems and a unified portal interface to a complete range of enterprise data.

Examples of this are salespeople who have a stand-alone sales force automation tool. They are busy following up on leads, qualifying prospects, making sales calls, proposing, and closing orders—the Sell stage activities. But there are many other factors that can affect the sales receptivity of a prospect or client. Every salesperson has had the disheartening experience of showing up for a presentation only to find out that the customer has had an ongoing service disaster with currently installed products. Or perhaps there is an active billing dispute, or an order has been lost in delivery. To be completely effective, salespeople also need access to production, financial, and service data.

The third purpose of the list is to illustrate how single roles are involved at many different stages of the cycle, but not in every stage. Instead of handling a process from end-to-end, participants in a relational organization jump in and out of a process's business cycle as required. Whatever IT systems are in place, they had better do an excellent job of getting these occasional participants up to speed quickly concerning what has happened since their previous involvement with a customer.

Finally, where are the divisions between back-office and front-office functions in this description of the business cycle? Most organizations consider back office and front office to be separate and distinct functional areas, each with their own systems and software. Enterprise resource planning (ERP) systems run the back office, and customer relationship management systems (CRM and eCRM) bring the front office to life. As the business cycle description shows, front-office and back-office roles are required at every stage of the cycle. To the customers, there is no front-office/back-office split. It's all one interaction process. Their attitude is, "Just find me somebody who can take the lousy $2.75 off of my bill. I don't care if it's the janitor."

Summary

Organizing a relational enterprise around roles and the business cycle introduced in this chapter creates three important service capabilities:

1. It enables one-role specialists to contribute wherever needed in the cycle.

2. It supports multirole generalists who stick with an internal or external customer from Sell through Analyze.

3. It provides the data needed by various roles when jumping into the middle stage of a cycle.

As we will see in the next chapter, real satisfaction improvements come about when internal or external customers can be served by the first person they contact. This requires all three of these service capabilities.

Learning Points

1. Customers, whether internal or external, want self-service. Perhaps this is a function of how poor service is in general, or maybe it's a matter of convenience.

2. There is a multistage business cycle that customers follow throughout an individual transaction with the organization. Back-office/front-office distinctions disappear in this cycle.

3. Self-service systems must be able to provide customers with information about all seven business cycle stages.

4. Once integrated information can be provided for customers, it is also available to all spider chart constituents. The problem is that organizations are stuck with functionally segmented systems internally, while customers demand a fully integrated self-service capability externally.

5. People must take on multiple roles during a single stage of the cycle, and individual roles are required across multiple business cycle stages. Systems must be created to facilitate this process.

NOTES

1. John Guaspari and Edward Hay, *TIME: The Next Dimension of Quality,* videotape (Watertown: American Management Association, 1993), 18 minutes.

2. Michael Hammer and James Champy, *Reengineering the Corporation* (New York: HarperBusiness, 1993), pp. 36–9.

CHAPTER 6

Maximizing Interaction Satisfaction

It is the ultimate negotiating challenge. You walk into a store intent on returning a gift you don't want—let's say it's that teddy bear sweater that makes you look like a middle-aged Grateful Deadhead. There is just one small problem—you don't have a receipt. So you go up to the clerk, mention that the giver bought the sweater here at the store, and tell the clerk you want your money back.

What is the response? Of course you can't have your money back. You don't have a receipt. It's the store policy, written for your convenience in English and posted right up there on the wall in print too small to see. Sorry . . .

So you ask for the department manager. After a few minutes wait, she comes and explains much more sympathetically and in much more detail why you can't have your money back. You are shocked at the larcenous customers this retailer has to thwart, and are a bit irritated at the implication that, by asking for something that is clearly not allowed, you too may not be totally honest. In a well-run store, the manager will offer you credit. In a bad one, you will be hit over the head with the return policy until you retreat bleeding.

So you decide to go to the store manager. What's interesting is that store managers nearly always offer to return your money. They listen politely to your story, find out what the sweater cost, and immediately instruct a nearby clerk to process the refund, thanking you for your business. Why the turnaround? Because store managers understand your lifetime value and figure that if you are angry enough to go to the top, then you are mad enough to never come back if you aren't satisfied.

I've told this story to thousands of seminar attendees, many of them working for retailers. Everyone is nodding at this point at what appears to be a perfunctory lesson in good service. But most miss the point. Do you, the customer, walk out of that store happy? Satisfied with the service? Thrilled and appreciative that you managed to get that sweater out of your life and receive cash in the amount of its worth? Or do you walk out victorious, thumping your chest with a Carol Burnett Tarzan yell saying, "Yessssss . . . I beat those [expletive deleted] into the ground. I showed *them*!"

This interaction was an ultimate disaster for the retailer. It not only lost the customer's satisfaction, it also lost the money. Don't alienate customers and then give them the money, too. If you're going to totally aggravate the customer, by all means keep the money while you're at it. Then tell them to get their bottom out of your store and don't ever try to cheat you again.

You see, there is only one way to gain customer satisfaction in this situation. Give the customer a full refund immediately, smiling until it hurts. You are buying goodwill. You will have lost the money, but you will have gained a sweater that some dazed middle-aged hippy might buy off the discount table, and you have earned the customer's continued satisfaction and (it is hoped) loyalty. This is a critical service concept—essential for a successful relational enterprise. (Stomp, stomp.)

The minute you force customers to escalate their requests, you have thrown away any chance of satisfying them.

At this point, *they* begin taking on responsibility for their satisfaction, with your organization viewed as their adversary. In this example, the customer adopts the attitude that his own negotiating persistence was responsible for getting his money back, not the retailer's desire for good service.

Only the first person (or Web site) that customers contact can satisfy them. It's bad enough that most phone calls start with a lengthy and irritating series of menu choices that all customers hate, guaranteeing that they already start out in a bad mood.

Once customers are transferred around, or have to make multiple visits and calls, and messages have to be left or e-mails sent, customers start taking ownership for the ultimate result. The relational service rule is:

> *The systems and processes of a relational enterprise must all be designed so that a single individual can take on as many different roles during an interaction as required to satisfy the customer.*

No transfers, escalations, or deferred responses are allowed. Otherwise, just keep their money and tell them to quit contacting you, you're not buying any satisfaction anyway.

Measures of Interaction Satisfaction

A highly satisfying interaction has three characteristics: first contact resolution, successful resolution, and minimum time to resolution.

FIRST CONTACT RESOLUTION

As Figure 6-1 shows, satisfaction is inversely related to the number of contacts required or the number of people talked to until an appropriate resolution is reached.

Note that Figure 6-1 illustrates a range from satisfied to dissatisfied. The customer exchanging the sweater probably didn't walk out angry at the store, whereas Mom was so far down in the dissatisfied range with SLMM that she was in revenge mode. The only way to maximize satisfaction is to take care of customers, whether internal or external, with the first person, the first time, every time. This may be impossible to achieve, but it is the target for every interaction.

This is such an important satisfaction factor that one of Hewlett-Packard's support centers didn't count a "first call resolution" if there

Figure 6-1. The credit line.

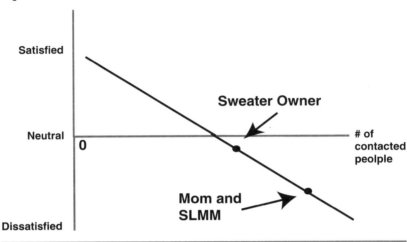

was a transfer to a second agent, even if the problem was eventually resolved in a single call. Hewlett-Packard's management recognized the reduction in satisfaction from having to repeat the problem to more than one person, regardless of whether resolution occurred during the same call.

SUCCESSFUL RESOLUTION

The second measure of a high-satisfaction interaction is *all incidents to resolution.* The driving force behind successful resolution of interactions should not be the persistence of a customer to keep nagging the vendor. Too many organizations operate in triage mode, overwhelmed with interactions and focusing only on customers who are deemed important or who are attracting an uncomfortable amount of attention from management. A relational enterprise should never let an incident hang on indefinitely, and it should never admit failure. Nothing should drop through the cracks.

Great Follow-Up Is the Only Recovery Option. A sub-issue is what happens when an incident cannot be resolved to the customer's satisfaction on the first call. Then the organization must follow through on whatever actions it promises to take in the interim. Customers should never make a second contact only to find out that no progress has been made. Service commitments should be kept every time, all the time. It's like the joke where an airplane hijacker tells the pilot, "Get this plane where it's supposed to go, and get us there on time!" Customers want organizations to keep their promises.

Follow-up as a critical satisfaction issue is supported by numerous customer studies. For example, a major commodity chemical manufacturer surveyed its buyers about what they wanted from the company. The list included all kinds of questions concerning sales calls, call frequency, service levels, additional consulting—that is, a long list of sophisticated services that the company might offer to create a competitive advantage. The company was surprised when "follow-up" was the number one customer priority. These chemical buyers didn't want to have to check up on commitments made by vendors.

An independent chemical industry survey had similar results. In 1994, *ChemicalWeek* and research firm IDSI tabulated questionnaires from 580 readers concerning customer satisfaction issues.[1] Although "Response to problems or requests" was ranked fifth in importance out of fifteen satisfaction criteria, it was one of only two items listed under "Areas for improvement: high importance/low satisfaction."

Follow-up has long been a priority for customers. In the late 1970s and early 1980s, *Purchasing* magazine published results of an annual contest where readers were invited to nominate outstanding sales representatives. Respondents were asked to identify the top three characteristics of these reps, and winners and their customers were later interviewed. A content analysis of the entries from 1977 through 1983 was performed, and the frequencies for traits listed by readers were computed. "Thoroughness and follow through" was the top rated attribute, mentioned by an average of 65 percent of buyers.[2]

A study of 249 purchasing, engineering, and operations buyers from the electric utility industry found that "Reliability" was ranked number one out of ten preferences for salesperson competence.[3]

In a 1993 survey of sixty medium and small sized industrial firms, managers who purchased industrial products and services in a major metropolitan area ranked "Follow-through skills" of vendors as the most important of ten possible attributes.[4]

In case we haven't beaten this to death, an analysis conducted in the early 1990s by Ameritech Information Systems' Sales Academy identified "Ability to carry out promises" as one the top four customer requirements its people needed to improve upon.[5]

This recurring high ranking suggests two things. First, customers believe follow-up is important. Second, they probably aren't getting acceptable follow-up performance, or else the item wouldn't consistently be a top priority for the last twenty-five years. Taking all interactions to resolution means that systems and processes are in place to guarantee that whatever role the incident requires can be fulfilled.

TIME TO RESOLUTION

The third measure of an excellent interaction is *time to resolution*. Internally this is a productivity measure of total amount of worker time needed to resolve the incident. This includes both contact time with the customer and any off-line work done between contacts about the incident. Externally, this is the clock or calendar time from the customer's viewpoint between the initial contact and ultimate resolution. A service agent might work on a particular incident for an hour, but the activities involved could take place over a period of weeks. The goal is always to spend less time resolving incidents, and to resolve them quicker for the customer. These are two separate measurements.

Satisfaction Through a Roles-Based Structure

For support or help-desk managers, so far this chapter is Call Center 101. Many of the satisfaction measures may already be in center performance reports, even if the organization's service systems and processes aren't built to optimize them. For the rest of the spider chart, this may be revolutionary. Within general service, there is an endless succession of unanswered phones, useless voice mail announcements, and unreturned calls, letters, faxes, and e-mails. As a result, service follow-up falls into an organizational black hole never to be seen again, and success comes only to the loudest and most insistent customers.

Overlay these satisfaction criteria with the business cycle of Chapter 5, where individual roles appear throughout the cycle and many roles are necessary at each stage of the cycle. How does this map to people? From a service standpoint, if indeed many roles are required at each stage and customers require first-call resolution, then it is clear that constituents in the spider chart are going to have to be able to take on multiple roles.

This creates brand new problems for the organization. Does St. Louis Merciful Medical want nursing or the patient's advocate writing off $2.75 bills? How about $275.00 bills? Even if they wish to allow any employee to write off bills below a certain amount, what systems will it take to enable them to do it?

The questions have already been answered in other industries. One major luxury hotel chain empowers *every* employee to issue up to $2,000.00 in credit to maintain guest satisfaction. It takes some training along with the authority. As management consultant Jim Robertson observes, "You don't give a shotgun to a six year old." Yet a front desk clerk can issue a room service food credit if it is required to maintain guest satisfaction. A cleaning associate vacuuming a hallway rug at this hotel chain can open the gift shop and record a cash sale. I've seen it happen.

Expand this concept throughout the relational enterprise. What does it take to make this level of service possible? Remember, the customers we are referring to are not just buyers of our products and services. They include everybody involved in the spider chart who is a beneficiary of any internal or external process. This could be employees, strangers down the supply-chain line who are using the portal for e-commerce, or sales partners interacting along the entire business cycle.

Summary

High satisfaction service goals are:

1. To complete all customer interactions
2. Within a single contact
3. As quickly as possible

Where single contact resolution isn't possible, follow-up activities must be completed, as promised, on time, and without the customer having to remind the organization or verify the results. Being passed on to multiple individuals, no matter how necessary, reduces or eliminates customer satisfaction. Why? Because customers start crediting themselves and not the organization with the success of the interaction, and time to resolution is extended.

Systems and processes in a relational enterprise must allow the first person contacted to satisfy customers, no matter where that contact resides in the organization. This isn't carrying a process through end-to-end a la reengineering, it is being able to contribute to a process anywhere along the business cycle, and in a variety of roles. This means that the relational organization must be stocked primarily with generalists, and the old departmental divisions of work and clear lines of decision-making authority are obsolete.

What is needed is a way to open up the entire organization, front office, back office, e-office, spider chart office, and so on, throughout the entire business cycle. The term often used to describe this is one of the most used and least understood concepts in business today, the "360-degree view of the customer."

Learning Points

1. The only person who can satisfy a customer, whether internal or external, is the first person contacted. After that, the customer starts taking credit for the service result.

2. It makes no sense to aggravate customers with a bad process, then give them what they asked for in the first place. Either serve immediately and buy customer goodwill, or reject immediately without spending any money. Living in the middle, giving poor service before ultimately satisfying, loses both the money and the goodwill.

3. Three goals for a high satisfaction interaction are: first-call resolution, all incidents resolved, and quick resolution.

4. Follow-up is a top priority with customers. If you promise it, it must happen as promised without fail, and happen without reminders from the customer.

5. The three interaction goals are impossible for a traditionally structured organization to meet. Appropriate systems don't

exist, and lines of departmental authority and responsibility keep workers from taking on multiple roles throughout the stages of the business cycle.

NOTES

1. Elizabeth S. Kiesche, "CW-IDSI Survey: Customers Satisfied—Barely," *Chemical Week,* April 6, 1994, pp. 68–9.

2. Alvin J. Williams and John Seminerio, "What Buyers Like from Salesmen," *Industrial Marketing Management,* 1984, pp. 75–8.

3. H. Michael Hayes and Steven W. Hartley, "How Buyers View Industrial Salespeople," *Industrial Marketing Management,* 1989, pp. 73–80.

4. S. Joe Puri, "Where Industrial Sales Training Is Weak," *Industrial Marketing Management,* 1993, pp. 101–8.

5. Jim Cusimano, "Ameritech Sales Training Turns Tradition Upside Down," *Marketing News,* September 14, 1992, pp. 34–5.

CHAPTER 7

A Second Generation Definition of 360-Degree View

I love to snowboard, because it's like sledding except that you don't have to walk back up the hill. This year we were riding the back bowl at a Colorado summit area resort, and found out they had a sno-cat that would take anyone up the backside of the bowl where there were no trails or lifts. At the end of the ride there was a thirty minute walk up across the ridges until we reached one of the highest points in the area. You had to be determined, because the air is thin at the 12,500-foot height of the path.

Once there, we were stunned, mostly by the foot-slogging, lung-searing hike but also by the vista. Talk about a 360-degree view. We stood there, turning around, seeing thousands of feet down in every direction. Highway 70 was a thin ribbon glimpsed between the slopes. We were glad that a couple of our friends had chosen not to join us. We thought it was exciting, but they would have needed tranquilizers and a ski patrol sled to get off the mountain. It was a spectacular view, but it would have been sensory overload for them. There was just too much mountain at too high a difficulty.

You can see where this analogy is headed. Put yourself in the "ski boots" of a customer interfacing with a financial institution like Bank of America, with its 156,000 employees. Where do you start? Whom do you seek out for service? If you are an employee, what is the right department to which to refer this caller? Once there, where do you start within this department?

With the advent of voice mail and the obsolescence of receptionists, figuring out the entry point in a complex organization is nearly impossible. And it is even more confusing when dealing with a spider chart of separate companies or agencies. Workers don't know their own organization and procedures well enough, much less those of other companies, and customers don't know enough to ask for the right directions.

A true relational enterprise provides customers and workers with the ability to see each other through every stage of the business cycle. Think of it as looking down the mountain and also looking up. The label used is a "360-degree view of the customer." This is one of the most overhyped and least understood concepts in business today.

A Bidirectional 360-Degree View

A 360-degree view, often equated with customer relationship management (CRM), is typically defined as "providing everyone in the organization with a consistent view of the customer." This is one of those definitions that sounds vaguely helpful but doesn't convey much. What does a "consistent view of the customer" mean? Should we be thinking only about a customer view? What about an enterprise view?

The first question to clear up when talking about 360-degree view is, whose eyes are we looking through? The most common definition is the one above, that we are referring to the enterprise's view of the customer. This requires effectively capturing customer data and sharing it throughout the spider chart. As we learned in Chapter 6, this single-enterprise view of a customer requires different roles to add value at various stages of the business cycle.

Some organizations, mostly those at the leading edge of Web technology, are focusing on the reverse, "a customer's view of the enterprise." Self-service Internet systems distill the entire enterprise into a single view, so that customers can work their way through the business cycle on their own. In addition, customers want a single point of contact within the organization who can take their issues to resolution on the initial contact.

These two viewpoints are both first generation customer concepts. By that we mean that these definitions of 360-degree view are relatively unsophisticated beginning points. Getting all customer data into one coherent system so that everyone can access it is an important starting point, but it doesn't provide much of a value-add to the organization. The real issue is what that view can help an enterprise accomplish. Providing consistent customer data is a feature, not an advantage.

(Stomp, stomp.) The second-generation definition is:

360-Degree View: *Treat customers throughout the business cycle based on their lifetime profitability.*

It's not enough to provide consistent data. So what? The leverage is in what the data enables workers to *do* while serving customers, and what it enables customers to do with self-service. In the search for revenue growth throughout the 1990s, many organizations lost sight of profitability.

Lifetime Customer Profitability

Lifetime customer value has been a fundamental building block of customer service systems for many years now. Carl Sewell of Sewell Cadillac in Dallas wrote about his typical $332,000 customer—the cost of twelve luxury cars plus associated service revenue.[1] Grocery retailers know that the typical consumer shops at three locations, and spends an average of $100 per week at a favorite store. With an average time between moves of seven years, the lifetime revenue of a grocery customer is over $36,000.

Note that the definition of 360-degree view focuses on lifetime customer *profitability*, not revenue or value. Revenue is the wrong measure. It's like the old New England farmer who was asked what he'd do if he ever won a million dollars in the lottery. "Well," he said, "I'd just keep on farming 'til it's all gone." As many Japanese companies found out in the 1990s, and the dot-coms found out at the end of the decade, the long-term pursuit of market share ultimately had to be supported by a profit stream.

Value is also the wrong measure. Look it up in the dictionary. Value focuses on worth or exchange. Profit is a measure of excess. Customers pay more for something than it costs to give it to them. (As comedian Yakov Smirnoff would say, "What a country!") The more profitable the relationship, the more vendors can do for customers.

There are three major goals of profitable relationships. The first is to make existing profitable customers more profitable. This is accomplished by one-to-one marketing in cross-selling and up-selling existing customers. The second is to acquire additional profitable customers. This is a function of customer profiling and target marketing. The third is to turn unprofitable customers into profitable ones. This can be accomplished again by cross-selling and up-selling. It also means doing analysis to understand individual profiles, and then identifying and chasing away (or sending to competitors) customers who will never be profitable.

This second-generation definition seems like a small distinction, yet defining "360-degree view" properly can prevent miscues. I had the chance to talk to two bankers while teaching a seminar in Australia. When we got to the lifetime customer profitability issue, they mentioned that their bank had just spent millions of dollars on a marketing campaign to acquire 10,000 new customers. The bank had met its goals with just one minor problem. The customers were mostly consumer accounts and, on average, about 60 percent of individual accounts are unprofitable.

Certainly, this bank had the opportunity to cross-sell and move as many of the 6,000 unprofitable accounts into profitability as possible. Yet it would have been far more beneficial for the bank to understand who its current profitable customers were, profile them, figure out to reach more of them, and then target a tailored campaign to attract them. The bank spent millions of dollars to increase their losses. And the marketing group probably received a bonus for meeting goals.

What were they expecting? Four thousand profitable accounts are more than offset by 6,000 unprofitable ones. As far as lifetime customer profitability, the two attendees said that the bank had no idea how many of the new customers would ever reach profitability. There had never been any data collected to use in making projections. It's like the old

Saturday Night Live TV commercial parody for the "Change Bank." How does a financial institution make money when its sole service is making change? Volume!

This focus on lifetime profitability rather than on value, revenue, or even a simple consolidated view, has at least four implications:

1. The first issue is personalization, which means more than adjusting to buying preferences. Different customers have different lifetime profitabilities, and therefore will deserve different levels of service from every person and each Web site in the enterprise.

2. Some sort of analytical system must be in place to individually project and measure profitability by customer.

3. This information must be delivered to everyone involved in the business cycle throughout the spider chart so that they can continuously make customer service decisions based on profitability.

4. The potential benefits in service and pricing when customers increase their profitability to the organization must be communicated to customers.

360-Degree View and the Business Cycle

The best way to understand the 360-degree concept is by linking it to the business cycle. Many system vendors are describing their offerings as giving organizations a 360-degree view of customers, when the actual coverage is far less.

A 1999 META Group survey of a hundred companies involved in customer relationship management found that although most organizations wanted to buy integrated systems, many were actually installing line-of-business point solutions.[3] There are a number of factors behind this. No software vendor can be best-of-breed in every functional category. Enterprise-wide integrated systems are extremely difficult to design and implement. And enterprise customers are still organized into line-of-business and departmental structures that resist the levels of integration required for a 360-degree view.

META Group found that a majority of organizations had implemented at least one customer relationship system, most often the service function. As Figure 7-1 shows, implementing any single CRM application—such as sales force automation (SFA), service/support, or field service—provides only a 30-degree view of the customer. This single application approach is called a "point solution"—meeting one department's needs without worrying about the bigger integration picture.

Our catch phrase for this approach is, "Point solutions—you get to do it right next time." Stand-alone solutions that address just a single stage in the business cycle provide only *localized value* to the enterprise. This is because they attempt to solve one problem at a time, often with

Figure 7-1. Local value 30-degree view.

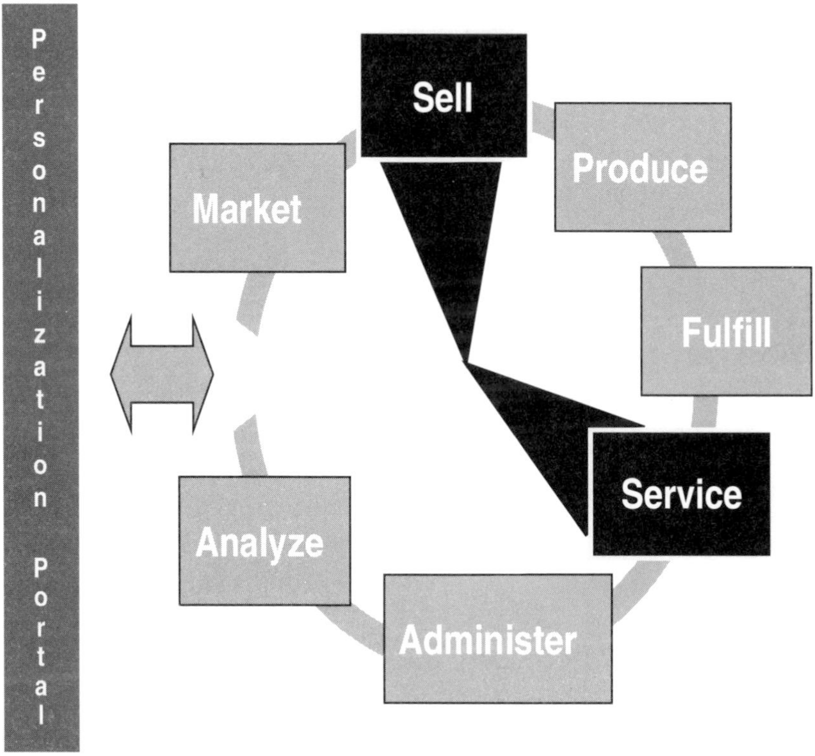

incompatible systems from different vendors. For this reason, analysts predict that most point solution vendors will either go out of business or become acquired, and existing process automation systems will have to be gutted within two years.[4]

As shown in Figure 7-2, even combined solutions such as marketing/SFA, or support/service offer only a 60-degree localized value view of the customer. While there is some synergy between pairs of applications, only a small portion of the business cycle is addressed by such a system. And a 360-degree self-service view is impossible because only a small portion of the customer cycle is addressed.

The current approach of software vendors is to offer a CRM application suite that is touted to offer a full 360-degree view of the customer. However, a CRM suite alone actually represents only a 90-degree customer view. As Figure 7-3 shows, CRM suites still cover only a portion of necessary business cycle stages.

This is why a stand-alone CRM suite delivers only *reactive value* to the enterprise. The problem is that the applications in a CRM suite

Figure 7-2. Local value 60-degree view.

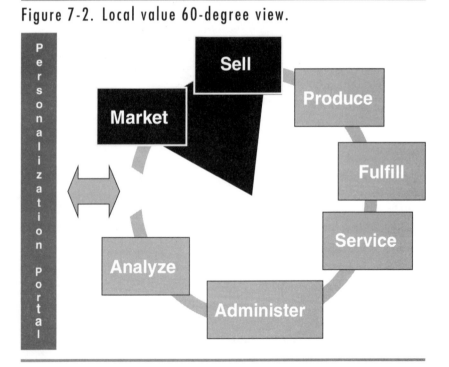

Figure 7-3. Reactive value 90-degree view.

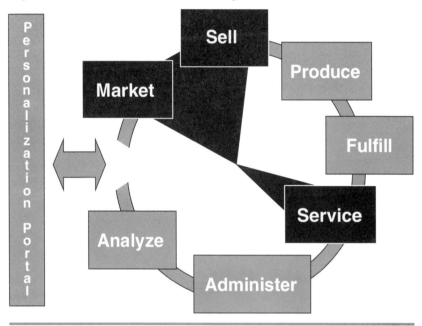

deal with "lagging data" in an after-the-fact manner. The first indicator is that most of the data is inputed by CRM end-users themselves. Recording the results of a sales call, creating a service trouble ticket, or providing quality improvement feedback are all examples of lagging activities. CRM helps employees deal with customer incidents after they have occurred. While the use of any CRM application will generate some operational benefits, business results will never be optimized solely through the use of a CRM suite. At best it provides only a 90-degree view and facilitates the ability to react to events after they have already happened.

A true 360-degree view is obtained by encompassing all stages of the business cycle as shown in Figure 7-4. This approach incorporates data from both the back office and front office, and then combines it with analysis so that employees can add *proactive value*. The result is that people in various roles can anticipate a customer's sales and service needs, leverage analysis information to target marketing campaigns, link to buying histories and billing information, and see the customer's entire relationship with the organization in order to make better service deci-

Figure 7-4. Proactive value 360-degree view.

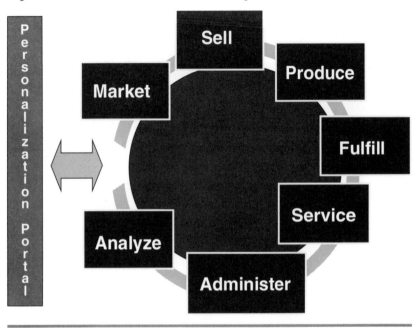

sions. A true 360-degree view also lets customers serve themselves throughout the entire cycle and take their own proactive measures.

Summary

"360-degree view" is one of the hottest concepts in the area of customer relationships. Everyone is talking about it, but no one really understands what "a consistent view of the customer" means. A better definition focuses on allowing everyone in the organization to be proactive with customers based upon their lifetime profitability. A 360-degree view is also required to enable what customers are demanding—self-service throughout the entire business cycle. Every constituent in the spider chart must be operating using the same definition of 360-degree view, whether from the organization out or from the customer in.

In this chapter we've introduced another term that is confusing to many people, customer relationship management. This, too, needs an updated definition, and it is the subject of the next chapter.

Learning Points

1. Today's organizations are overwhelming to customers. Figuring out how to interact with an enterprise is like starting novice skiers out on double black diamond slopes.

2. A 360-degree view goes both ways. Every constituent in the spider chart should be able to see customer information from every stage of the business cycle. Conversely, customers should be able to find their way around any part of the relational enterprise at every business cycle stage.

3. A 360-degree view is far more than making customer data available to whomever. Every action taken by the organization (or customer) must be based upon the lifetime profitability of the relationship.

4. While automating any stage of the process provides some value, true 360-degree views maximize profitable relationships throughout the cycle.

5. The goal is to create systems with proactive value rather than lagging (reactive) or localized (departmental) value. The only way to do this is by providing integrated functionality at every stage of the business cycle.

NOTES

1. Carl Sewell and Paul B. Brown, *Customers for Life: How to Turn That One-Time Buyer into a Lifetime Customer* (New York: PocketBooks, 1990), pp. 161–2.

2. META Group and IMT Strategies, "Customer Relationship Management (CRM) Study 1999: Sponsor Report," September 22, 1999, p. 9.

3. META Group, "META Group CRM Conference," February 21, 2000.

4. Jeff Sweat, Rich Whiting, and Beth Bacheldor, "Analysis: The Missing Piece of the Puzzle," *InformationWeek*, April 17, 2000, p. 28.

CHAPTER 8

Expanding the Definition of CRM

Teaching seminars is a lot more fun than giving speeches because a training session allows two-way communication. I frequently learn as much from my audiences as I hope they do from me. Plus, if they make an insightful comment or funny ad-lib, I can steal it and use it in succeeding seminars and everyone will think I'm that much more clever. (Remember, if Robin Hood had been a consultant, he would have stolen from the rich and *sold* to the poor.) It's easier to find a new audience than new material.

In one session I was extolling the necessities of a relational enterprise, talking specifically about the changes in customer relationship management. A curmudgeonly executive sitting there with a sour look on his face finally said, "Look, I don't need a group hug with vendors. I just want to buy something and be left alone."

Fortunately, everyone in the session laughed, giving me a few moments to sort through the real issues. It was clear that my response had to leverage the concept of a 360-degree view throughout the entire business cycle. I replied, "So you've bought your product. Would you like to know about related items that might make your purchase more useful? Do you want the right product delivered on time? Do you want to be billed correctly? Would you like to get discounts because you're a frequent buyer? What happens if it doesn't work? Would it be nice to know how to reach a real person who can handle any problem on the first call, or find a Web site so that you can take care of it yourself? If so, then you had better buy from someone with a true CRM system."

Over the long term, CRM is not an option. Much like TQM, it will be a requirement to stay competitive, a ticket to get in the game. The differentiator will not be who is doing CRM, but who's doing it best. This is why META Group and IMT Strategies discovered in their 1999 study that nearly two thirds of firms implementing CRM had no clear measurements in place to assess their installation.[1]

Part of this is because CRM is still very early in the adoption cycle. A 2001 survey by Data Warehousing Institute of 1,516 business executives and IT managers found that only 7 percent of respondents had a "mature" CRM system in place. An additional 8 percent had recently completed implementations. The remaining 85 percent ranged from having no plans to deploy CRM, to being in various stages of planning, development, or rollout.[2] Many organizations have CRM in their business plan, but are struggling to make it happen and then figure out what it has done for them.

In-Use Definitions of CRM

Before getting too much further into CRM, it's time for a very basic checkpoint, because there is confusion as to exactly what CRM is. The META/IMT Strategies report pointed out that respondents had no consensus definition of CRM, with individuals from even the same company holding inconsistent or contradictory views.[3] According to the report, the respondents held six different views of CRM:

- **360-Degree View of the Customer.** META/IMT Strategies uses a second-generation definition of CRM: "enabling a better understanding of customer lifecycles and profitability." It is important to note that this definition is held by less than one-third of respondents, so there is extensive education required to get the entire organization thinking in terms of lifetime profitability.

- **Quality of Interaction.** This leverages classic TQM principles concerning customer service. The theme is that every interaction should meet customers' needs and expectations. This should be done across all possible contact channels.

- **Tools and Technologies.** Some viewed CRM as a set of features and functionality that delivered improved service and efficiencies. This is the systems view, with the tools including processes and front-office applications to serve customers.

- **Organizational Shift.** This group saw CRM as a shift in philosophy from a product or internal focus to a customer orientation. This includes everything from organizing around customers rather than product lines to shifting the focus from physical assets to customers as assets.

- **Pushing Customer Data.** This is a tactical view of customer information delivery. The goal is to get the right data out to customer-facing employees at their points of interaction. This is akin to our first-generation definition of 360-degree view of the customer.

- **Buzzword.** A skeptical few saw CRM as the latest fad, at best a new label for database marketing. Their view was that relational information provides the value and that current systems already exist to accomplish this.

Table 8-1 shows the percent of respondents using each of the above definitions. Notice that no single definition has even a majority usage. So the first thing organizations have to do when talking about CRM is to make certain everyone is working from the same conceptual base. Settling on the 360-degree view and its profit implications is a good start, but now it's time to explore CRM in further detail. Again, we will use an absolutely-on-target META Group definition, and it holds a number of surprises in its scope.

Table 8-1. Definitions of CRM.

DEFINITION	PERCENTAGE OF RESPONDENTS USING
360-degree view of the customer	29%
Quality of interaction	27%
Tools and technologies	22%
Pushing customer data	14%
Organizational shift	20%
Buzzword	6%

Source: META Group/IMT Strategies, 1999.

Three Kinds of CRM

CRM addresses elements of five of the above customer definitions: lifetime value, quality service, systems, customer data, and leadership attitudes. But CRM is now much more than that. We have used the term "business cycle" to refer to an end-to-end transaction relationship. META Group uses the term "customer lifecycle" for the overall interaction relationship over time. Managing both is necessary to maximize lifetime customer profitability.

META has developed a conceptual framework called the "CRM Technological Eco-system."[4] This framework, shown in Figure 8-1, consists of three categories: Operational CRM, Collaborative CRM, and Analytical CRM. This definition is becoming accepted in the industry and is starting to be seen as an acknowledged standard in the trade literature.[5]

- **Collaborative CRM** consists of technologies to ensure enterprise/customer interaction across all contact channels, such as in-person, phone, electronic, and wireless. The collaborative infrastructure provides access to people, processes, and data across the entire spider chart.

- **Operational CRM** provides the biggest surprise, with its inclusion of back-office and legacy applications under operational

Figure 8-1. Three types of CRM.

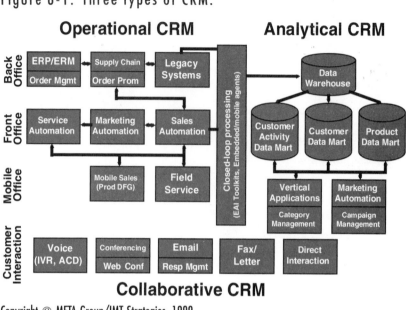

Copyright © META Group/IMT Strategies, 1999.

CRM. Customer relationship management and front office have always been considered synonymous, with the two terms being used interchangeably. META Group is now saying that front-office and back-office distinctions disappear when considering the entire customer lifecycle. They are all elements of an overall customer-facing system.

- **Analytical CRM** is what delivers the profitability payoff. Analytics takes the mass of relationship data throughout the relational enterprise and puts it into a form that can be used to add proactive value. This means that operational results, product information, and marketing data must be integrated using data warehousing and reporting tools.

There are parts of Figure 8-1 that have not been addressed—a single box and the connector lines. Although not labeled as a separate function, integrating the three types of CRM is an essential requirement. Enterprise application integration (EAI) tools are needed to connect front-office applications to each other, to ERP systems, to legacy systems, to the collaboration infrastructure, and to the analytics engine.

Consolidation Into RM

What are the implications of defining CRM using META Group's technology eco-system? Right now the main requirement is for integration of diverse systems. If the application scope consists of the entire business cycle throughout the extended enterprise spider chart, then the distinctions between internal/external and front office/back office go away. As both ERP and CRM applications mature and move towards commodities, a new class of solution that addresses all relationships will emerge. Figure 8-2 shows the conceptual roadmap. The various customer initiatives of the past twenty years are heading towards a single philosophical and technological toolset.

It all started with customer service and support (CSS) approaches. This includes adopting a customer satisfaction focus as a core competency, instituting TQM's continuous quality improvement of processes

Figure 8-2. Relation management.

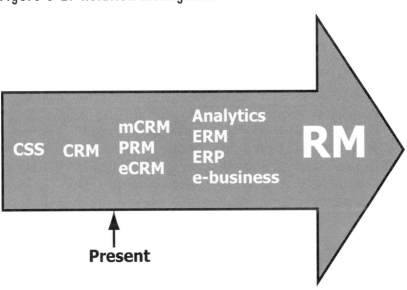

to raise satisfaction, applying value-added flow analysis, and implementing reengineering to improve processes. This also encompasses specific, local value customer service applications, such as customer hotlines or scheduling field service calls. These systems were forerunners of multifunction CRM applications.

The next stage is customer relationship management (CRM). This term is generally applied to both point solutions that offer comprehensive functionality for a single CRM application (sales force automation, marketing, support, help desk, field service, and quality) and to suites that integrate these front-office applications. Based upon the Data Warehousing Institute study mentioned earlier in this chapter, most organizations are currently somewhere between CRM point solutions and integrated suites.

There are a number of other *RMs being discussed, and organizations are making forays here and there into the technologies. Mobile CRM (mCRM) addresses extending CRM functionality to the variety of present and planned mobile devices, such as Palm Pilots and mobile phones. Partner relationship management (PRM) extends CRM functionality out to sales and fulfillment partners. E-business CRM (eCRM) puts customer functions on the Web, thereby enabling self-service and wider access to information across the spider chart.

At a more global level, organizations are focusing on CRM analytics as a tool to provide actionable data that can help drive increased profitability. As the scope of CRM expands, vendors have coined terms such as enterprise relationship management or extraprise relationship management (ERM) in an attempt to create a label for addressing what we have been calling the relational enterprise or spider chart. Enterprise resource planning (ERP) is being integrated into CRM as it expands to address the end-to-end customer business cycle. Finally, e-business applications, typically being implemented separately from these other systems, are developing alongside CRM initiatives.

The final step is simply *relationship management* (RM). Organizations are currently in a race to implement all the acronyms in the arrow chart, Figure 8-2. The next challenge will be to play connect-the-dots and get all of these point solutions talking to each other. The long-term implications are clear. As customer-facing systems mature and become more like commodities, a new class of enterprise application that encompasses all three types of CRM is going to emerge.

On the hard-easy scale, getting to RM is extremely difficult. Some analysts have estimated that enterprise CRM projects (meaning front-office suites) are three times more complicated than ERP projects. This can be terrifying to organizations that have seen a major ERP implementation drag on for two or three years.[6] Some buyers have not even been able to get their ERP project completed before the next version of the software is released. One of my clients dubbed this "continuous obsolescence."

If implementing an enterprise-wide front-office suite is three times more difficult than implementing ERP, then getting to relational enterprise RM is a monumental undertaking. Yet this is not a go/nogo participation decision, it is a matter of when. In the past, organizations could afford to fall a few percentage points behind in back-office productivity as long as revenue was growing. Staying competitive with customer-facing systems is not an option any more than improving product quality was in the 1990s. Falling behind with customers means that the company can be lost, with thousands of employees holding pink slip parties.

Summary

CRM is an often-used term that is rarely understood. Organizations are well along the implementation cycle without everyone really agreeing on what CRM means. CRM is no longer a feel good treatment of customers or software for running a call center. It is not putting an e-store on the organization's Web site. CRM is not just a point solution or even a suite of customer-facing front-office applications. CRM is the umbrella under which nearly every other process and organizational structure initiative fits.

In the context of the spider chart extension of the enterprise, of portals making everyone a customer, of the alternative workforce, and of role-based relationships throughout the entire business cycle, CRM becomes the pathway to a new class of system simply called relationship management.

A good place to start in understanding this new definition is with collaborative CRM. A CRM system isn't going to add much value if customers can't access it the way they need to or want to, or if the interaction is ineffective. Looking at channels and integration is our next task.

Learning Points

1. RM isn't a choice, it's a mission. Treating the customer right isn't an option, it will be the ticket to survival. RM is the ultimate competitive advantage.

2. Organizations are implementing CRM with no clear definition of what it is or what value it is expected to deliver. Efforts to date, the few that there are, have been made on a "leap of faith." Ultimately, organizations are going to have to develop a CRM measurement system that will let them know how they are doing versus competitors.

3. There are six definitions of CRM in common usage, with only one of them close to being right: the 360-degree view of the customer lifecycle. The first order of business is to get everyone to agree as to what CRM means to the organization.

4. A holistic view of the CRM technology eco-system recognizes that there are three categories of CRM: operational, collaborative, and analytical. Everything drives analytical CRM, which provides the big payoff.

5. Front-office and back-office distinctions are disappearing. It's just going to be "office" as organizations move beyond point solutions or narrow suites into a full-blown extended enterprise RM system.

6. Getting to relationship management (RM) is going to be the hardest thing organizations have ever attempted. CRM is three times more difficult than ERP, which many organizations couldn't successfully install. Implementing an integrated RM system is going to be perhaps three times harder again than CRM. Imagine tackling a project that is many times more difficult than ERP with the current organizational setup. It's not going to happen without a dramatic change.

NOTES

1. META Group and IMT Strategies, "Customer Relationship Management (CRM) Study 1999: Sponsor Report," September 22, 1999, p. 4.

2. Rick Whiting, "CRM's Realities Don't Match the Hype," *InformationWeek*, March 19, 2001, p. 79.

3. META Group, "Customer Relationship Management (CRM) Study—1999," p. 3.

4. Ibid., p. 7.

5. Chuck Trepper, "Match Your CRM Tool to Your Business Model," *InformationWeek*, May 15, 2000, p. 74.

6. Scot Petersen, "Conway: We're Redefining ERP," *eWeek*, July 17, 2000, p. 20.

C H A P T E R 9

The Expanding Range of Collaborative RM

In Spring 2000, I had an opportunity to attend the American Management Association's 32nd Global Human Resource Management Conference in Nice, France. (Tough duty, but someone had to do it.) One of the best features of the trip was getting to mix with other consultants and see a number of leading-edge speakers. I rarely get to hear anyone else present unless they are on right before me or right afterwards.

A speaker who evoked a strong emotional reaction in the audience was Dr. Patrick Dixon, one of the world's leading trend researchers.[1] At one point in his talk, Dixon held up his hand, placing his index finger and thumb about one centimeter apart. Although it wasn't visible, he was holding a device about the size of two grains of rice. It contained a miniature processor, memory, and transmitter. Next, he held up a large syringe barely smaller than a turkey baster with a needle thick enough to see from where we sat 30 or 40 rows back. Dixon explained that the syringe could inject a transmitter under the skin, usually in the neck area, and that this device was often used by the wealthy or famous to be able to track their children in case of an emergency. This is currently available technology, not something coming in the future. It makes the classic Star Trek communicator badge look like a 1950s transistor radio.

Dixon went on to explain what a world adapted for everyone having such a personal storage and transmission device could look like. Imagine being able to:

- Have the toaster (or any appliance) know exactly how you want your meal prepared.

- Sit in a car and have it automatically adjust the seat position and steering wheel tilt, and load your personal driving habits and vehicle handling preferences in the car's on-board computer.

- Have a personalized "you are here" map from anywhere in the world at any time.

- Walk into an airport, be mechanically greeted by name at the door, have the computer know your flight details and offer directions to your gate, then have your credit card automatically billed when you confirm your presence by walking on the plane.

- Walk down the aisle of the grocery store and have the display box on your cart offer you specials geared towards your personal buying habits as you pass each relevant department.

At this point in the talk, audience members were visibly uncomfortable, squirming in their seats. At lunch later that day, several of the eastern European attendees told me that they had found it frightening. The whole concept was enough to set the nerves of privacy advocates on edge, yet it was totally within the realm of current technology. Talk about a new method of accessing an organization. Forget hand-held, this is embedded in your body!

In addition to new channels, Dixon spoke of using existing channels in new ways. Once Web bandwidth is capable of decent quality real-time video, buyers could interact with the production processes of vendors from whom they've ordered. Imagine using Web video to watch your special-order auto being made on the factory floor, and talking to the robots making it in real time to find out what's going on. The Produce stage of the business cycle has always been assumed to be back office only, but will now be another customer-facing system.

Integrating the spider chart across all today's channels is difficult enough. The job will be complicated by the new channels that are being discussed, and by unforeseen interaction channels (such as the injected device) that are not yet on any RM vendor's radar. It all begins by understanding the importance of customer touch points.

Characteristics of an Effective Channel

A book that is assigned reading in all our RM and leadership training is Jan Carlzon's *Moments of Truth*.[2] As the new president of a struggling SAS Airlines, Carlzon focused on improving what happened during the 50 million "moments of truth"—10 million fliers each interacting with an average of five SAS employees.

This is the heart and soul of collaborative RM. No matter what the medium, each interaction must satisfy the customer, the first time and every time. To achieve that satisfaction, there are channel realities that must be accommodated.

THE CHANNEL MUST WORK

This is one of those "Well, duuuh!" recommendations, but it is a major problem area. Don't think that this is too basic to discuss. Customer-facing systems are full of channels that seemed purposely designed to frustrate customers. Ask any group, and every single person will be able to cite a recent personal example, situations such as the following real occurrences:

- Working your way through a long series of automated phone menu prompts only to find out that there is nothing at the end but a dial tone. My favorite one was a system that ended with, "Press 8 to hear a quacking sound." At least the service people had a sense of humor.

- Circular systems where the support line phone message tells you to visit the Web site and the Web site instructs you to call support.

- Faxes, letters, e-mails, or Web site messages that fall into inter-dimensional space or go on some other one-way trip and remain unanswered.

- An e-store that takes you all the way to the final order confirmation screen, then gives you an error message that everything isn't filled out even though it is. There is no one to call for help and no way out other than to leave the site.

- Unanswered voice messages. Evidently many companies operate without any human habitation.

- Calling for support at 4:30 P.M. and being told the wait is forty minutes, then being disconnected at 5:00 P.M. when the support hours end.

- Calling the same number over the weekend and being put permanently on hold, with horrible music, and never being told that the offices are closed. You could hold until Monday morning if you wished.

- Frequently-asked-questions (FAQ) support sites with no FAQ's in them.

- (Insert your favorite here . . . you've got one, don't you?)

We could fill the book with horror stories about broken communication channels. It's funny that everyone is talking about mind-boggling communications infrastructures, multimillion dollar computer telephony integration (CTI), channel integration with everything except two cans and a string, sending signals to other star systems in search of intelligence, etc., but we can't figure out how to return a call or set up a phone menu system. Customers may end up like the two (four?) aliens in Figure 9-1. It makes us wonder whether vendor executives in the above organizations have ever actually tried to use their own systems.

An exercise we particularly enjoy assigning in our classes is to have attendees pair up during break and attempt to reach their partner at the office. Attendees then detail their travails through their cohort's communications obstacle course in trying to talk to an actual human being. They also describe what they were able to find out about where their partner is and when they could expect a return call. The stories paint an ugly, but entertaining, picture and are certainly enlightening for the attendees.

Figure 9-1. Rudy Park.

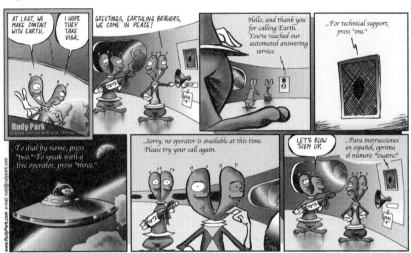

Copyright © 1999 Darrin Bell and Theron Heir. Reprinted with permission.

The moral of this section is, "If they don't work, it doesn't matter how many channels you have." This is pretty basic stuff, but something that few organizations seem to be able to figure out. It's better to kill a broken channel than to aggravate a customer.

CHANNELS MUST ALLOW CUSTOMERS TO CHOOSE

When I was in London on a European teaching swing, an attendee from the continent made an interesting comment. "You Americans think everyone lives in Silicon Valley and is into technology. Our culture is different. We are more people oriented. We enjoy seeing people, talking to people. We don't want to do the bulk of our business over the Web and we never will."

Customers want to contact organizations the way they want to contact them. Preference is the number one satisfaction requirement. For example, a February 2001 survey of small and medium-size companies found that 70 percent prefer to communicate with their employees by intranet versus 21 percent who prefer communicating by e-mail.[3] With this difference of opinion, a multichannel strategy might work better.

In addition to satisfaction, a multiple channel approach can be good for revenue, especially at retail. A Fall 2000 report found that retailers employing retail, catalog, and Web channels sell more per channel than single-channel retailers. Even pure Internet retailer Amazon.com mailed out catalogs during the Christmas 2000 season, and it also offered a toll-free number for placing phone orders.[4]

Organizations also want to minimize service costs. They want customers to use fax-back services or Web support sites rather than talking to a call center agent. The economics are compelling. An average telephone call costs at least $5 while a Web site visit can cost an organization 25 cents or less. Right now, organizations seem to be winning, with the loser being the customer who would rather talk to someone.

The operating principle is:

> *If a customer wants it done* and there is profit in it, *then someone is going to do it. It had better be you before your competitor.*

J. C. Penney, founder of the retail chain whose name we forget, had a related customer service sign on the cash register of his first store, "Either you or your replacement will greet the customer." Providing the preferred access channels offers the same opportunity.

Relational organizations must integrate all the channels that customers want to use. A Web shopper comparing costs on pricewatch.com isn't likely to walk into a store to buy the item at retail. Customers will either buy through the preferred channel from their favorite vendor, or buy from a competitor that offers that channel. And the channel preference may not be consistent from transaction to transaction, so it takes more than one channel to satisfy an individual customer.

CHANNELS MUST BE APPROPRIATE

Tom Thomas, president of Vantive before it was acquired by PeopleSoft, used to talk to audiences about the plastic gizmo that a major oil company offers to consumers. It's a little knob that fits conveniently on a key chain and is magnetically coded with account information linked to the consumer's oil company credit information. All the customer has to do is to pass the knob over a reader panel on the pump or in the store, and a credit card payment is automatically processed. Give one to your teenagers and they need never again run short of gas or junk food.

Thomas would pose this question: "Is this e-commerce?" Most listeners would agree that it was, since there was no physical interchange in an electronic transaction. Then he would ask, "What happens when it doesn't work?" After some discussion, the answer was that they would have to call the oil company. The final question was: "Then is this still e-commerce, or is it plain old call-center service?"

The message here is that there are very few single-channel interactions. Even the pure dot-coms have discovered that they need an old-fashioned call center because customers want to talk to human beings. If I'm out of gas and out of cash, I can't exactly drive home and fire up my trusty home PC to register my problem with that magnetic gizmo on my key chain.

I may be willing to buy casualty insurance at discounted rates over the phone or on a Web site, but I don't look forward to standing outside my house as firemen try to bring the blaze under control and saying, "Dear, we've got to send an e-mail to our agent about this."

Channels must be appropriate to their function. Too many organizations are trying to force fit their processes into existing channels.

CHANNELS MUST BE USED APPROPRIATELY

Another reason for integrating multiple channels involves the content of the message. A terrible old joke talked about the bicycle messenger who comes to deliver a telegram. The customer had always wanted to receive a singing telegram, and insists that the messenger sing the contents to him. The messenger begs to not have to sing, but after a long argument and a drawn-out joke build up, the messenger warbles, "Tadadadedum, tadadadedum, tada, tada ta ta . . . Your uncle died."

Pretty dumb, but this is a perfect example of the message not fitting the medium. In particular, bad news needs to be delivered very carefully. For example, organizations should not use print channels such as letter, fax, or e-mail to deny a warranty claim. Psychologically, it is much easier to upset a person in writing than in-person or by phone. No matter how well written, paper is impersonal. It is also persistent and potentially permanent. Paper sits on people's desks to be read frequently and irritate repeatedly. It can be copied, passed around, posted on the bulletin board, and stuck in files to be used years later in delayed retribution. A bad piece of paper can hurt for a long time. (Ask Ollie North about those e-mail printouts.)

The Web seems to be a great boon to mankind until you consider typing skills. There is a sheer volume problem. It is estimated that we think at 10,000 words per minute, we have five terrabytes of data streaming in our eyeballs, and we speak at 150 words per minute. Unfortunately, few people can type more than ten to fifteen words per minute. Communicating by keyboard over the Internet for most people is like driving down the street while looking through a soft drink straw. There's too much information and too little data transmission capacity.

Some channels can't convey the entire content of the message. In his popular (and often misquoted) study, Albert Mehrabian researched how much nonverbal and verbal communication contribute to the understanding of attitudes. He found that body language contributed 55 percent, voice contributed 38 percent, and words contributed 7 percent.[5] Channels providing visual and audio information will always be more effective than text in dealing with sensitive interpersonal situations because they convey the bulk of the emotional content.

Again, these are simple truths that are evidently not so simple to implement. Effective collaborative RM provides the channels that customers want to use, makes certain they work as intended, then uses channels appropriately depending upon the content.

The State of Bandwidth

With the mention of audio and video, this is a good time for a quick comment on communications bandwidth. In 2000 I had the opportunity to tour a communications center in Dallas that was incredible. The building was hardened so that a tornado could pass right over without inflicting damage. It was powered by two substations, with a battery room the size of my home. There was row upon row of racks, each containing stacks of eight-way RAID-enabled servers. (The IT readers are enjoying this part.) There was a multimillion dollar row of Cisco switches stretching off across the cavernous room. It was like walking through HAL 9000's brain, assuming HAL was a block square. I've toured massive electric generating plants and am not easily impressed, but I was impressed here.

There are over twenty such installations in the United States, with expansion underway in Europe and Asia. The company is laying its own transoceanic cables, and there were pictures of machines working their way across the Nebraska prairie laying fiber optic cable bundles to connect U.S. cities. The host of the tour explained that bandwidth will soon be in as much surplus as long distance phone service. We asked how they hoped to make money in this environment and the answer was, "We're figuring that bandwidth will increase faster than prices will go down." The message is that acceptable quality voice and video over the Internet will soon be available in major metropolitan areas, with general consumer access (in one form or another) to soon follow.

Wireless technology is also moving forward rapidly. The second-generation (2G) digital-cellular networks are giving way to new 2.5G networks and third-generation (3G) networks that are to be built shortly. Even now they're talking about 3G-1X, 3G-1XEVDO, and 3G-1XEVDV. (Don't ask.)[6] Something loosely called 4G is in discussion for delivery by 2010. IDC expects the wireless market to increase from 7.4 million wireless subscribers in the United States to 61.5 million by 2003.[7] The prediction is for one billion mobile phones (and an estimated half-billion Internet accounts) in use worldwide by 2003.[8]

These technological advances will cause a blending of channels. For example, research firm Ovum, Ltd., estimates that by 2006, nearly one-quarter of all Internet users will make phone calls from their PCs.[9] This represents some 166 million users worldwide and will be a $6.2 billion industry in 2005 as phone applications merge into computers.

Devices themselves are also converging, particularly in the mobile market. One example is the Smartphone, a hybrid of a mobile phone and a personal digital assistant. There is a phone keypad and an imbedded Palm organizer screen. The two functions are integrated, so that a call can be initiated by tapping a phone number in the address module of the Palm Desktop. Visor has taken the opposite approach with its VisorPhone expansion module by adding mobile phone capabilities to its Visor Palm-compatible digital assistant.[10] Users are likely to see continuing convergence as bandwidth capabilities increase.

Collaborative RM Channels

So as the months roll on, bandwidth is going to be less and less of a problem, particularly for mid-size and large organizations. What is

going to present problems is the wide range of possible interaction channels, differentiated in three ways.

First, channels are differentiated by the content they can carry
(text, visuals, voice, video).

Second, channels that carry the same content can require their
own specialized presentation format. For example, Web applications
must be formatted differently for the variety of presentation devices, such
as a personal computer monitor, hand-held computer, home TV, Palm
Pilot, or digital phone. The displays present different sizes, color capabilities, and screen resolutions to the application. There is now even a
wearable computer that fits on a belt buckle and allows voice input,
3-D mouse, or Twiddler keyboard (three rows of four keys) input.[11]

Figure 9-2 shows an example of a sales force automation (SFA)
contact access sequence as displayed on a wireless access protocol phone
device. Compare this to the amount of information that can be displayed to a PC client by the same SFA application as shown in Figure

Figure 9-2. WAP phone SFA.

9-3. Relational systems have to be able to present the same information readily across devices this diverse.

Third, channels have different interaction capabilities and capacities. A pager or a messaging phone may allow for text in but not out. A phone or personal information manager may have very limited keyboard capabilities for entering text, and so on. This is what contributes to the great variety of interaction choices.

Following are the major collaboration channels. This list is by no means exhaustive, and there are certain to be surprise devices (such as the body nodule) that new technology springs on unsuspecting organizations.

In-Person

- Direct contact . . . face-to-face

Telephone

- Phone . . . Watson, come here
- Voicemail . . . We're not in right now . . .

Figure 9-3. Sales portal.

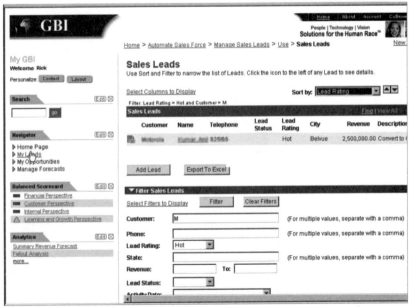

- Interactive voice response (IVR) . . . Press 1 to listen to another menu
- Voice recognition . . . Dave, stop Dave . . . please Dave, stop . . .
- Fax/faxback . . . How do you uncurl that roller paper?

Paper
- Mail . . . snail mail
- Overnight . . . fast snail mail
- Telegram . . . converted to snail mail

Electronic
- E-mail . . . EARN PROFITS NOW!!!!!
- Web applications . . . www.[yournamehere].com
- Web site messaging . . . Please describe your problem in the box below
- Interactive Web chat . . . Let your fingers do the talking
- Web conferencing . . . Voice (and someday video) over Internet protocol (VOIP)
- Newsgroup . . . Re: Re: Re: Re: Poor service
- Listserv . . . e-newsletters

TV
- Cable . . . The promise of convergence
- Satellite . . . Another promise of convergence to come

Mobile
- Mobile phone . . . Please set your phone to not play classical music when it rings
- Pager . . . Text messaging
- PC wireless modem . . . Full computer wireless access
- Handheld PC . . . Windows CE devices
- Wireless access protocol (WAP) devices . . . Phone standards for mobile Internet devices

- Personal digital assistant . . . PDA with wireless access
- Tablet-sized personal computer . . . a la Microsoft's Tablet PC
- Proprietary devices . . . a la Research in Motion (RIM) Blackberry handheld or Charmed Technology's CharmIt
- Hybrid devices . . . Smartphone or VisorPhone PDA/mobile phone combination

There are tremendous potential benefits in integrating as many of these channels as customers demand. Sales researcher Neil Rackham explains a simple rule of thumb, "For every dollar you can gain within a channel, there are at least five to be gained across channels."[12] This is because customers want to use the channel of their choice and slide seamlessly between channels as desired. If one vendor can't accommodate this, then customers will find another one who will.

Note that although a number of the above channels are Internet based, there are numerous traditional channels. Business and technology trade press is focused on Web, Web, Web. If you believe the hype, human interaction is going to be replaced by e-business transactions. The Internet is certainly a defining technology for our times, but the right attitude is:

The Internet is not the channel, it is a channel.

According to META, e-mail volume is growing at the rate of 12 percent per year, while voice is up only 2 percent year to year. Not too long ago, voice was *twenty times* the volume of e-mail.[13] This is now changing.

As for the future, Dr. Jon Anton, Director of Research at Purdue's Center for Customer Driven Quality, and one of the world's foremost experts on customer interaction centers (CICs), has projected the shift in channel usage.[14] Table 9-1 shows usage will move away from phone, but phone will still represent a significant channel of interaction.

Summary

Organizations are supposed to make certain that (1) customers can interact using any desired channel, (2) all of them must work, and (3)

Table 9-1. Customer-to-business contacts by channel.

	1999	2002 (PROJECTED)
Phone	75%	32%
Web	11%	38%
E-mail	8%	22%
Other	6%	8%

Source: Dr. Jon Anton, Director of Research, Center for Customer Driven Quality, Purdue University.

the content must be appropriate for the channel. Customers will either interact with organizations over their channel of personal preference, or they will find a competitor who can.

Seeing this list, the complexity of implementing a multichannel strategy is readily apparent, and most of the task lies ahead. Once multiple channels are in place, customers face the challenge of integrating channel interactions, which is our next topic.

Learning Points

1. The days of communicating primarily in-person, by phone, by mail, or by fax are long gone. Customers now have a wide range of interaction channel options with various organizations.

2. Each customer touch is a "moment of truth" that affects lifetime customer profitability. Ineffective channels impair that moment no matter how good the systems are and how well employees communicate.

3. Channels must work as advertised. They must allow customers to choose among them and still complete any interaction. They must be appropriate to the task. They must be used appropriately. The track record for this in most organizations is pitiful.

4. Sooner or later, and probably sooner, bandwidth for multimedia is going to be available. Get ready for integrating audio and video communications in your organization.

5. There are 27 channels listed, with more assuredly on the way. Each has different content and presentation characteristics. Systems and processes are going to have to accommodate as many of the channels as customers want to use and as can be delivered profitably.

6. Don't get starry-eyed about the Internet. Sure, it's a big deal. But it is *a* big deal, not *the* big deal. Don't lose sight of the traditional channel interactions that still need improvement.

7. The first step is to implement a multichannel strategy. Then the challenge is to integrate the channels.

NOTES

1. Patrick Dixon, "Virtual People—The Impact of New Technology on Human Resources," Talk to the 32nd Global Human Resource Management Conference, Management Centre Europe/American Management Association, Nice, France, April 11, 2000.

2. Jan Carlzon, *Moments of Truth* (New York: Perennial Library, 1989).

3. Sarah L. Roberts-Witt, "Intranet Lowdown," *PC Magazine,* April 3, 2001, p. 73.

4. Jessica Davis, "Catalog Distribution May Signal e-Tailers Are Getting With the Program," *InfoWorld,* November 13, 2000, p. 114.

5. Albert Mehrabian, "Significance of Posture and Position in the Communication of Attitudes and Status Relationship," *Psychological Bulletin* 79 (1969): 359–72.

6. Ephraim Schwartz, " 'Telephone Ladies' Turn Into Entrepreneurs; and Will Silicon Valley Change Its Dress Code," *InfoWorld,* April 2, 2001, p. 59.

7. Carol Levin, "Happy E-Customers," *PC Magazine,* May 9, 2000, p. 92.

8. Carol Levin, "Broadband Wireless at Home: Mobile Net Surge," *PC Magazine,* July 2000, p. 81.

9. eFiles column, "E-Calls Common Within 5 Years," *eWeek,* January 15, 2001, p. 65.

10. Mike Langberg, "Smartphone Combines Cellular With Handheld," *St. Louis Post-Dispatch,* March 28, 2001, p. E3.

11. Ephraim Schwartz and Jennifer Jones, "GTIA Wireless Show Ablaze With Gadgets and Glitter," *InfoWorld,* March 19, 2001, p. 27.

12. Neil Rackham, "Learn From Past Mistakes," *Sales & Marketing Management,* December 2000, p. 40.

13. META Group, "META Group CRM Conference," February 21, 2000.

14. Todd Coopee, "E-CRM Calls Customer King," *InfoWorld,* June 26, 2000, p. 78.

"You can't aggravate customers into profitability."

CHAPTER 10

Transitioning to a Customer Interaction Center

As unbelievable as bad service stories are, they have to be true because it's impossible to make this stuff up. The Wednesday before a Saturday graduation, my family decided to go watch an in-law get her diploma at Missouri University. We knew getting a room in Columbia was going to be a problem because ceremonies from the different schools were scheduled all throughout the weekend. We called numerous 800 numbers and found a hotel chain, let's call it Motel 2, that said its Columbia site had rooms available.

We had to call this local Motel 2 directly because it was a franchise and did its own bookings. When we reached the front desk we were told we couldn't have a room for just Saturday, that we had to rent for Friday and Saturday as a package. The motel was evidently determined to squeeze every penny out of the busy weekend. We argued that, at this late date, they should be booking anything they could get, that it was unfair gouging, that we weren't going to be there Friday . . . anything we could think of. The front desk manager was adamant—both days or nothing at all.

As we were about to hang up, the most bizarre conversation began.

The manager said, "By the way, if you'd like to join our frequent guest program, you can get a 10 percent discount on your rates at Motel 2 anywhere in the nation and earn credits towards a free stay."

You can imagine our incredulous response. "You mean you refuse to rent a room to us when we're *begging* you to let us stay, and you have the gall to try to sell us a frequent guest program? Why would we *ever* want to stay at a Motel 2 with this kind of service?" (silence . . . click.)

Here's a second incident with the same RM-related symptom. I was experiencing crashes with a critical PC program. I called the vendor's 800 help line, worked through a series of menu choices, then settled in for a cozy wait listening to elevator music interspersed with friendly sales announcements. I finally reached a technician who, fortunately, was very competent. It took us about ten minutes to resolve the issue and I was on my way. Before I could depart, the representative asked, "Would you like to hear a sales message about a service that might be of interest to you?"

"Sure," I said cheerfully. As a relational enterprise consultant I was curious about what they wanted to sell me and how they were going to do it.

"Really?" the tech blurted in total shock. I must have been the first person in the universe who had actually volunteered for the sales pitch. I found out why, because the call rapidly went downhill from there.

Once connected I heard, "Your phone number please." No greeting, no welcome, no introduction, just a demand for my phone number. It was a bad start.

"Actually," I said, "Before I give you my phone number, why don't you tell me what the offer is. I don't just give out my phone number for no reason."

"Sir, we need your phone number to determine if you quality for the offering."

"Great," I tried again. "Tell me what the offer is and I can save you a bunch of time by telling you right away if I'm interested or not."

We tried this a few more times until I finally said, "OK, can you guarantee me that the phone number I give you will not be shared with any other department or organization, and that it will be used only to determine if I qualify for this top secret offer of yours?" (long silence)

"Sir, I need your phone number. . . ." At that point I hung up, disappointed and disgusted, but also fascinated because this is a great example of what's wrong today with organizations trying to turn their call centers into customer interaction centers (CIC).

Defining the Customer Interaction Center

The first step is to lock down the terminology surrounding service centers, because terms with different meanings are often used interchangeably, and the same thing is called different names. For example, Gartner calls the ultimate center a "contact center,"[1] while Giga calls it a "call center within a customer interaction framework."[2] Author Paul Greenberg uses the more common term, "customer interaction center."[3] What we need here is a to agree on a terminology that will help differentiate the levels of service center functionality. Here is how to define the various kinds of service centers.

CALL CENTER

A call center is the classic, single-purpose phone service center. Groups of agents sit in a giant room with tiny cubicles, wired up somewhat like real humans were in the film, *The Matrix*. Both customer access to the center and agent response to the customer are primarily, if not solely, by phone. The call center is designed to resolve customer cases, as shown in Figure 10-1. Internal communications stay within the department and include other agents, case specialists, and supervisors or managers.

Managing a call center is a real challenge. Handling hundreds of callers per day can be a horrible job, with customer after customer coming in an unrelenting stream. Agents feel as if they can check their brains at the door, their options being limited by what the system lets them do and what information they have available. Repetitive stress injuries (RSI) are a constant concern, along with eye strain, carpal tunnel syndrome, back problems, circulatory difficulties, and plain old emotional stress lurking around the corner.

Keeping the call center staffed with agents is a never-ending challenge. The job is low-status, low paying, and not very stimulating—a trio of bad characteristics. Consequently, agent turnover can be 300 to 400 percent per year. A collections holding company with 7,000 agents told us that their collectors take five weeks to train and average thirteen

Figure 10-1. Traditional call center.

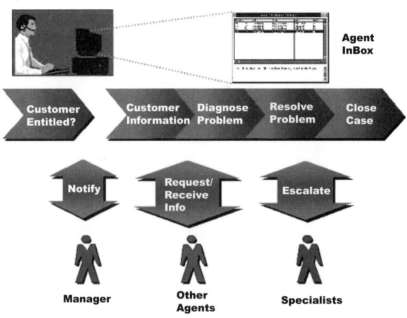

weeks on the job. This is why call centers will take anyone who can work a phone. Walk through a center and you'll see every style of dress imaginable, multi-colored Mohawk haircuts, people lying on the floor with the keyboard in their lap talking to customers, you name it. All that matters is keeping the phone lines covered, so the company is delighted to have anyone there. It's a tough business.

Call centers are focused on the telephone as the primary channel. For customers, writing a letter or faxing documentation can be a chancy proposition. The pages may reach the right person, or they might not. And any other agent contacted about the case may not have access to the physical documents transmitted. Those will likely be back in a pile somewhere on the originating agent's desk. Electronic communications such as Web messages and even e-mail may never reach the agent, because those are handled by another department—if they are handled at all. Many call center agents don't even have an e-mail address.

CONTACT CENTER

A contact center adds the element of channel communications, i.e., moving data in and out of the center through as many of the channel alternatives listed in Chapter 9 as possible. Most organizations currently have only two or three channels integrated, usually phone, mail, and perhaps fax. Information coming through other channels is on its own.

This channel integration is no trivial task. Letters have to be opened, recognized, routed, scanned in graphically or textually through OCR, and linked to the specific customer or case. A fax server must capture the facsimile pages and similarly get their contents into the proper records. E-mails, call back requests, voice messages, and all the other channels must be similarly linked to the call center operations system. Then customers must be contacted on the outbound link through whatever channel they have requested, which may not be the same as the inbound request.

Service centers currently aren't very far along in this process. It almost seems as though channels are being created faster than systems can integrate them. Organizations are just getting e-mail and fax integrated while customers are already moving on to data-enabled mobile phones, wireless PDAs, and tablet PCs. The extent of this challenge is clear from Chapter 9's extensive list of channel options.

The contact center is also moving towards a front-office suite, integrating customer-facing applications—such as marketing, inside sales, outbound sales, support, and field service. Help desk could be in the mix somewhere, but is typically an employee-facing application.

CUSTOMER INTERACTION CENTER

The goal of every call or contact center is to become a revenue generating customer interaction center (CIC). As illustrated in Figure 10-2, this means CIC systems must allow first touch resolution:

- Across all channels
- From the point of view of any role
- From anywhere in the spider chart
- Throughout the entire business cycle

CIC systems that deliver this functionality will enable organizations to turn service agents into sales agents. However, these requirements create both systems problems and service problems. Let's talk first about service.

Figure 10-2. Customer interaction center.

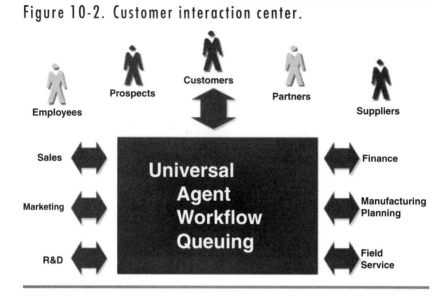

Levels of Service

There are many models of customer satisfaction performance, such as the satisfaction pyramid, which describes what is required to generate customer loyalty that also can be turned into increased profits. We prefer the simple service quality arrow model presented in Figure 10-3, which lists the four levels of service—respond, resolve, satisfy, and please—in increasing order of effectiveness.

- **Respond.** At the lowest level of performance, centers are focused on merely trying to keep up with the volume of customer contacts. Anyone who has waited on hold for service, been told the lines are full and to call back later, had voice messages unanswered, or had e-mail ignored is experiencing *respond* level of service. Trying to get service from this organization is like attempting to be the tenth caller to a radio program. It's pure luck when you get through, much less having your problem resolved satisfactorily.

- **Resolve.** At the *resolve* level of service, the focus is on handling all contacts and carrying cases to a conclusion. It may require

Figure 10-3. Profitability.

Please
Satisfy
Resolve
Respond

customers calling multiple centers, getting passed around to find the right person, or finding out a solution is not available, but the case is ultimately resolved and taken off the active list.

- **Satisfy.** There is a major jump in center sophistication required to reach the *satisfy* level of service. Here, not only are cases resolved, they are resolved to the customer's approval. As we have seen, satisfaction requires first-call resolution, short calls, multirole agents—that is, the beginning of the transition to a CIC capability.

- **Please.** The maximum profit potential comes at the *please* level of service. Not only must the systems work properly at this level, the comportment of agents and personalization of service must be outstanding. Only when customers hang up with that sense of "Wow!" will they be in a buying mood, particularly when they may have originally called about a problem.

(Stomp, stomp.) The most frequently occurring problem in organizations trying implement a profitability philosophy in their 360-degree systems is this:

Most organizations are trying to take a system operating somewhere between "Respond" and "Resolve" and turn it into a "Please" profit center without doing the intermediate steps.

This effort is doomed. What results are situations such as the two stories at the beginning of this chapter. Motel 2 was barely at the respond level of service. Someone must have had the bright idea at Motel 2 headquarters to offer anyone who called the chain a frequent traveler membership and eke a bit of additional loyalty and future revenue out of the transaction. What they forgot was that the initial stay has to be a positive experience before a loyalty program is attractive. Perhaps a better time to make the offer would have been at checkout.

The software vendor mentioned at the start of this chapter was at the resolve level of service. My problem was taken to resolution by a competent agent within an acceptable timeframe. I wasn't dissatisfied, but I wasn't pleased at having to spend unproductive time getting my software back online. The point at which someone has just experienced service downtime caused by a product is not the ideal time for an opt-in sales pitch. Then the inflexible process and chippy agent turned the entire experience into a dissatisfier.

Here was an organization cleverly snatching defeat from the jaws of victory by turning a successful service interaction into an aggravating sales situation. Instead of leaving satisfied, I hung up mad. Every child over the age of four knows the best time to ask mom or dad for something. Managers at these two organizations must have forgotten this principle sometime in the intervening years.

It's easy to find out how a service center is doing.

1. *Get a pair of headphones and sit in with call center agents for a couple of hours.*
You will learn more about customers, service, and processes than you ever imagined. At one financial institution, it is not unusual for call center agents to come back from lunch and find the president manning a phone. He says it helps him better understand customers and how the bank is doing with them, and he makes his top executives spend a similar session on the phones once per month.

2. *Create interactions across your contact channels and see what kind of responses you get, if you get any at all.*
We often do that before we make presentations to clients in order to better understand what their customers enjoy/endure.

3. *Check out call center reports.*
There is a thick stack of them printed daily. They are hard to

understand, but they somewhere contain switch data that tells you about rejected calls and wait time, and system reports on resolution and notification statistics. The results are always interesting to general management, and often terrifying.

CIC Universals

CICs are all about integration, be it channels, roles, the business cycle, the spider chart, whatever. There are additional issues of functional integration in CIC systems, specifically the three "universals" that appear in the middle block of Figure 10-2.

UNIVERSAL AGENT

Universal Agent is the term applied to an agent in a full-function CIC. With a true 360-degree internal and external view portal system, the universal agent can handle any interaction from any constituent in the spider chart. The long-term trend is that the multiple call or contact centers that an organization has today will be consolidated into a single functional entity. This means that an individual agent might consecutively handle an employee benefit inquiry, a client service request, a PC usage question, a partner inquiry, a customer order, a production status check, and a field service dispatch—all from the same agent portal.

UNIVERSAL WORKFLOW

Workflow is the term used to describe processes that are embedded in systems. This can include processes such as service escalation requirements as specified in client contracts, best-practice sales techniques for identification and qualification of prospects, or employee hiring policies and steps.

With universal workflow, different roles can tap into existing processes already within the system. This means that everyone is hiring the same way or that the same client support escalation can be used for a field-service incident. Universal workflow enables the universal agent.

One common objection is, "What about the PC help desk inquiry? It requires technical IT subject matter expertise that is far beyond the capabilities of a general purpose CIC agent." This can present a problem, and it certainly suggests that there will always be PC help-desk agents ready for referrals (perhaps as outsourcers). But an interesting statistic from help desks is that as many as 80 percent of all PC trouble calls concern one problem—forgotten passwords. This is a problem any agent can help address.

Another objection concerns how one agent can master so many diverse processes. The answer is that CIC systems are going to provide much of the process knowledge embedded in the system. Where interaction is required, the system will assist agents with the process. One such capability is called "branch scripting," in which the system displays a branching structure of prepared prompts that are activated by the customer's response to questions in the script. The path through the script can be evaluated and scored giving the agent expert feedback on how hot a prospect this caller is. So agents will need to be masters of the system, not masterful content experts.

UNIVERSAL QUEUING

Universal Queuing is directly related to channel integration and personalization. Universal queuing dumps every contact, no matter what channel of origin, into the same line for service. Once customers all make it into the same queue, relational organizations can begin personalizing service regardless of the channel. Without a universal queue, maximizing profit through personalization is impossible.

In most current systems, service priority is determined by channel rather than by importance of customer. Phone calls receive the highest priority treatment, because they are typically managed best. We're all programmed to answer our phone within three rings. Service centers have thick switch reports summarizing to the hundredth of a second how long callers wait and how many hung up after waiting how long. Call center systems are mature and managers are experienced at measuring service levels from computer telephony integration equipment and software.

Electronic interactions seem to get the lowest priority. For instance, META Group estimates that 50 percent of all cases submitted by e-mail go unresolved.[4] Mail, fax, and voice messaging get varying levels of attention—if they are attended to at all. Why? Because there is no one looking at e-mail, mail, or fax service levels, no stack of reports detailing response times, no managers living or dying on first contact resolution, as is the case in the call center.

What happens with segmented queuing is this: If the president of a major client sends an e-mail with a question, and the same company's front desk receptionist calls for help, who gets the best service? The secretary does because the request came over the top priority channel—a phone. With a universal queue and the right kind of identification hardware and profiling software, the president's e-mail would immediately be given to a premium service agent for immediate response. More sophisticated systems will apply intelligence to the routing decision by identifying the president, keyword searching the title and perhaps the text, checking the interaction database for active or related issues, then routing the information to an agent computed to be best qualified to handle the e-mail.

A CIC can only be implemented with universal agents utilizing universal workflow for clients consolidated into a universal queue.

The e-CIC

Some of the channel issues we talked about in Chapter 9 are going to cause dramatic changes in the physical look of service centers. In particular, rising bandwidth may make the call center building obsolete with its hundreds of cubicles arrayed across a cavernous office. Once voice over Internet protocol (VOIP) becomes a practical reality for users, service center agents can be physically located anywhere where there is a reliable high-speed connection. The day of the virtual call center is not too far off, and it offers tremendous potential advantages and also a few challenges.

Costs per agent have the potential to go down dramatically in a virtual model. Agents can work from their home office, or anywhere there is a PC. Coverage can be specifically targeted. Call center volumes are very cyclical, depending upon the application. Volumes often peak at noon and end-of-workday. For example, phone orders for a soft-drink bottler form a bell curve surrounding lunch, the time when most small accounts are in operation. Rather than staffing all day for periodic peak volumes, a CIC could staff for consistent needs and have virtual agents scheduled for peak times in a core/just-in-time employment model. Agent locations can also follow the sun. Instead of paying a premium to fill a second shift, virtual agents in the U.S. could support European clients. So it is important to think of a CIC not as a physical grouping of agents, but as individuals who can be located anywhere in the world.

The last point to make about a CIC is the role of self-service. As we have mentioned, the same technology that enables a call center agent to become a CIC universal agent enables a customer, partner, or employee to become a universal self-agent. The same portals, workflows, and scripts that provide expert support for agents can be used by those initiating the interaction to resolve their own inquiries. This creates another opportunity for reducing costs.

The second component going virtual is the universal CIC agent. Technology now exists to create virtual service agents that can answer questions online.[5] Instead of having to track down supervisors for help with difficult situations, CIC agents can enter in questions and receive immediate answers from an online system. One automotive customer expects to raise the number of calls handled per agent from seven to ten customer inquiries per hour to thirty to forty calls per hour. This same virtual agent technology can then be utilized on self-service Web sites.

Ideally, the transition from a call center to a CIC should happen in concert with the transition from a content/messaging Web site to a true self-service Web portal into the organization.

Summary

The relational enterprise cannot be implemented without the transition from a call center level of service to a full CIC capability. Profitability will never be maximized with a call center because customer interactions can only be resolved, rather than customers being satisfied and ultimately pleased. The key to the CIC is universal functionality that allows prioritization within the universal queue, expert systems support for all processes, and first contact resolution of all interactions.

This takes care of the who and the where of service. The next step is to examine what the new processes will need to be.

Learning Points

1. Organizations can't bad-service their way into increased profitability.

2. To generate pleased customers who can be sold to, call centers are going to have to grow through contact centers into customer interaction centers.

3. CICs are all about integrating the entire extended enterprise into a single 360-degree view.

4. Functionality therefore has to be universal by agent, workflow, and customer queue.

5. The CIC will potentially consist of agents physically located all over the globe.

6. The same technology that supports universal agents in a CIC enables customers to serve themselves. This ultimately creates the universal customer.

NOTES

1. C. Amuso et al., "Customer Service and Support: Morphing the Call Center to a Contact Center," *Gartner Group Strategic Analysis Report*, November 16, 1998, p. 6.

2. Elizabeth Herrell, "Redefining the Call Center as a Portal to the Enterprise," *Giga Planning Assumption*, P-0100-001, January 4, 2000, p. 2.

3. Paul Greenberg, *CRM at the Speed of Light* (New York: McGraw-Hill, 2001), p. 178.

4. META Group, "META Group CRM Conference: Opening Remarks," February 21, 2000.

5. Jennifer Maselli, "Virtual Agents to Answer Online Queries," *InformationWeek*, April 16, 2001, p. 75.

*"You can't get good service from
a bad process."*

CHAPTER 11

Effective Relational Processes

S ometimes processes that seem logical at the start can take on a life
of their own, or perhaps good ideas get warped beyond reason by
overzealous managers. We recently purchased several ceiling fans made
by the same manufacturer, let's call it Ralph Waldo Fans. (We can no
longer afford the utility costs to change the air temperature, so we're just
going to move the old air around.) Included with each fan was one of
the most brazenly intrusive product registration cards we've ever seen.

The card requests the typical contact information, then asks another thirteen questions about the fan purchase. The level of detail of
the fan-related questions was extreme but at least relevant, asking about
pricing, purchase location, competition, rooms, past fan purchase history, installation plans, the decision maker, and so on. Things got out
of hand with questions 18 through 30, where Ralph Waldo wanted to
know sensitive information such as:

- Vocations and income
- Age and sex of buyer, partner, and children
- Education levels

- Credit cards owned
- Plans to have a baby, get married, move, buy a car, and so on
- Pet ownership
- Charitable donations
- Phones and computers owned
- A list of 52 hobbies or interests to check off

In all, there were twenty-three separate data fields and 223 individual check box possibilities for data entry. The incentive for completing and returning the card was an entry in a $100,000 drawing with a chance to win up to $50,000. But there was a price. At the bottom of the second side of the card, in print tiny enough to require taking my glasses off and holding it up close to read, was a paragraph that included the following statements:

"Your answers will be used for market studies and reports. They will also allow you to receive important mailing and special offers from a number of fine companies whose products and services relate directly to the specific interests, hobbies, and other information indicated above."

The paragraph ended with two very small opt-out checkboxes for receiving regular mail and e-mail from these other "fine companies." At least Ralph Waldo Fans was honest about the whole exercise, even if they still don't get the opt-in philosophy of Seth Godin's *Permission Marketing* book.

"*Allow* me to receive"? The only conclusion is that Ralph Waldo Fans must think customers are idiots. Who in their right mind would share all this intimate data with strangers intent on selling every bit of their personal information to as many different organizations as possible—all for buying a fan? Similar to the discussion in Chapter 10 about organizations trying to make call centers profitable without doing the service work in between, Ralph Waldo's marketing folks must have read the first few pages of Peppers & Rogers' *Enterprise One-to-One* and decided to wring every last dollar out of the fan-buyer contact they'd managed to capture.

The effect was to make this customer's paranoia meter jump off the scale because Ralph Waldo Fans looks so greedy. "A number of fine companies" in fifty-two areas of interest? My data isn't going to be shared with another department or a few business partners, it's going to the entire Chamber of Commerce. It's as if ceiling fans are a loss leader for the junk mail division. We wouldn't call Ralph Waldo Fans on anything but a public phone while using a voice disguiser for fear of inadvertently giving them information that they'll run off and sell. And we certainly won't buy any more of their fans.

Value-Added Processes

The Ralph Waldo Fans registration process is a great example of what can go wrong when setting up customer-facing processes. Organizations are intent on maximizing profitability, but ignore the realities of customer reactions. A good starting point is understanding why the concept of "value-added" is a familiar business term that very few people can define.

There are commonly three types of value-added activities, and we're going to add a fourth.

CUSTOMER VALUE-ADDED

The best definition of customer value-added (CVA) comes from the AMA video, *Time: The Next Dimension of Quality*.[1] Consultants Guaspari and Hay recommend three measures:

1. *Does the customer care?*
If the customer doesn't care about the process step, then it is not value-added. Fan buyers aren't looking to sign up for a mass marketing blitz, they're just buying a fan. The entire "allow you to receive" opportunity is great for the fan company, but not very desirable to the buyer. We didn't buy a fan in order to have a chance to request marketing materials.

2. *Is it done right the first time?*
In true TQM tradition, rework can never be value-added. Checking up on work previously done can't be value-added. Processes are supposed to be so well designed that they eliminate defects and minimize check steps.

3. *Does it physically change something?*

Moving data from one place to another doesn't add value. Getting an approval, making a copy, or archiving doesn't add value to customers. If no work has been accomplished, no value has been added.

BUSINESS VALUE-ADDED

There are a number of activities that aren't of interest to buying customers, but are necessities for organizations. Billing is one example. Customers would actually be more satisfied not to receive a bill, yet the seller needs to get paid. Invoicing is therefore business value-added (BVA). Customers don't care about the vendor's tax situation, yet this is certainly BVA. So there are certain things that customers don't really care about, but still add value to the organization.

NON-VALUE-ADDED

Those activities that do not meet the three criteria for a CVA activity, or are not BVA organizational needs, are non–value-added (NVA). NVA activities are ideal candidates to be nuked. If it doesn't add value, get rid of it.

CUSTOMER VALUE-SUBTRACT

Customer value-subtract (CVS) is our addition to the list. Going back to the fan example, my signing up for Ralph Waldo's spam list is BVA to them, but it is worse than NVA to me. The over-the-top request for information in return for a measly chance at some sweepstakes that might not even be legal in my state is a dissatisfier—a CVS.

It's one thing to have NVA activities that raise costs and slow down service. It's a far more serious problem to have formal relationship processes that actively turn off customers, a sort of anti-loyalty program. Imagine, Ralph Waldo Fans has formalized a process that aggravates customers. Some poor factory worker actually gets disciplined when he or she forgets to include a registration card that scares away repeat customers.

With these concepts about value-add, it is relatively simple to list out the steps of a process in a value-added or process flowchart and apply the three rules to determine which activities are truly value-added to customers.

GOOFY/HINDER QUESTIONS

Another great analysis tool is to simply ask people, "What hinders you in your job? And what do you do that's goofy?" It's much like Art Linkletter interviewing the row of grade schoolers appearing on his *House Party* show, all of whom have been prepped by relatives not to spill the family secrets on national TV. He would instantly destroy any conditioning by innocently asking, "What did mom or dad tell you not to talk about today?"

This is a great discovery method. I was walking through a small sales call center one afternoon with the center manager, who was not happy that the president had sent me down for the tour. As we passed by an available agent, I asked the goofy/hinder questions. She told me, "What hinders us? Well, every afternoon about 3:00 p.m., our busiest time, the system goes down. We have to take down the orders by hand and then rush to get them input before the deadline for next-day shipment." When I asked how long this had been going on, she told me, "Two years."

"And you know what's goofy?" she continued. "When the phone lines get full, a red light goes on in the supervisor's office."

"What happens then?" I asked.

"Nothing, just the light goes on to tell her we're busy. It would be great if we could actually get some help."

At this point, the manager was sputtering. He had worked there for years and was unaware of any of this. Front-line agents know what's wrong with processes. They battle the problems every day. This is why we include goofy/hinder questions in quality climate surveys that we require clients to complete before starting any business process redesign project.

A good rule of thumb is that up to 75 percent of the process time can be saved by eliminating the NVA steps. The best way to identify these steps is to create a value-added flow chart listing the steps an object undergoes throughout its life in a process. Table 11-1 shows a "before" value-added chart that lists step descriptions, durations, and value-added status for a simple donation request process. This is a typical submit, approve, and pay process that took seven to ten elapsed working days to complete.

Table 11-2 then shows the "after" version generated by eliminating as many NVA activities as possible. The process improvement team

Table 11-1. Value-added flow chart—donation request "before."

ACTIVITY	DURATION	VALUE
Customer calls/visits to make request.	1 day	CVA
Give executive with responsibility the request.	1 day	NVA
Executive makes decision.	1-2 days	NVA
Customer inquires for answer.	1 day	NVA
Send request to bookkeeping.	1 day	NVA
Bookkeeping not there in afternoon.	1 day	NVA
Check mailed or customer picks up.	1-3 days	CVA
TOTAL	7 to 10 days	

was able to reduce elapsed time to one to three days by setting up a pre-approved list and eliminating the executive's NVA involvement for each request. Overall organizational time to process the request was reduced, and a decision was delivered much quicker to the customer.

The donation example is an actual process from one of our sessions. We have introduced this value-added flow chart improvement technique in a few minutes to workers, and had them redesigning live processes before they left the room. They are always amazed to find how many non-value-added activities are embedded in their processes.

Systematizing Relational Processes

This brings up the million-dollar question: So which processes do you automate?

1. Do you limit effectiveness and competitiveness by systematizing current processes that were designed for a different technology and contain significant NVA or CVS activities?

Table 11-2. Value-added flow chart—donation request "after."

ACTIVITY	DURATION	VALUE
Executive with responsibility pre-approves donations for this budget period based on previous year's roster, current plans, and this year's budget.	Once	BVA
Customer calls/visits to make request.	1 day	CVA
(1) Secretary checks against roster and amount, and immediately approves if listed.	0 days	CVA
(2) Or secretary offers lesser pre-approved amount.	0 days	CVA
(3) Or if not on list, lets customer fill out a request for the next budget period.	0 days	CVA
Bookkeeping writes check and hands to customer or mails.	0-2 days	CVA
TOTAL	1 to 3 days	

2. Do you use a new RM project to redesign processes and so complicate the conversion and installation project with unproven procedures that it has reduced chances for success?

3. Do you try to do a little bit of both in order to keep the project manageable and yet get some benefits from improved processes?

The concern is not to automate your own incompetence, something META Group labels a "recipe for failure."[2]

Facing these options, some vendors suggest installing their solutions unchanged out of the box. Their philosophy is, "We've done the best practices research and we're the expert, so our processes are better than yours anyway." The vendor decision then becomes a massive feature comparison checklist with the best feature set winning out. This simplifies installation and supposedly delivers improved application processes.

The weakness of this approach is that of reduced effectiveness and competitiveness. Organizations have spent decades learning how to beat their competition. These tailored processes are then thrown out in the interests of smoother systems installations. Next, using the same software out-of-box as a competitor delivers no advantage. For example, IBM recently "standardized" itself and its partners on a single SFA package. It is helpful for IBM, perhaps, to move as many of its partners as possible to the same selling system. But it delivers little value-add to the partners who might someday be using the exact same sales technology and processes as thousands of their IBM partner competitors.

The other end of the spectrum is to go with more of a toolkit that allows total customization of a system. Some years back one of the major automotive companies bought only the tools portion of a major CRM system and used it to program a totally customized service application. This was a massive undertaking, but resulted in a system exactly tailored to the complex needs of the manufacturer.

The best approach is somewhere in between, with the initial emphasis on business needs. An insurance company executive explained how his company worked to be certain that a credit card payment process improvement team (PIT) was effective. "The mandate for every PIT starts with clearly shared objectives emphasizing a 'business first' value system. . . . Because credit card billing touches virtually every process of the company, we started by resolving the interlocking business, administrative, and technical processes that would be required to support credit card transactions."[3]

The insurer's focus was on business process first, then technology. The quote also shows that it recognized the importance of a company-wide solution to this specific "moment of truth." The effectiveness of the customer experience was the prime concern.

An insightful quote about process came from a META Group conference speaker on operational CRM. "Organizations should not be automating the sales force. They should be automating the sales process."[4] As the first three chapters explained, the direct sales force is only a small part of the sales process and represents a subset of the channels. Doing

SFA is at best a partial solution. The correct approach is to look at sales *process* automation (SPA) across the entire relational enterprise.

Who Owns the Process?

The problem with adapting a SPA-style philosophy is, Who owns the sales process? The marketing department conducts research and executes on campaigns. Inside sales does lead management. Outside sales make calls and closes sales. A dedicated IT group maintains the e-store with input from product managers. Parts sales come and go through the inventory department, with orders taken through the call center or on Web site pages that inventory creates and maintains itself. Partner sales are completely automated through the supply-chain system, maintained by a dedicated group. Operations controls parts charged through billable field service calls. There are separate on-quota specialists who sell service contracts to the existing client base. And a vice president, who is number two in the company, is pushing to make all this happen on a consolidated corporate Web site. SFA? It's a minor issue in the pantheon of SPA concerns.

For that matter, who owns any process? By ownership, we mean someone who is in charge of how the process is supposed to work, and who is responsible for its continuous improvement. If Philip Crosby's version of quality is, "Do it right, or change the way it's supposed to be done," then who has the right to change processes?[5] When there are ambiguities or disagreements about how to accomplish something within the process, who makes the decision?

Processes can occur by default. Organizational policy is often set by some programmer deciding on IF statement arguments. Sometimes processes evolve beyond the reasons for their existence. During a BPR assignment, we talked to an administrator who received five copies of a report. He described where four of them went and didn't mention the fifth. When we asked about it, he explained that he put it into a desk. Then what? When the desk became full, he threw the copies away to make room for more. (Goofy) Why? Because he had been trained to do it that way.

The question isn't, "How could this happen?" The real issue is,

"Who could have changed it once it was recognized?" While quality professionals call this the process owner, financial professionals call this the *system of record* owner. Many organizational process failures can be linked to the fact that there is no process owner, and there is no system of record to own.

One executive, tired of finding only gum wrappers in suggestion boxes mounted on walls around the plant, scrapped the entire idea program. Instead, process owners who had in-depth operational knowledge were selected and a chart with the process name and the owner's name, picture, and department was mounted on the wall of a main hallway.

Those individuals' performance plans were modified to include the responsibility to improve the processes they had been entrusted with, and employees were urged to share all improvement ideas directly with the appropriate process owner. Owners actively solicited ideas and comments from coworkers, and were specially trained to facilitate improvement efforts using teams. This organization turned a lifeless formal suggestion program into a lively, front-line oriented improvement process that invited cooperation and communications.

Summary

Without process owners and a formal system of record, processes are in the same situation as traditional customers of a hierarchical organization. When everyone is responsible for improving processes, no one is responsible.

One of the top five goals for IT managers in 2001 is to streamline business processes.[6] The only way to guarantee continuous process improvement is right out of Management 101. Give people the authority, responsibility, resources, and then get out of the way. That means designing solutions to business problems first, then adopting the technology to implement them. This design begins with the data that is collected, and is the subject of our next chapter.

Learning Points

1. Pigs get greedy, hogs get slaughtered. Organizations can't act like a starving used-car salesperson spotting the first person to walk on the lot in a month.

2. You can't fool customers into loyalty. Calling a mass spam campaign an opportunity just makes customers doubt everything else you say. You'll have better luck convincing children to enjoy their medicine.

3. The goal is to pare processes down to primarily CVA and BVA activities. The benefits can be enormous from this simple improvement approach.

4. Goofy/hinder questions are great tools for uncovering broken processes.

5. Don't automate your own incompetence. Solve business problems first and then implement the technology.

6. Every process needs an owner who is responsible for its continuous improvement. Every process should have a system of record for reference.

NOTES

1. John Guaspari & Edward Hay, *Time: The Next Dimension of Quality*, videotape (American Management Association, 1993), 18 minutes.

2. META Group, "META Group CRM Conference: Value Management," February 21, 2000.

3. John Kador, "Leveraging Process Improvement: Four Strategies to Squeeze Success From Process Improvement," *InfoWorld*, March 19, 2001.

4. META Group, "CRM Conference: Opening Remarks ," February 21, 2000.

5. Philip Crosby, *Quality Is Free: The Art of Making Quality Certain*, (New York: Mentor, 1979), p. 15.

6. InformationWeek Research, "Streamlining Business Processes," *InformationWeek*, April 2, 2001, p. 6.

PART THREE

RELATIONAL
ENTERPRISE SYSTEMS

CHAPTER 12

New Relational Data Types

Sometimes the little things will trip you up, and they often come from the most unexpected places. The corporate business development group of a major bank had been working for months to secure a multi-hundred million-dollar treasury management agreement with a major manufacturer in its city. The deal was ready to close and had been passed on to the company's president for approval.

On the following Monday the bank's account manager received a call from her contact at the client and was told that the deal was off, that the manufacturer was going with a competing local bank. Stunned, she asked what happened, since the deal was supposedly all but signed. The answer was, "Over the weekend our president had dinner with his son who just graduated from college. It seems you turned his son down for a car loan and our president was furious. I had a message waiting for me first thing this morning, 'If my son's not good enough for them, then neither is my company. Find another bank.'"

Fair? Maybe not. Understandable? You bet. Top executives aren't used to being told "No" on anything, and often have high dominance personalities. But, you say, one banking interaction involved corporate finance and the other was consumer banking. These are totally separate divisions within the bank, so there is no way anyone could be expected to connect the two situations. True, except that they weren't different to the customer. It was the same bank.

It's easy to point the finger of blame in this situation at the retail banker or the treasury sales group, but it's not really their fault. The problem is that there was no capability to capture data that would allow either department to associate the two transactions in the unique way required. I've never seen a loan application that asks, "Do you have any important relatives who are currently prospects for any of the bank's corporate, retail, or trust services?" Even if it did ask, chances are the son wouldn't have known that there was a big treasury management deal pending at dad's company anyway.

Contrast this with the Ritz-Carlton hotel chain, a past Malcolm Baldrige Quality Award winner. The Ritz systematizes its customer data gathering to collect a wide range of unique information that employees can use to increase satisfaction and effectiveness. It gives every employee "Guest Personal Preference Communique" forms to record guest preferences. When we last did a best practices benchmarking of Ritz-Carlton for another client, there had been preferences of 120,000 individual guests recorded over a three-year period.

The Communique is not a part of any standard service process, it is completed at the initiative of employees. Whenever they encounter anything of interest, they may fill out the short form and put it in a centrally located box for later entry into the Ritz's system. For instance, if you don't like a pickle on your sandwich, that might be recorded. Then any room service meal you order in *any* Ritz-Carlton hotel worldwide will not have a pickle on it because the kitchen staff sees preference information attached to your order screen. If you took your spouse to a Ritz-Carlton on your anniversary and happened to mention it to any of the staff, if you ever again stay at a Ritz on that same day, the wake-up call will be, "Good morning Mr. Cooper, this is your wake up call. Happy anniversary . . ." Any special days, birthdays, spouse's birthday—that is, anything you mention—is recorded and available to everyone in the hotel looking at your record on the system.

Do practices such as these get results? Again, at the time of our benchmarking visit, the Ritz-Carlton quoted business results such as:

- Published satisfaction rating of 94 percent versus the nearest competitor at 54 percent
- Complaints per hundred comments reduced 27 percent
- Improved key account retention by 20 percent
- Highest market yield (revenue per available room) in the industry

Certainly, not all of these results are due to the guest preferences database system, but it is this type of process that contributes to competitive advantages and keeps one department from undoing another department's good work.

New Data Types Are Required

It is not so much that we need to know far more about our customers, it's that we need to know more of the right information. A point solution, localized-value approach to customer interactions is supported by a similarly focused data schema. The best example is in the call center, which, as we saw, requires a fundamental change in its most basic informational structure to make the transition to a CIC.

In looking at data, the question is, "What is the primary unit of measure from the organization's standpoint?" The answer is *case* or *incident*. Think of this as the root data structure of the entire service database. Let's take an example of a customer situation that is going to require some follow-up.

A customer calls in about a problem and reaches a call center agent. The agent enters the pertinent information, determines that there can't be an immediate resolution, promises a follow-up action, and then sets up the appropriate notifications and escalations. The last thing the agent tells the customer is, "Let me assign you a case number. If you have any questions or want to check on the status, just give the agent this number: 150.00012175. This will get right to your data next time and you won't be charged for a separate incident."

How does the customer refer to the incident? "This is my third call about . . ." or "I've got a couple of issues I need to ask about. . . ." Customers measure service based upon conversations. They don't make distinctions between cases and departments and agents. As we saw in Chapter 10, they don't want to ask about one issue, then hang up and call another department about something else. It's all one combined service experience, just like the bank was both a commercial bank and a consumer bank to the manufacturing executive at the beginning of this chapter. This says that the most fundamental, basic unit of a call center database may be obsolete. This is the death knell for point solutions, because they don't capture the proper information.

In relational systems, the measure is not the case or incident, but the *interaction*. Customers don't want to know solely about calls concerning a single issue, they want to know about their interactions across the entire enterprise. Therefore, organizations need to be able to see each touch, every moment of truth with the customer—no matter which department was contacted or for what reason. This is the only way to avoid the bank situation where the treasury sales team was inadvertently sabotaged by consumer lending. Every salesperson who has optimistically walked into a sales presentation only to find a customer furious over a billing problem understands this need.

These new information requirements are far more than filling in some reserved data table with new records, and then splashing them up on a screen. Changing the base unit of record-keeping and data presentation from a case to an interaction is a fundamental extension of the functionality and workflow of RM applications. This data has to be integrated across all roles that might possibly be affected by interactions. As Figure 12-1 shows, this is only one of the new types of data that is required for profitable relationships.

People-Oriented Data Elements

There are new data elements that must be added in relational systems, many of these depending upon the vertical application. Following are some of the common elements that typically don't appear in existing RM solutions.

INTERACTION

Finance and insurance industries were among the first to recognize the importance of switching over to this data element as a basic unit. Interaction views summarize all customer touches regardless of channel.

Figure 12-1. New data objects.

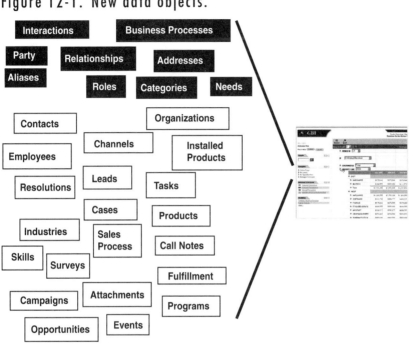

The insurance example in Figure 12-2 shows a phone call interaction being recorded by a service center agent. Notice the list on the lower left side of the screen displaying this client's history of all interactions from multiple channels, in this case phone calls in and a letter sent out.

Information about multiple products are indicated with circled P's in the box on the upper left side of the screen. A single insurance agent visit or phone inquiry can cover several policies, so getting a consolidated cross-product-line view of the customer is also necessary in servicing and selling customers. The policy maturity dates can be used to begin the selling up process for additional or extended coverage. All this is impossible with only a case-by-case or policy-by-policy view with no information to link the breadth of customer relationships with the insurance company and the insurance agent sales partner.

RELATIONSHIP
It no longer makes sense to focus just on who is buying products. First, both the spider chart's organization and redefinition of customers

Figure 12-2. Interaction data object.

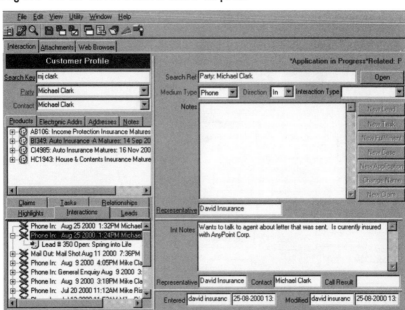

show that everyone is a customer of one sort or another. The customer box is only one of many that can generate profit for an organization. "Customer" can now refer to people in complicated chains, such as suppliers' customers or customers' suppliers or outsourcers' employees or partners' suppliers' customer. It's incredibly helpful to know where in the world some of these people come from. Systems must be able to keep track of these convoluted connections and help any enterprise constituent leverage the unique opportunities these relationships represent.

Second, there are other individuals in the buying process who may have a significant influence on the sale, but are not represented in the database. If a salesperson is facing a "see my mother" close, then mom is a key factor in the sale and should have a spot somewhere in the database to indicate it. Business owners may have asked their lawyer, accountant, broker, or consultant to act as their adviser and get involved in a buying decision. While these service professionals are not customers, they may be more important to the ultimate sales decision than customers themselves.

Another example of an influencer is the low-level PC evaluator buried like Gollum in the Misty Mountains of the IT department. This person will never sign a P.O. or in any way appear on a list of customers, yet is likely to be one of *the* key decision makers in determining the choice of a PC vendor for corporate standards. Transactional systems will never recognize this caller as important. An RM system with the relationship data type can code this person as a high priority contact and provide premium service for any hardware questions or problems. Literally thousands of sales units could be depending upon the recommendations of this so-called noncustomer.

Third, relationship is a valuable piece of data in prospecting for additional customers. People often buy based on the recommendations of their family, friends, and coworkers. Organizations may want to target offerings to groups of people living on the same block, belonging to the same church, or involved in the same hobbies. A credit union that allows family members to join may want to market to relatives. Organizations may have special discount offerings for partner employees. The box in the lower left of Figure 12-3 shows an example relationship tree containing information on family, business, and social connections. This is the screen that could have told that loan officer from the beginning of this chapter to *give* the prospect president's son a car, if necessary.

ROLE

There may be a variety of individuals who are given permission to act for the customer or who are integral parts of the transaction. This can include lawyers, trustees, investment managers, financial planners, agents, family members, guardians, justice system authorities, step-parents, those with power of attorney, licensees, and so on. In a real estate transaction, for example, a multitude of roles can be involved: builder or seller, seller's agent, buyer, buyer's agent, appraiser, building inspector, pest inspector, banker, and a title company. There is only one "buyer," yet any one of these individuals is interacting throughout the transaction or can kill the deal. A transactional system needs this data type and the associated business logic behind the scenes to leverage it.

ALIAS

Traditional transactional systems have difficulty dealing with overlapping data. An alias data element is useful for situations where an

Figure 12-3. Relationships data object.

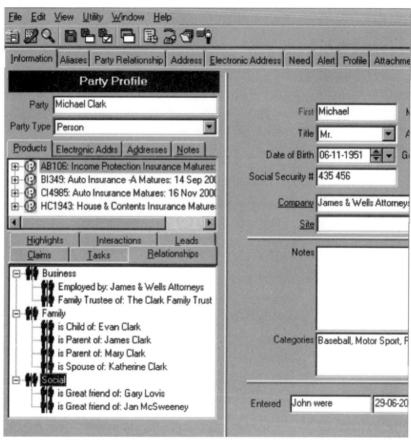

individual or organization may be listed under a variety of labels or names depending upon the timeframe. Examples are a woman getting married and changing her last name, a child being adopted, a subsidiary of a bigger company, or a corporate name change. The historical records for these entities are listed under two different before-after names, which causes difficulty in accessing the entire record of interaction.

Figure 12-4 shows an example of an alias screen, which lists Michael Clark's legal name, other names he may have used on applications or interactions, and any casual names or nicknames. A woman could marry, marry again, then return to her maiden name. The same thing can happen to businesses. A company can be bought out, or a self-

Figure 12-4. Alias data object.

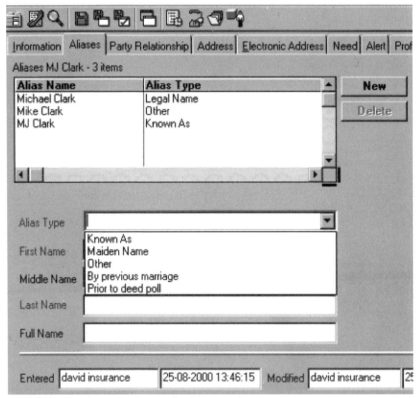

employed professional could be working under a registered fictitious name. This data element allows all the related interactions to be grouped into one summary screen.

PARTY

This data type is what this insurance system uses to identify individuals. More of a global label, it recognizes the variety of people that could be involved in processes. This might include a customer, lawyer, accountant, investment advisor, trustee, relative, and so on.

ADDRESSES

This would appear to be a familiar data type. Addresses have existed since people have had homes (for example, Thog, third cave from the left). The difference is that, in a relational system, there may be more than one address per party, and more than one party per address.

Figure 12-5 shows four possible addresses for Michael Clark: a home, a post office box, a business address, and an inactive home address. In this age of home-office workers, it is not unusual for a party to have both a home and local office address, as well as apartment and office addresses in the headquarters city. Many transactional systems would account for this as four separate customers. Compound this process across all the possible roles in the real estate example mentioned above, and the problem becomes a system killer.

NEED

There are a number of new data types that enhance the revenue opportunities of an organization. Need is an item that rarely appears in existing sales and marketing systems. This isn't necessarily a follow-up

Figure 12-5. Addresses data object.

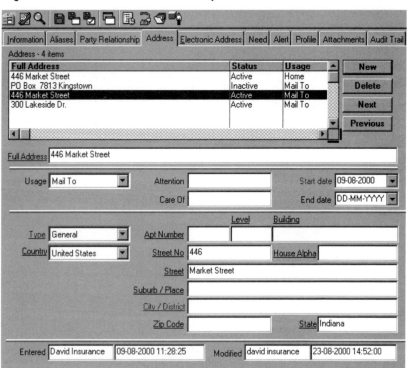

request. It is similar to an explicit need as described in Rackham's *SPIN Selling* book.[1] As the example in Figure 12-6 shows, need can create workflow notifications for later action, and can be linked to products, sales reps, or parties.

ALERT

Alert is an all-purpose data type that can be utilized for helpful information that service personnel (or business logic) should know about. The screen in Figure 12-7 illustrates an overdue payment situation with Katherine Clark, Michael Clark's wife. This is an excellent illustration of integrating data types, such as relationship and alerts, with a workflow process that adds value. When Michael calls in about his policy, the agent is alerted to several important facts:

- Michael is profiled as a high profit Very Important Customer.

- His wife's payment is overdue.

Figure 12-6. Needs data object.

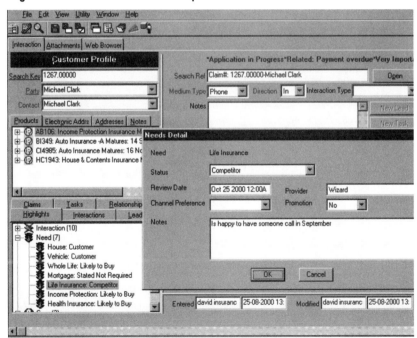

Figure 12-7. Alert data object.

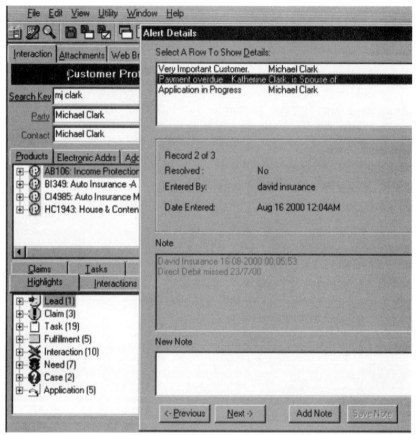

- The company made a mistake and missed a direct debit payment, so there has been a problem in the past.

- There is a policy application currently in the system that hasn't yet been finalized. It could be at risk if there are any more problems.

This alert information allows the agent to provide better service by reminding the client of the potential payment problem before a lapse warning is sent, and to take actions commensurate with the client's product ownership status and sales situation. This makes for a more satisfied client and a happier agent partner, David Insurance.

Product-Oriented Data Elements

There are also a number of relational data elements that are product oriented.

- **Package.** A package is comprised of one or more components. So an asymmetric digital subscriber line (ADSL), high-speed Internet access service order might include modem hardware, wiring, Internet access, a router/hub, self-install or field service, and feature decisions, such as static or dynamic IP addresses.

- **Feature.** Feature is a subcategory that represents a valid component of another product or service that cannot be ordered directly. For example, a PC consists of case, motherboard, memory, CPU, drives, and software, none of which may be ordered separately by a department store electronics buyer.

- **Feature Group.** A feature group is a collection of features where, if included or required, one of the features from the group must be ordered. This is an important data type of e-store or ordering systems, where buyers must select at least one item from each list of options.

- **Attribute.** Attributes describe other data objects, such as employee, party, product, or company. An employee could be a telecommuter, have a company car, be vested, and have an expense account. These attributes then come into play in interactions concerning work records, expenses, or benefits. Figure 12-8 illustrates how an e-mail account might have multiple name, account type, and password attributes specified.

These are some of the major data types that must be added to create RM applications that allow both people and system objects to relate as needed. Client companies can have multiple *Sites*. Relationships might have multiple *Classifications*, such as "business affiliate" or "family affiliate." Vertical applications require specialized data types and workflow. Banks, for example, need a *Signature* data type to keep track of who is allowed to withdraw from accounts. There can be literally hundreds of new data types that must be created, then supported with

Figure 12-8. Attribute data object.

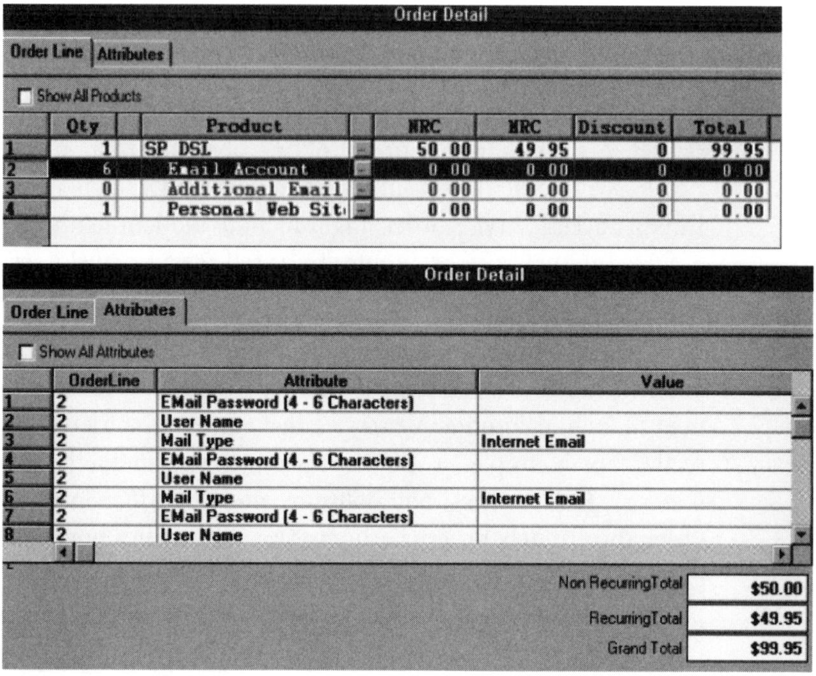

	Order Detail					

Order Line | Attributes |

☐ Show All Products

	Qty	Product		NRC	NRC	Discount	Total
1	1	SP DSL		50.00	49.95	0	99.95
2	6	Email Account		0.00	0.00	0	0.00
3	0	Additional Email		0.00	0.00	0	0.00
4	1	Personal Web Sit		0.00	0.00	0	0.00

	Order Detail	

Order Line | Attributes |

☐ Show All Attributes

	OrderLine	Attribute	Value
1	2	EMail Password (4 - 6 Characters)	
2	2	User Name	
3	2	Mail Type	Internet Email
4	2	EMail Password (4 - 6 Characters)	
5	2	User Name	
6	2	Mail Type	Internet Email
7	2	EMail Password (4 - 6 Characters)	
8	2	User Name	

Non RecurringTotal	$50.00
RecurringTotal	$49.95
Grand Total	$99.95

the proper workflow to implement the corresponding business logic and processes.

Once these data objects have been created, they can then be used by service agents in systems, such as those we've seen so far in this chapter, or they can be used to provide functionality to other relational enterprise constituents. Figure 12-9 shows an insurance agent (sales partner) portal screen that includes new data types such as Party. Figure 12-10 illustrates how the same technology can be used to create self-service capabilities such as this policy application screen for customers.

This has not been intended as an exhaustive list of relational data elements. That can vary greatly by company or vertical industry. For example, the insurance company mentioned in this chapter has had the following added to the CRM suite upon which it is based: 26 new data tables, 14 new elements, 67 new forms, 4 new groups, 111 new procedures, and 16 new action triggers. All of these must be supported by associated workflow rules and processes.

Figure 12-9. Partner portal.

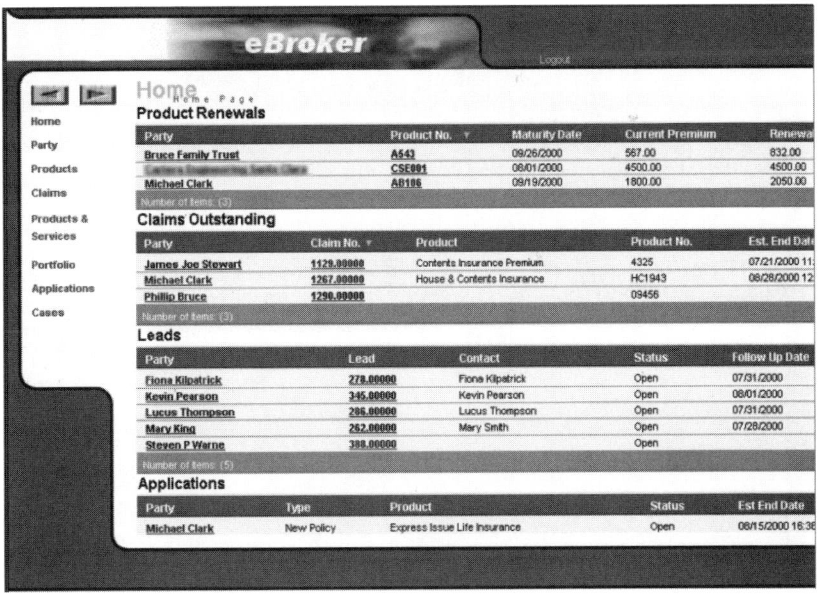

Summary

Traditional customer-facing systems create two concerns. (1) They typically do not contain the full range of data elements required to implement an enterprise-wide RM system. (2) They do not contain the data elements required for CIC agents to provide the best service. The new data elements described in this chapter show what is required to truly maximize customer service, satisfaction, and profitability of a relational enterprise. Our next step is to explore the applications themselves.

Learning Points

1. Traditional CRM applications and point solutions don't contain the data types necessary to maximize customer service and profitability.

2. A customized and focused database structure can provide a significant competitive advantage. Just ask Ritz-Carlton.

Figure 12-10. Customer self-service.

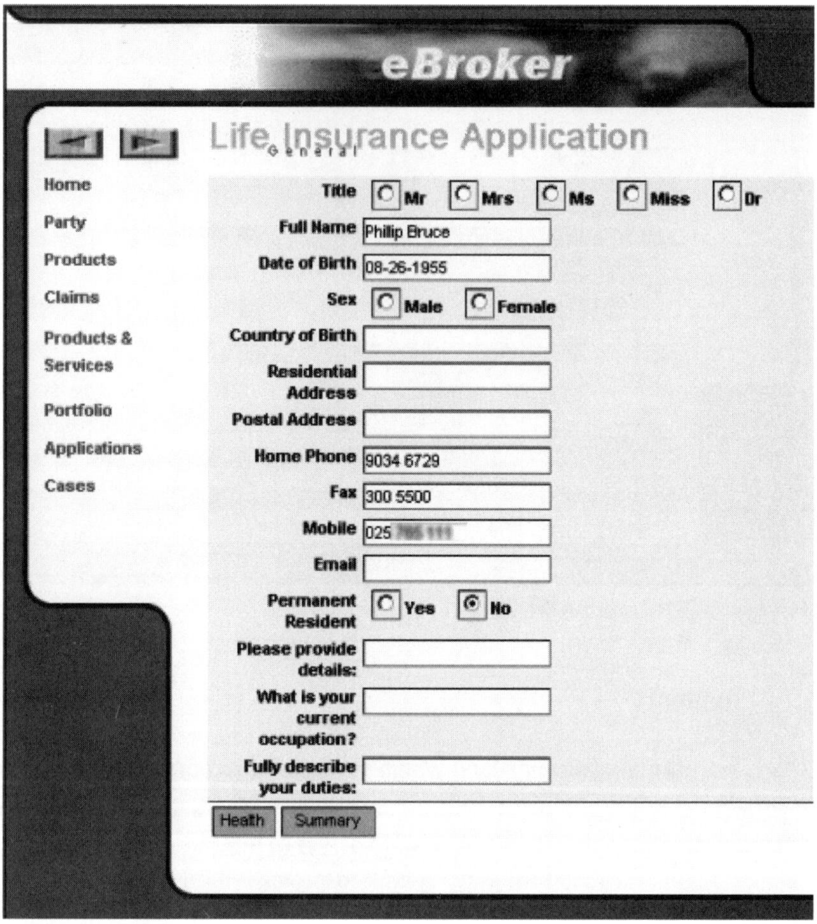

3. To become a CIC, the primary data unit of a call center—the case—needs to be supplemented with a new fundamental unit—the interaction. Only an interaction summary that includes information from all contact channels and touch points can provide a 360-degree view throughout the entire business cycle.

4. There are lots of new data types required in a relational enterprise. A few of the people-oriented types are interaction, rela-

tionship, role, alias, party, addresses, need, and alert. Product-oriented data elements include package, feature, feature group, and attribute.

5. A tailored industry solution is more than just adding a few data tables and displaying them somewhere on a screen. As an example, the data elements in this chapter are just a few of the 238 additions that an insurance solution required to be added to a standard CRM suite.

NOTES
1. Neil Rackham, *SPIN Selling*, (New York: McGraw-Hill, 1988), p. 58.

CHAPTER 13

Understanding Relational Systems

There is a common process that organizations go through in selecting a relational system. First they conduct a preliminary market review and create a list of potential vendors. After initial sales calls, six to eight vendors are invited in for a "how we see things" presentation. The goal is to find out what's going on in the market and what the various solution approaches are. Then the list is pared down to four or five main vendors for a generic product demonstration. At this point the buyer goes away and writes a request for proposal (RFP), selecting two or three vendors it is willing to have sign a nondisclosure agreement and turn loose to do research in the organization. The goal here is a customized demonstration, built to the RFP's requirements, and a written proposal. Then a final decision is made.

Like the old joke, this is a great trip, but the first step is a killer. Decision-makers who have sat through the two-day marathon of initial vendor pitches say it is one of the most confusing things they have ever been subjected to. In the words of one RM buying-team member, "It's like talking to the IT group and knowing less walking out than I did going in."

The problem is that all the vendors appear to have the exact same messages: Customer service and satisfaction are critical. Multichannel access is provided. Everyone is moving to the Web. The systems architecture diagrams look exactly the same. There is an applications suite. All the functionality is customizable and easy to integrate with other systems. It's almost like the sales reps are interchangeable, with any of them being able to give the others' pitches. Differentiating between vendors is little more than, "Let's pick the folks wearing suits." There's got to be a better way.

Relational Systems Architecture

The place to begin our understanding of relational systems is with its architecture. We've literally spent an entire week training technical salespeople on this topic alone, so this section is intended only as an overview. The goal here is to become familiar with some of the key terms, and to explore how vendors explain their architecture.

Vendors love to talk about tiers. There are two-tier, three-tier, or so-called n-tier architectures out there. A *two-tier architecture* consists of a server and a client. Business and application logic resides in both locations, meaning that any changes to application code or screen presentation have to be propagated out to all users. Two-tier client code can be as large as 50MB, so this can put a burden on network systems for local users and is extremely difficult to distribute in a remote environment where it might take five hours to download an update. Depending upon the database used, it can be a challenge to scale two-tier systems for a large number of users.

A *three-tier architecture* places an application server on the network in between the client and database. This allows a client to hold minimal or no application logic, which makes upgrades far easier. The application server provides many advantages including increased scalability, easier upgrading of applications, more security for the database, and easier integration.

Finally, in a multichannel environment, there may be another level, such as a Web server, fax server, mobile server, or "something new" server between the application server and various channel clients.

Putting this all together results in an architecture that looks like Figure 13-1. In this scheme, the separate application server continues to deliver great value.

A key factor in performance, reliability, and ease of upgrading is how and where the various types of data—such as application logic, user interface layouts, and data table definitions—are stored. A term that

Figure 13-1. Relational systems architecture.

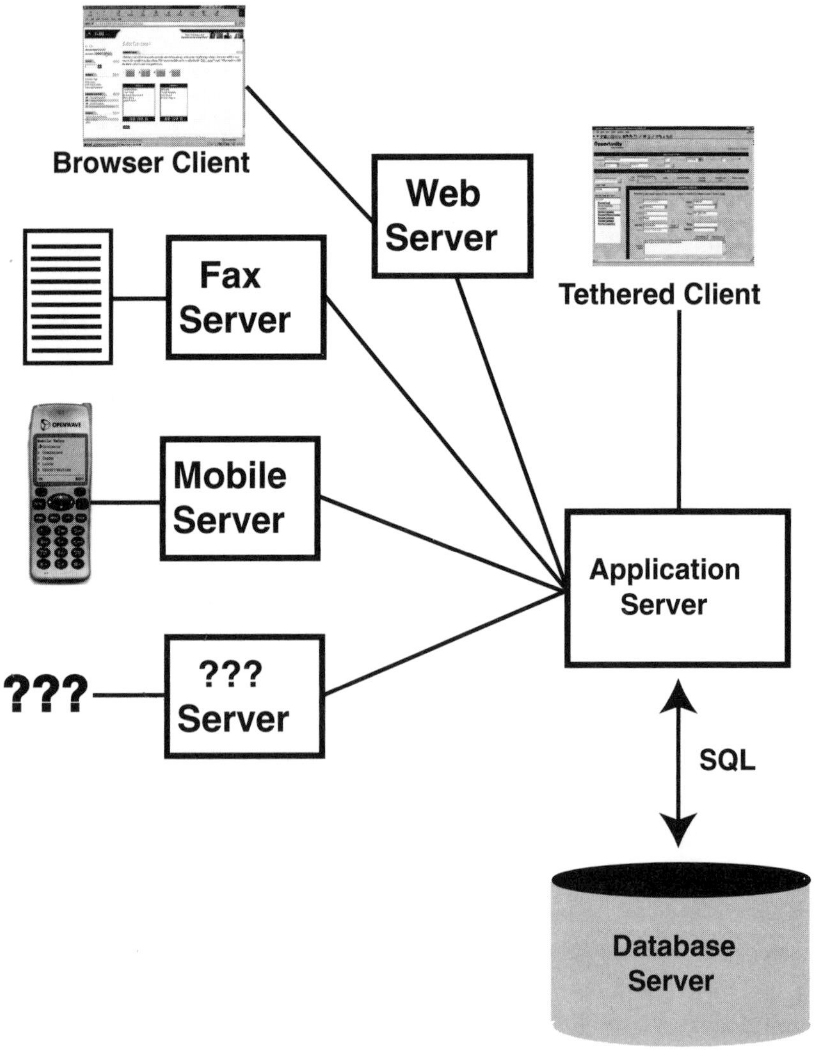

comes up frequently is "metadata"—data that describes other data. Metadata is not defined using application code, so a metadata interface file doesn't contain an actual screen layout, only a description of that screen. This greatly reduces the volume of information that must be transmitted at runtime, and it streamlines technology upgrades.

All this may be confusing, but the reason for discussing it here is that the architectural story of some vendors tends to get fuzzy. Although everyone shows a similar three-tier diagram, the terms can be misleading. There will be an "application" layer mentioned so that the diagram looks three-tier, but this will be a logical function in a two-tier system and not a physical server. Another fuzzy area is in so-called Web-enabled applications. As we will show, there are a variety of ways to bring applications to the Internet—all with different value propositions.

This is why the involvement of IT is so important. Sorting through the vagaries of vendor propaganda is not for technology neophytes. Sometimes it takes real digging to understand the true architectural base for a vendor's system, and to grasp the differences between what they are currently delivering and what is coming RSN (real soon now).

Types of RM Applications

The issue of feature-by-feature application comparisons is going to be covered later, in Chapter 16. What is needed at this point is to understand the various application technology levels and what they offer organizations. It will be useful to glance back at Figure 13-1 as you read through this section to determine where each of the five possible approaches fits in the overall architecture.

1. STAND-ALONE APPLICATIONS
There are a number of single application solutions for small to mid-size companies and workgroups. These consist of everything from SFA packages that can be purchased at the local computer retailer to Web-based application service providers that can have multiple users of an organization up and running in minutes. These are available, but are not really suitable for the organization wishing to become a relational enterprise.

2. TETHERED NETWORK APPLICATIONS

This is the technology commonly used for PC clients connected locally over a network in both two-tier and three-tier architectures. Applications can be Win16 clients running under DOS/Windows 3.1 or Win32 clients running on Windows 95 or higher. The screens typically have a classic database application look and feel, although several vendors have created a browser-like look for their Win32 interfaces. While some buyers may feel this is "outdated" technology, many organizations are still implementing these systems due to their mature feature set, proven reliability, high productivity, object-oriented tool sets, and capability to scale to tens of thousands of simultaneous local users.

Figure 13-2 shows an example of a typical tethered client sales opportunity screen. Note the uncluttered layout and graphic elements. Win32 interfaces are typically easy to customize without having to be a

Figure 13-2. Win32 client.

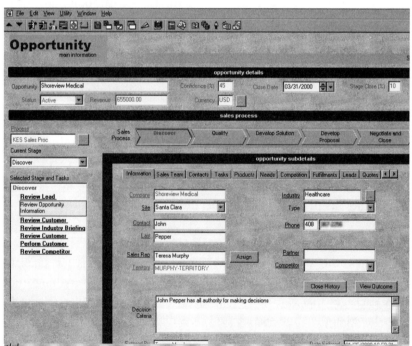

programmer. This technology can present quite a sophisticated inter-face, and utilizes familiar Windows constructs such as drop down boxes, buttons, and hyper-linked text. Also note the tabs across the Opportunity Subdetails section. This provides what is called a "flat and wide" interface. Users can use the tabs to quickly see related screens. This makes Win32 applications very easy to use and navigate with either mouse or keyboard. Win32 applications also use screen space quite efficiently. A Web browser layout, whether a Win32 or browser client, gives away as much as 40 percent of the screen real estate to navigation areas across the top and down the left side.

In formal RFP demonstrations of CIC systems, center managers will sit in the back room with a mechanical clicker, counting every keystroke and mouse click of the required demo sequence for each vendor. Operations costs are a critical issue, and additional keystrokes or reaching for a mouse hurts agent productivity. If one vendor requires 10 percent fewer keystrokes or mouse clicks for the demo, this can contribute significantly to better agent utilization.

Finally, the brightly colored Web implementations of some vendors can grow tiresome to a center user who is an all-day every-day agent, just like a Windows user gets bored with the same desktop wallpaper picture. The Win32 client is not so distracting.

Although some vendors will claim that these systems are out-of-date, organizations with an immature intranet infrastructure or high scalability requirements will find Win32 solutions to be a high productivity approach for heads-down agent applications. But these applications potentially are not as useful for periodic users or remote users who are not connected to the network.

Periodic users may need the more intuitive interface of a browser application and usually prefer a more visually stimulating look and feel. Remote users may find it easier to operate an online application rather than working offline and having to do daily batch synchronizations of their database with the master file. And Win32 clients require at least some form of client software to be loaded. True zero-client applications can be accessed from any Web client containing a compatible browser.

3. WEB PORTS

These are applications that retain their complete Win32 client look and feel, but are ported to the Web. In the early days of the Internet, this was a fast way for vendors to get applications online, and it provided a consistent interface to remote and local users. Figure 13-3 shows an example of an inquiry message screen that was created with this approach.

4. HYBRID APPLICATIONS

The next stage was to create separate Internet applications that run on top of or beside existing Win32 applications. Interface customizations could be made with simple Web design tools. In some instances, the Web application took the Win32 application output and then sent it to the Web using HTML. In other cases, the Web application took its data directly from the application server without requiring the equivalent Win32 application to be installed. Figure 13-4 shows a Web-based SFA

Figure 13-3. Web port client.

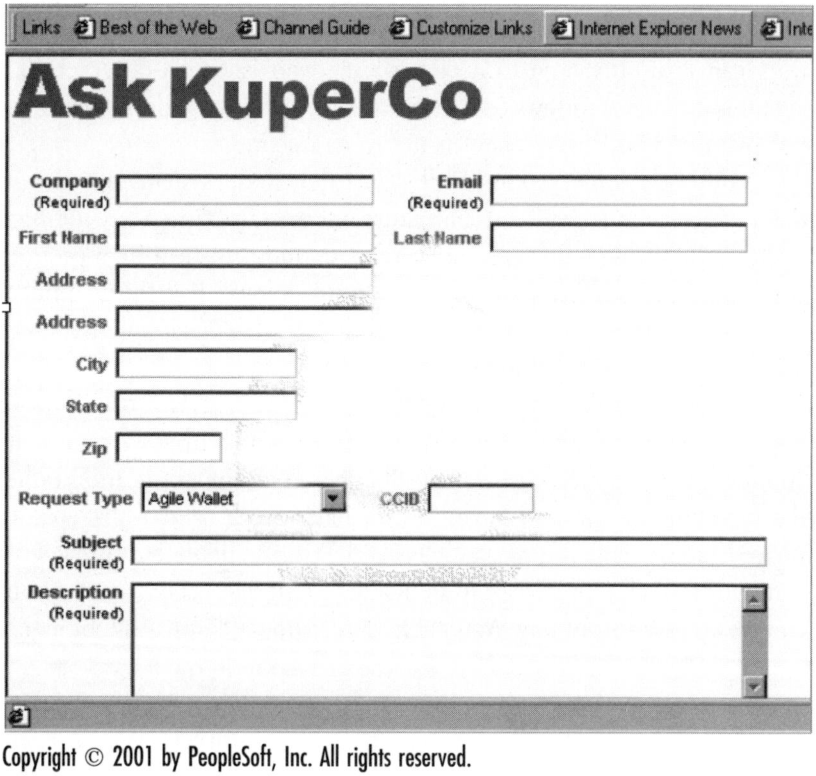

Figure 13-4. Hybrid client.

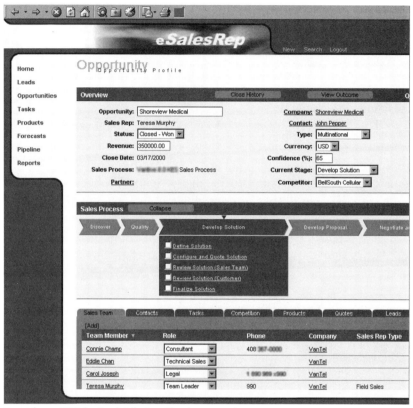

application that used the first approach. The outside salesperson could be looking at active service cases using a browser on a remote laptop while talking on the phone to an inside salesperson looking at the same information on a Win32 application.

5. PORTAL-BASED ZERO CLIENT BROWSER APPLICATIONS

The most effective approach to relational applications is to leverage the best features of all the above technologies. This requires blending portal concepts with Internet-based application functionality. The result is easy access to a variety of applications so that workers can quickly shift roles between helping themselves, handling interactions with others, and accessing the data they need to make decisions.

Figures 13-5 and 13-6 illustrate portal versions of the sales opportunity screen from Figures 13-2 and 13-4. Now users can access information from any browser-equipped device, such as a laptop PC, handheld PC, personal digital assistant, or tablet PC. The interface is very economical in its use of screen space, yet retains the Web's intuitive operation and ease of use.

This approach provides a system that is suitable for both outside periodic users and inside heads-down agents. The single platform also greatly simplifies the development effort. Multi-interface approaches force organizations to maintain parallel systems. Changes have to be posted separately to all systems using different tool sets and design skills. This is no longer necessary.

Portal-based Web applications provide the ultimate in role flexibility, ease of use, productive interface, application functionality, and

Figure 13-5. Zero-client browser client.

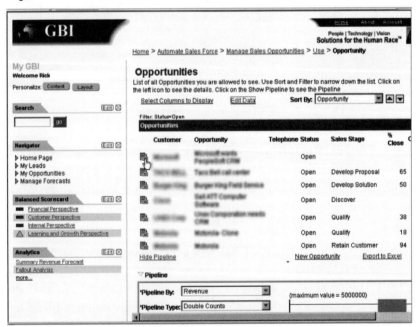

Figure 13-6. Portal client.

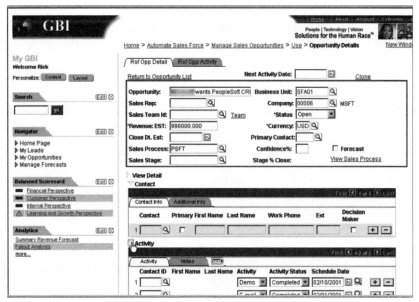

self-service. This is the type of system relational enterprises need to install in order to deliver the level of service and support all constituents of the relational enterprise demand.

An Employee Example

As we saw in Chapter 3, the Web portal approach works across the entire spider chart. One of the biggest user satisfiers is that portals allow everybody to customize their view of the enterprise. Figure 13-7 shows a sales employee portal customization screen where the user can select information to be displayed on the Home Page upon login. The four major sales sections are accessible from a menu on the left that sits above balanced scorecard and sales analytics functions.

The body of the screen lists possible content from both inside and outside the organization. This is not some manager or programmer centrally choosing what everyone is uniformly going to be able to see.

Figure 13-7. User personalization options.

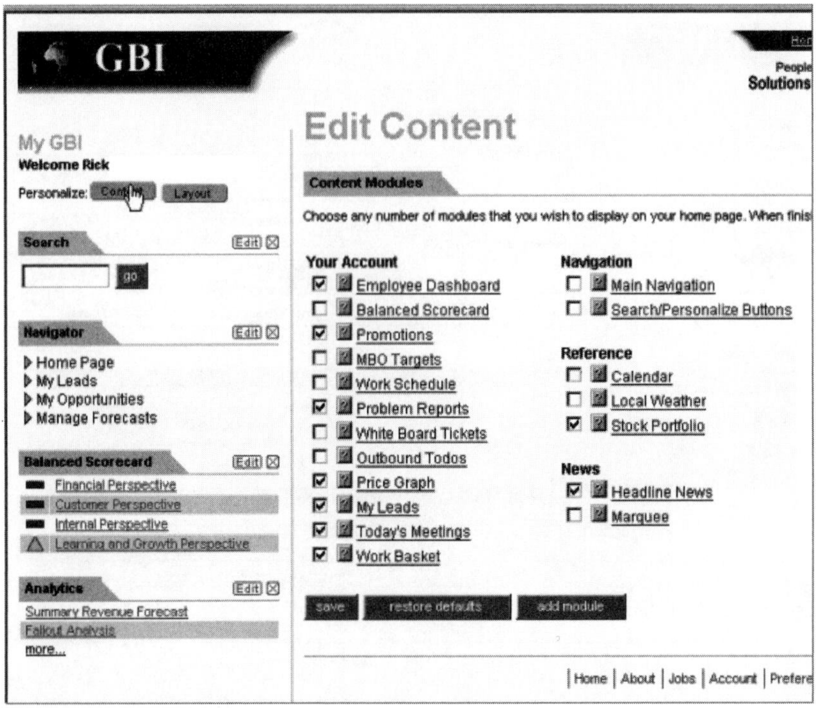

Each individual user can personally select from a wide range of functions. This turns what would have been a simple sales application in the past into a totally individualized and integrated sales, employee, and consumer portal under the complete control of the user.

Once content is selected, users should be able to arrange the actual interface to suit their unique needs as in Figure 13-8. Again, satisfaction and productivity are the primary goals. The system should present information the way users need it rather than users learning how to coax information out of the system.

In this example, the user has put employee information into column one on the screen and needed sales information into column two. This might be advantageous for someone who has a PC to the left of the phone and wants to be able to glance over during calls and pick up information from the right side of the screen. A user with a different

Figure 13-8. User layout options.

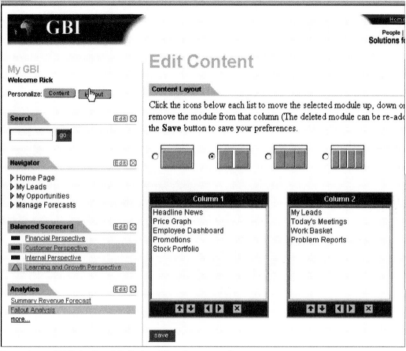

cubicle layout might arrange things differently. That's the type of flexibility that maximizes the productivity of a system and increases end-user acceptance. So the user now has the custom interface shown in Figure 13-9. Note that the system takes care of arranging everything without the user or IT having to do any programming or development work.

Now that the interface is customized, the user can access whatever information is required throughout the workday. In the employee role, this user might want to access the back-office payroll system to track down some overtime information, as illustrated in Figure 13-10. He or she might want to take a look at the screen in Figure 13-11 and see how much business he has at each stage of the sales cycle to determine what he should do next.

Done right, this customization capability should extend throughout the entire system. Now that our fictional sales rep has seen what

Figure 13-9. Personalized portal client.

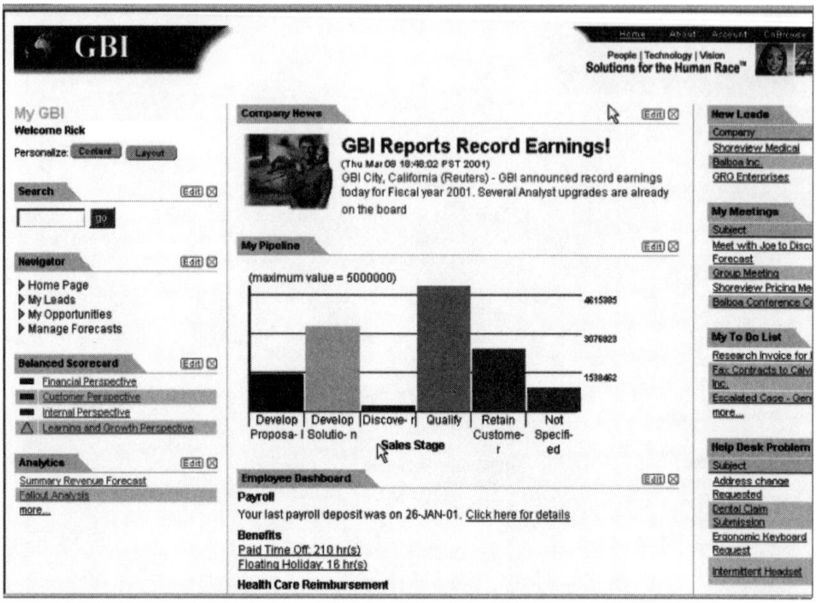

business is in the pipeline, it's time to pick up this week's new leads and initiate contacts. Figure 13-12 shows how even this lower level of data can be individually tailored for the user's preferences *at that moment*. Once users get accustomed to the flexibility that can be built into these systems, they will literally change functionality on the fly as needed. It only takes a few moments to modify display preferences for the specific task at hand, and then they are back to work. Users may create four or five different interfaces in moving from task to task in a single day's work.

Summary

There was a contest on the radio where callers were asked to submit a famous saying that still made sense after dropping a single word. One of the winners was, "Beauty is only skin." In the case of relational

Figure 13-10. Employee functions.

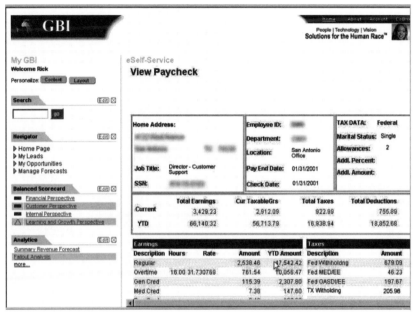

applications, beauty has to run throughout the entire architecture to provide the level of functionality relational enterprises require. Web-based application design has finally caught up with organizational requirements, such as the spider chart, multiple roles, first-call resolution, everybody's a customer, access to front-office and back-office applications, integrated channels, value-added processes, personalization, customization, and all the other agenda items we've discussed.

Once all this is in place, organizations are poised to deliver the big payoff—analytics. That is what we must study next.

Learning Points

1. On the surface, different relational systems all seem to promise the same advantages. The first step is to understand where they fit on the six-step application evolutionary ladder.

Figure 13-11. Sales functions.

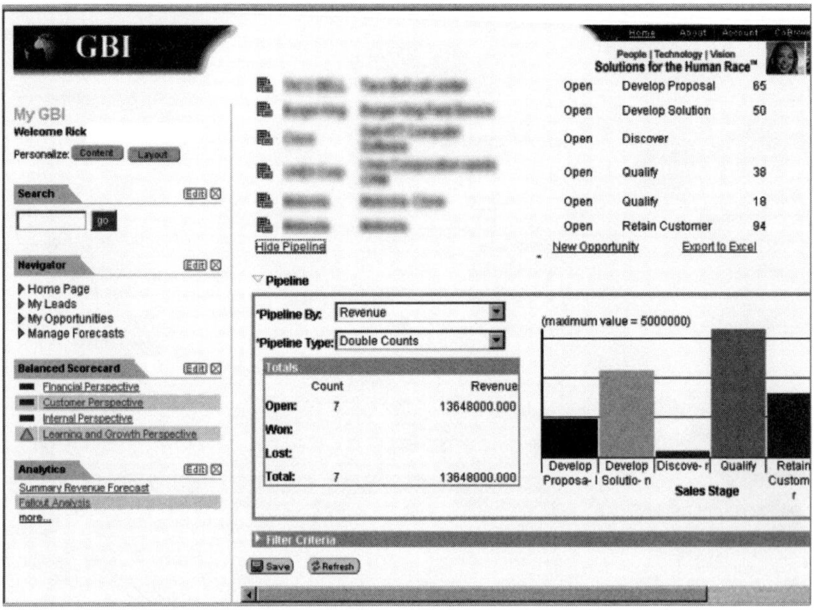

2. Architecture is important, but it's a specialty in and of itself. Get IT involved to sort it out for your decision-makers.

3. Remember that, in an Internet world, scalability is going to be more important than you thought because almost anyone might someday be using your system.

4. There are five different RM system approaches out there, but the one that will maximize profitability is leveraging portal functionality into integrated Web-based solutions.

5. Customization and personalization are critical to maximizing user productivity and acceptance of a relational system.

6. The examples in this chapter show why it is so important to provide a multirole view of the entire business cycle for every constituent in the relational enterprise. None of these examples could work without it.

Figure 13-12. Detail personalization.

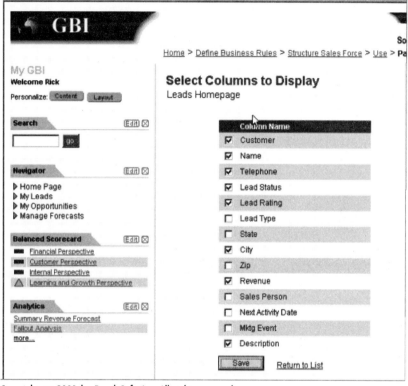

"Power lies not with those who have all the answers, but with those who have all the questions."

CHAPTER 14

RM Analytics

Just as the technology roller coaster eased over its apex at the end of the first quarter of 2000, there began to be these surreal articles talking about how long various dot-coms had until their cash was gone. One group of Web retailers listed in a *USA Today* feature were losing between $4 million and $70+ million per month. The author ranked these companies by survival time, with entrants having anywhere from four to fifty-seven months until their money ran out.[1] It was a case of last one out, turn off the lights.

The weird part is that for many of these companies, employees seemed surprised when the doors closed. People were still coming in to work, not looking for other jobs, focused on the next innovation or release. The numbers were staring them in the face, jumping out from their company reports and plastered all over the business press. What exactly did these dot-commers think was going to happen?

The bottom line about the bottom line is that organizations that ignore the bottom line get kicked in the bottom. Success today is all about what you know and what you do with it. The period of trying to grow through negative cash flow is over. The age-old game where profit is how you keep score is back. From the first touch in the 360-degree business cycle to the last strategy decision concerning next steps, every employee should be treating all customers according to their lifetime profitability. Organizations can't do that without analytical systems that provide profitability information.

The Analytics System

The full explanation of analytical architecture, as they used to say about proofs in the mathematics textbooks, would take many pages. This a complex and massive undertaking, with all sorts of technologies, such as data warehouses, data marts, data mining, data modeling, data enrichment, behavioral modeling, intelligence, insight, OLAP multi-dimensional cubes, and ROLAP cubes. For most people, the more they hear about it the more their IQ drops.

For our purpose, a functional analytics architecture is shown in Figure 14-1. Data comes into the system from a variety of internal and external sources. It is placed into a data warehouse, where it is combined, organized, and transformed into a format that feeds the analytics reporting functions. Users can then look at data reports, analysis that provides insight into the data for evaluating next steps, and balanced scorecards that highlight key strategic indicators.

Analytics is a critical systems requirement for becoming a relational enterprise, and is a hot software market. Unfortunately, the big benefits of analytics can only be obtained with a big developmental effort. The best hope is to look for vendors who have already integrated their operational front-office and back-office applications with their CRM analytics. The people who understand all this are saying that implementing analytics is not an option, it's a requirement.

The Importance of Analytics

Take a look at the strong language industry analysts use when talking about analytics (the emphasis is mine):

Figure 14-1. Analytics architecture.

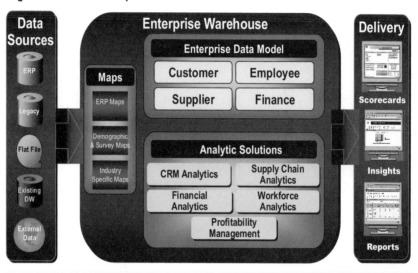

Analysts say CRM is **useless** *without data analysis, as is analysis if it isn't translated into action.*[2]
and
Organizations that don't embrace analytical CRM are going to **fail** *in their CRM projects.*[3]

The second quote is from Steve Bonadio, an analyst at META Group. (Remember, when META Group talks about CRM, their definition includes front-office, back-office, integration, and collaborative functions.)

This is very plain talk. The message is clear. Without analytics capabilities, operational and collaborative RM efforts are wasted. The opportunity is missed to leverage the new collection of data objects to improve service, competitive position, and profitability.

Some vendors recommend that customers *start* their product evaluations with relational analytics and work backwards to the applications that drive them, rather than focusing on the applications and then seeing what analytics can be generated. Focusing on analytics for effective decision-making rather than on transaction processing for efficiency is a major shift in organizational thinking.

Analytics vs. Accounting Systems

Analytics systems are very different from the reporting functions of departmental accounting or organization-wide ERP. In traditional systems, it's as if performance is measured by looking out the back window of the car and seeing where you've been—called "lagging indicators." In a relational enterprise, the goal is to provide insight that drives forward-looking action—called "leading indicators." Employees in all roles are to treat all customers according to their lifetime profitability—present and future. Since the relational systems that support this consist of many new types of data across a wide range of functions and roles, a forward-looking analytics system can be one of the most complex applications in the organization.

Table 14-1 summarizes the differences between a traditional reporting system and an analytical insight system. Traditional systems are tactical. They gather separate transactional information, such as support cases, sales calls, or purchases. The primary goal of back-office applications is reducing costs. Reports contain backwards-facing, historical data, summarizing how efficient a department or work area was in the past. Employees process transactions, and managers make all the decisions. Front-line workers can check their brains at the door.

In an insight system, analytics is used as a strategic application. The critical data has been identified, extracted, organized, and evaluated

Table 14-1. CRM analytics systems.

TRADITIONAL SYSTEMS	INSIGHT SYSTEMS
Tactical solution	Strategic solution
Data about transactions	Rules-based data transformation
Goal is cost reduction	Goal is value creation
Efficiency measures	Effectiveness measures
Lagging indicators	Leading indicators
Management decides	Responsible role decides
Operations training	Interpretation education

according to specific rules before being presented to an enterprise constituent. Decision-making is at the role level, and employees learn how to interpret data and take more effective action based upon it. The goal is maximizing lifetime customer profitability, and enterprise constituents are focused on how effective their future actions will be. An analytical insight system provides the payoff for the operational and collaborative systems.

From TCO to Transition Costing

This shift in the use of data creates the need for new accounting approaches. A CooperComm study of technology and process accounting for a major computer hardware manufacturer found that the traditional total cost of ownership (TCO) model was obsolete. Instead, we proposed a transition cost model (TCM) that reflects the new business realities.[4] This TCM model can be used to better evaluate regular business processes in addition to hardware and software purchases, such as relational systems.

Table 14-2 summarizes the differences between the two models. First, timeframes have changed. With the current rate of technology innovation, a five-year TCO computation is of little use because no system is going to be in place over the entire five-year life of the study. Customers are looking at shorter useful lives. One client insists that every system

Table 14-2. New accounting philosophies.

TOTAL COST OF OWNERSHIP MODEL	TRANSITION COST MODEL
5-year life	3-year life
Classical accounting	Activity based costing
System based	Person based
Single technology	Transition of technologies
Uniform cash flows	Adjusted over time
Exact results	Best projections

justify itself within eighteen months because it feels that any projections beyond that are pure speculation.

Classical chart-of-accounts accounting no longer reflects the total spectrum of expense, because too many of the costs do not appear anywhere as identifiable line items. A better analysis method is activity-based costing (ABC). ABC takes a look at the total costs for a complete activity end-to-end, and is similar to putting a cost to each step of a value-added flow chart. When you read that paying an invoice costs organizations $150 from receiving the bill to reconciling and archiving the endorsed payment check, you are seeing an ABC computation.

For example, a large chemical company determined that each general e-mail notification it sent out cost $100,000. These were the "our server system will be closed Sunday from 10:00 p.m. to 12:00 a.m. for maintenance" kind of no-brainer messages. This cost seemed ridiculously high until IT realized that 50,000 employees read the e-mail. Some accidentally delete it and ask for it again. Some call IT with questions. Others put comments on it and forward it to coworkers. By the time this simple e-mail had rippled its way through the system, the company has spent six figures on it—an amount no accounting system ever identified. Without an ABC model, nobody would ever have known. As a result, the number of notification e-mails was cut back dramatically.

Analytics is based upon activity-based costing. By definition, ABC models follow processes across departmental boundaries. Without a fully integrated RM system in place, true analytics is impossible.

The TCO model focused on systems and seats (number of end-users.) The transition cost model focuses on people in roles. The problem with focusing on systems and seats is that a RM system may be comprised of dozens of individual applications accessible through a single employee portal.

This is one reason why it's becoming impossible to cost out a single technology at a time. Another reason is that technologies are no longer stable. Instead of a TCO model for a single system over five years, organizations are looking at the costs of specific functions provided by an ever-changing assembly of systems and hardware. Just look at the channel agenda from Chapter 11. How are organizations going to project collaborative channel costs over the next five years using that list?

The days of the old engineering economy, net-present-value-for-ten-years style of study are over. Cash flows are not going to remain uniform over any such period. A major analyst has published five-year

TCO figures for end-user computing alternatives that were calculated down to the dollar, which seems too precise to be credible.[5] The TCM model is more concerned with best projections of alternatives rather than exact costing of single options. The future is a bit too unpredictable for that, and the analytical system must be able to handle this uncertainty.

Use of Balanced Scorecards

In 1992, Robert Kaplan and David Norton introduced a new way of giving managers performance measurement data, a "balanced scorecard—a set of measures that gives top managers a fast but comprehensive view of the business."[6] The goal is to provide a complete view of the organization in a single report. A scorecard tracks the key performance indicators (KPI) of an organization from four perspectives: financial, internal business, innovation and learning, and customer.

A major benefit of scorecards is that they counter the tendency of organizations to suboptimize within their islands of operations. By presenting integrated operational data, decision-makers can get a global view of the results of their actions. The authors have since further refined the scorecard concept and showed how to build one.[7] Their next step was to define a company-wide strategic management system that could be used throughout an enterprise.[8] The goal there was to link an organization's long-term strategy with its short-term actions. The three articles mentioned in this section are highly recommended reading for anyone wishing to fully understand analytics reporting.

Figure 14-2 shows an example of an advanced enterprise balanced scorecard. The buttons in the three columns are colored green or red to denote either meeting or falling short of goals. This makes it very easy to focus in on exactly what requires attention. The associated component list is hyper-indexed to allow drilling down multiple levels to get more detail. The menus on the left provide access to other parts of the analytics system, such as ABC data, warehouses, KPI administration, and various views of the scorecard's data.

More focused reporting is available from a customer scorecard, a sample of which is shown in Figure 14-3. Note that customer information is available for all four scorecard perspectives. Each subcategory is

Figure 14-2. Enterprise balanced scorecard.

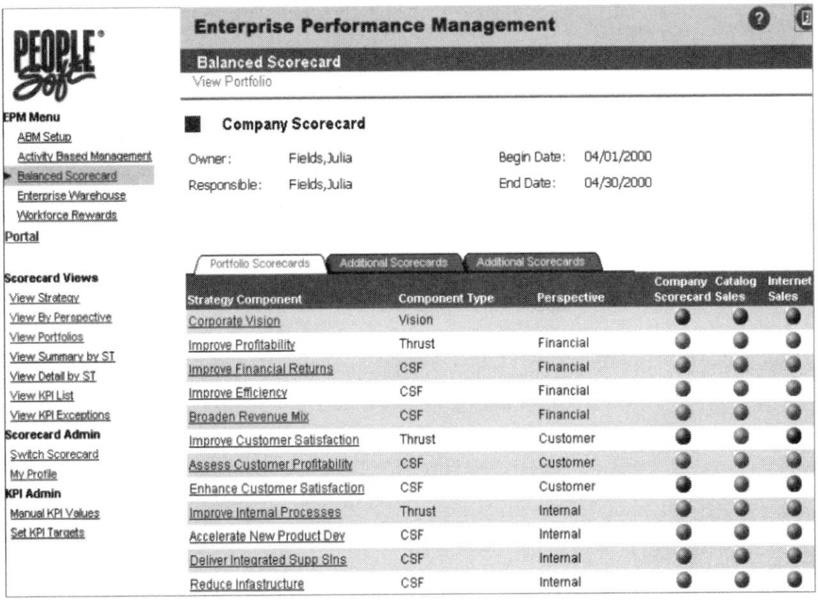

then rated with a plus, triangle, or minus, which are quick indicators of position to goal. Again, the listed items can be clicked on to drill down for more details. As in 14-2, additional scorecard information is available in menus on the left of the screen.

In Figure 14-3, the scorecard process owner, Julia Fields, has clicked on the profitability of a certain router model shown in the customer perspective as being below goal. Figure 14-4 shows the monthly performance compared to target, and highlights a trend line. This still doesn't provide Ms. Fields with the information she needs to take corrective action, so she clicks on a summary financial forecast to look at future sales estimates and to see where orders are going to come from.

Once at the level shown in Figure 14-5, Ms. Fields can begin looking at the data in different ways to determine the best next steps. While the initial scorecards help identify *where* to look, this multiview look at the data allows users to develop insight into *why* things are happening and determine *what* to do about it. This process can be completed very quickly. Ms. Fields could easily have looked at five to ten screens of information in less than the time it took to read about it here.

Figure 14-3. Portal customer scorecard.

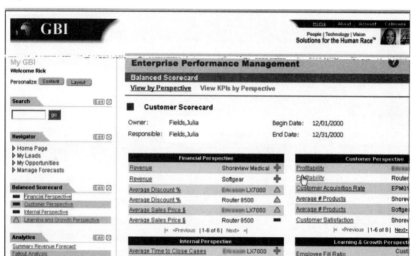

Balanced scorecard systems help organizations identify and track KPIs, then provide the analytical information and insight engine to allow employees to take action that brings performance back up to goals and beyond. This is the true difference between efficiency and effectiveness.

Employees Must Be Able to Use Analytics

There is another mid-1990s fad that unfortunately faded from management consciousness before the technology could catch up. In 1989, author John Case coined the term "open-book management" (OBM) to refer to the revolutionary practice of sharing performance numbers not just with managers, but with employees at all levels. Organizations that were able to open the books and empower employee

Figure 14-4. KPI detail.

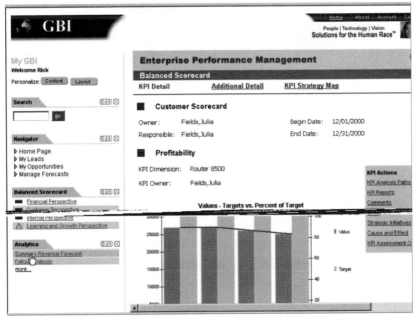

decision-making saw tremendous increases in business results. In his 1995 book, Case described the three features of OBM:

1. Every employee sees—and learns to understand—the organization's financials, along with all the other numbers that are critical to tracking the business's performance.

2. Employees assume that, whatever else they do, part of their job is to move those numbers in the right direction.

3. Employees have a direct stake in their employer's success.[9]

The goal is for workers to have the information to act like owners and begin playing what author and OBM practitioner Jack Stack calls "the great game of business."[10]

The problem is that many organizations could not make the necessary changes in reporting and decision-making from a management

Figure 14-5. Market detail.

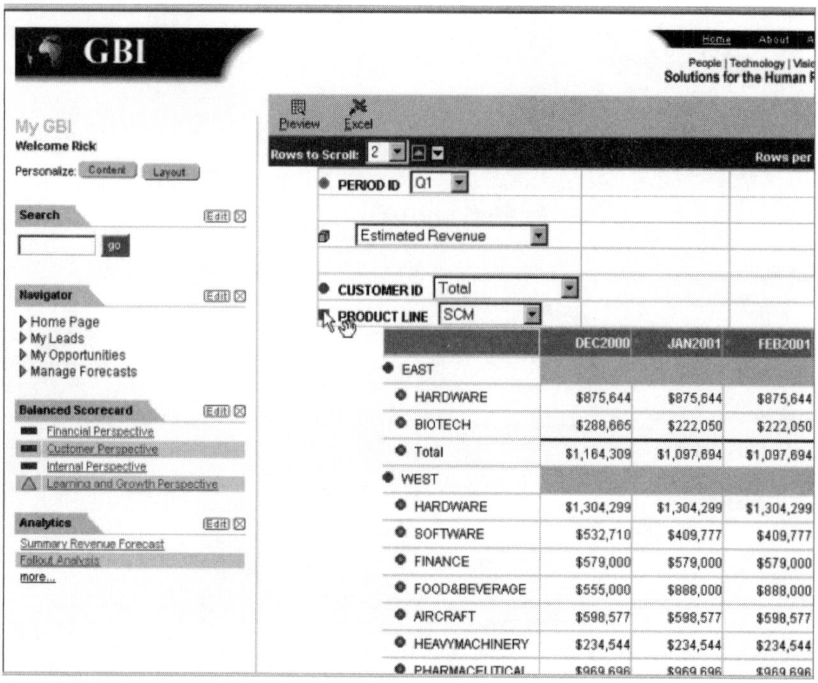

		DEC2000	JAN2001	FEB2001
EAST				
	HARDWARE	$875,644	$875,644	$875,644
	BIOTECH	$288,665	$222,050	$222,050
	Total	$1,164,309	$1,097,694	$1,097,694
WEST				
	HARDWARE	$1,304,299	$1,304,299	$1,304,299
	SOFTWARE	$532,710	$409,777	$409,777
	FINANCE	$579,000	$579,000	$579,000
	FOOD&BEVERAGE	$555,000	$888,000	$888,000
	AIRCRAFT	$598,577	$598,577	$598,577
	HEAVYMACHINERY	$234,544	$234,544	$234,544
	PHARMACEUTICAL	$969,696	$969,696	$969,696

prerogative to an employee responsibility. Management-only decision-making defeats the purpose of OBM. For analytics to add value through-out an organization, leaders are going to have to make the same data-sharing and decision-making process adjustments as they would for OBM, and then make certain that constituents in roles throughout the enterprise can complete the analytical process illustrated in Figure 14-6.

The first activity, Measure, is a conventional reporting step. What begins to differentiate analytics are the next four steps, Analyze, Discover, Strategize, and Plan. Analytical data helps users develop *insight* into the data and turn facts into *business intelligence*. This information then leads to *action*. This is the big payoff.

Leveraging the data and reports into more profitable operations requires more than just training people to use the system. It requires each role to master a new set of analytical concepts and analysis skills.

Figure 14-6. The analytics process.

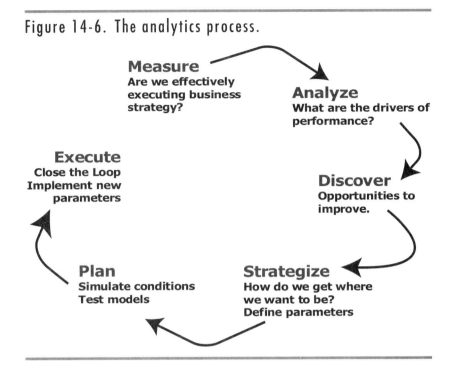

Roles-Based Analytics

In the relational enterprise, users of the analytics system will be performing specific roles. So the system must present analytical data that supports the operational portion of CRM systems. As an illustration, someone in the sales manager role may have a number of sales effectiveness questions:

- How can we drive more revenue/sales per salesperson?

- Where should we allocate our sales resources?

- Where do salespeople encounter difficulty in the selling process?

- Are salespeople turning in accurate forecasts?

- Is our sales process on track to achieve forecasted revenue and profitability goals?

A list of the insight reports a sales manager might wish to see is shown in Table 14-3. Note that even though this is a sales role, information is needed from four different front-office systems to answer the above questions.

Figure 14-7 shows an example of a sales-deal analysis report. It could be used to analyze deals by customer to figure out which clients are more profitable, or it could be redisplayed by territory to see whether certain salespeople are leaning too heavily on price discounting to close deals. Once the more profitable customers have been identified, they could be profiled to determine why they are willing to buy at a higher price. Then future marketing campaigns could be designed to attract more such customers.

A sample forecast accuracy report is shown in Figure 14-8. Here the manager can look at time to close and sales price deal by deal if necessary. It's also possible to drill down into the details of any one deal. With this, managers can detect problems that salespeople are having in moving from any one selling stage to another. This example focuses on customers that are in the retention stage and looks at the revenue generated and time to close—data that is helpful in managing salespeople and campaigns.

In another illustration, someone in a marketing role may be concerned about the following questions:

Table 14-3. Sales manager role analytics.

INFORMATION NEEDED	INSIGHT REPORT
Profit and loss by customer	Customer profitability
Pipeline accuracy	Sales effectiveness
Forecast accuracy	Sales effectiveness
Deal analysis	Sales effectiveness
Fallout analysis	Sales effectiveness
Attainment analysis	Sales effectiveness
Cycle time and analysis	Sales effectiveness
Revenue analysis	Sales effectiveness
Campaign effectiveness	Marketing effectiveness
Case analysis—open cases	Support effectiveness

Figure 14-7. Sales deal analysis report.

	Product	Customer	Territory	Sales Team	Close Date	List Price	Actual Selling Price	Average Selling Price	Deviation from ASP	Deal Value	Actual Discount %
1	Stat2001	C-One Boston 1	East	E1	12/27/99	18,000	11,000	15,054	(4,054)	11,000	39%
2	Stat2001	C-One Boston 2	East	E2	12/27/99	18,000	11,000	15,054	(4,054)	11,000	39%

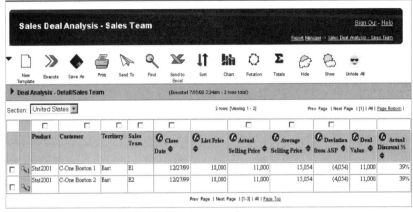

Figure 14-8. Forecast accuracy report.

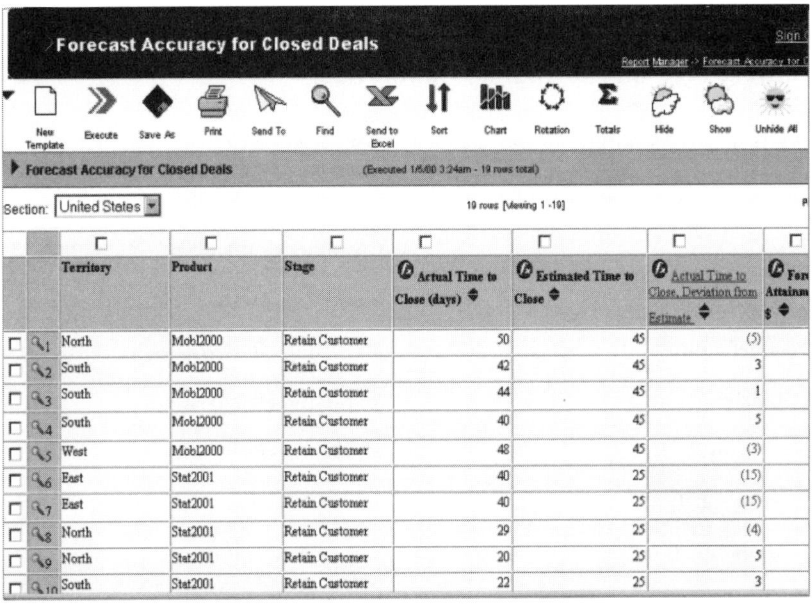

	Territory	Product	Stage	Actual Time to Close (days)	Estimated Time to Close	Actual Time to Close, Deviation from Estimate	For... Attainm... $
1	North	Mobl2000	Retain Customer	50	45	(5)	
2	South	Mobl2000	Retain Customer	42	45	3	
3	South	Mobl2000	Retain Customer	44	45	1	
4	South	Mobl2000	Retain Customer	40	45	5	
5	West	Mobl2000	Retain Customer	48	45	(3)	
6	East	Stat2001	Retain Customer	40	25	(15)	
7	East	Stat2001	Retain Customer	40	25	(15)	
8	North	Stat2001	Retain Customer	29	25	(4)	
9	North	Stat2001	Retain Customer	20	25	5	
10	South	Stat2001	Retain Customer	22	25	3	

- Which lead profiles have responded to campaigns?
- Is the campaign on a path to success?
- Is the campaign being managed successfully within its budget?
- What is the forecasted cost to complete the campaign?
- What is the current return on the campaign?

Some of the corresponding insight reports that could provide answers for these questions are shown in Table 14-4. As with all roles, again note that the marketing professional requires information from multiple customer systems. This is a factor in all analytics applications, and it is what separates them from the simple reporting that is included with point solutions.

The campaign effectiveness report in Figure 14-9 is a good example of the detail an individual role can obtain when drilling down for specific insight into current performance. The results to date can be examined by campaign, program, and event, and compared to goals. The remaining leads budgeted can be identified, and plans can be made to find and convert them based upon the campaign success to date.

Table 14-4. Marketing role analytics.

INFORMATION NEEDED	INSIGHT REPORT
Profit and loss by customer	Customer profitability
Product mix	Customer profitability
Campaign effectiveness	Marketing effectiveness
Product affinity	Marketing effectiveness
Campaign forecast	Marketing effectiveness
Campaign ROI	Marketing effectiveness
Revenue analysis	Sales effectiveness
Discount analysis	Sales effectiveness
Customer purchase analysis	Sales effectiveness
Product quality	Support effectiveness

Figure 14-9. Campaign effectiveness report.

		Product	Campaign	Program	Event	Event Date	Event Time	Territory	# Accepted	# Rejected	# Qualified	% Qualified	# Target / # Leads	# Rema
		STAT	Sell 1Q00	Discount Coupon	HealthClub Handout	7/3/00		West	1,867	381	1,486	80%	3,000	
		STAT	Sell 1Q00	Cable Infomercials 7/26	Infomercial 7/26	7/26/00	20:30	West	20	-	20	100%	10,000	
		STAT	Sell 1Q00	Cable Infomercials 7/30	Infomercial 7/30	7/30/00	13:00	East	1,099	88	1,011	92%	3,500	
		STAT	Sell 1Q00	Cable Infomercials 7/4	Infomercial 7/4	7/4/00	13:30	West	1,105	25	1,080	98%	5,000	
		STAT	Sell 2Q00	Cable Infomercials 8/23	Infomercial 8/23	8/23/00	20:30	West	-	-	-	0%	10,000	
		MOBL	Aware1Q00	Sponsor SF 10K	Banner at Start	7/22/00		West	75	5	70	93%	100	
		MOBL	Aware1Q00	Quokka Ad	Website Ad	7/1/00		All	50	45	5	10%	100	

Analytics information can also be made available outside the balanced scorecard framework. Figure 14-10 shows the possible analytics functions available through Chuck's personalized employee portal. The Scorecard tab at the upper left provides access to the standard balanced scorecard perspectives, and the tabs down below list the individual reports that Chuck is permitted to view. Chuck can even be assigned to-do activities linked to the reports, in this case reviewing sales and marketing insight reports.

In the main portion of the screen, Chuck sees some important product profitability information that is highlighted rather than embedded in the scorecard. The portal also has an "employee dashboard" function. This is an overview of key employee measurements that can be scanned, much like when a driver glances across the dashboard of a car to get a quick view of the engine's condition. In Chuck's case, he can access personal information, such as payroll status and open expense report submissions, and he can also see how he is doing compared to his travel budget. This presents a window into all the relevant performance information Chuck needs, and is extremely easy to access and navigate.

Figure 14-10. Portal analytics.

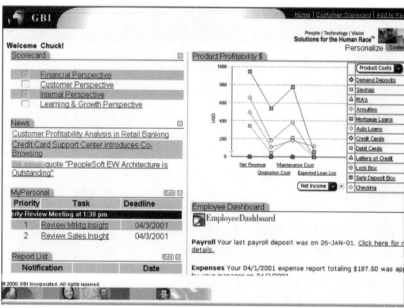

The final example, shown in Figure 14-11, illustrates how analytical information can make its way into individual applications. Here, the marketing-manager-role view in an eCRM application suite is presenting forecast accuracy information similar to the scorecard screen in Figure 14-8. This application version is very navigable, with the ability to click on regions for additional detail and to examine forecasts deal by deal.

The functionality shown in Figures 14-2 through 14-11 is what separates CRM analytics from typical reporting options within individual applications. To provide the views each role needs, data from all across the relational enterprise has to be brought through the architecture illustrated in Figure 14-1. Then individuals have to be educated by role in the use of the system and in the subtleties of gaining useful insight from the reports.

Summary

As Calvin Coolidge succinctly observed, "Business will be better or worse." Analytics is all about telling organizations which of these

Figure 14-11. Application analysis.

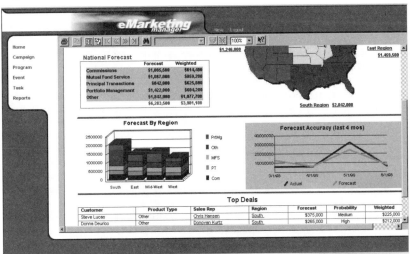

alternatives is occurring. Yet that is only one-third of the famous three "what questions" . . . What? So What? Now What? Analytics closes the loop on "Now what?" by helping organizations not only account for what is happening, but figure out what it means and what to do about it. This is the value of analytics that makes analysts say RM is worthless without it. What are the benefits of systems that have it? That's the subject of our next chapter.

Learning Points

1. Watson, the game is afoot. But it's not about playing until the money's gone. It's about effectiveness.

2. Kids, we're trained professionals—don't try this at home. Look for a vendor that's already integrated the analytics chain from base application to portal scorecard.

3. Analytics is not an option. Remember the highlighted words from analysts . . . CRM would *fail* and be *useless* without analytics.

4. Don't think you have an analytics system just because you receive accounting reports. The information you require needs to be actionable.

5. The static TCO model is obsolete. Everything is in transition from here on out. Analytics represents cross-functional activities, not chart-of-account line items.

6. Organizations are adopting balanced scorecards to manage their operations. A good analytics system helps deliver that functionality.

7. All this data and technology are useless if the people in those roles don't know how to use the information to *take action*. Open-book management is still a great idea.

8. Examples show how analytics requires data from throughout the business cycle and across the relational enterprise. Remember, no customer process stays in one department.

NOTES

1. Matt Krantz, "E-Retailers Run Low on Fuel," *USA Today*, April 26, 2000, p. B1.

2. Jeff Sweat, Rick Whiting, and Beth Bacheldor, "Analysis: The Missing Piece of the Customer Puzzle," *InformationWeek*, April 17, 2000, p. 28.

3. Jeff Sweat, "Oracle Rolls Out Business-Intelligence Products," *InformationWeek*, May 1, 2000, p. 28.

4. CooperComm, Inc., "A Transition Based End-User Computing Model: Replacing Total Cost of Ownership," *CooperComm Briefings*, November 2000, p. 25.

5. Lauren Gibbons Paul, "Finding Your Way in TCO Maze," *PC Week*, June 25, 1997, pp. 7, 25.

6. Robert S. Kaplan and David P. Norton, "The Balanced Scorecard—Measures That Drive Performance," *Harvard Business Review*, January–February 1992, pp. 71–9.

7. Robert S. Kaplan and David P. Norton, "Putting the Balanced Scorecard to Work," *Harvard Business Review*, September–October 1993, pp. 134–47.

8. Robert S. Kaplan and David P. Norton, "Using the Balanced Scorecard as a Strategic Management System," *Harvard Business Review*, January–February 1996, pp. 75–85.

9. John Case, *Open-Book Management: The Coming Business Revolution* (New York: HarperBusiness, 1995), pp. 37–8.

10. Jack Stack and Bo Burlingham, *The Great Game of Business: Unlocking the Power and Profitability of Open-Book Management,* (New York: Currency Doubleday, 1992).

PART FOUR

RELATIONAL
ENTERPRISE LEADERSHIP

*"The value of computers is what
you are willing to pay
for results."*

—ROBERT A. STRASSMANN

CHAPTER 15

Benefits of Relational Systems

The speaker had everyone's rapt attention. He was an operations research analyst from a U.S Air Force base near our college, and he was giving a lecture describing a massive research project his group had just completed. The year was 1970, and his base was the dispatch point for all medical airlifts worldwide. Every day, multitudes of wounded personnel had to be transported. It was extremely complicated. There were restrictions on crew flying time, stopover options depending upon medical condition and local base hospital facilities, medical equipment availability on flights and layovers, the number and size of available aircraft . . . and many other factors.

It turns out that this was a massive nonlinear programming problem. With the computing power of that era—a time when today's thirty dollar TI calculator used in Junior High math cost our industrial engineering department $2,500—this was an enormously complex task. For nearly two hours we learned how the Air Force had developed a model and specialized computational solution techniques to create schedules before each day's flights began. Total R&D cost for the system? $1 million in 1970 dollars.

As we sat, impressed, my advising professor held up his hand. He was a real character, a prototypical Texan, and had a unique view of systems and processes. He asked the researcher how the Air Force had scheduled medical airlift flights up to now.

Evidently there were two grizzled old sergeants who had been dispatching these flights for years. They would arrive in the wee hours of the morning, look at the transportation needs reports, go up to a gigantic wall map with pegs in the locations of the various bases, then begin planning flights. This consisted of taking colored strings, one for each available airplane, in a length that approximated the allowable crew flight times, and wrapping the strings around the map pegs to represent each plane's route. The sergeants kept in mind which facilities could handle which patients for transport, stops, and overnighters, and placed strings on the map until everyone had gotten where they were supposed to go.

When this was done, the sergeants took a Polaroid picture of the map, pulled off all of the string and measured its total length with a yardstick on the wall—much like a clerk measures off fabric in a store. The length of the string indicated total flying miles. The sergeants tried it again, and again, working on alternatives until they ran out of time. The sergeants had been doing this for years and had evidently developed a real feel for it. The Air Force then used the photo with the shortest amount of string, representing the lowest flight costs, to dispatch its crews and equipment. Compared to the sophisticated nonlinear programming system just developed, it sounded pretty archaic.

Then my professor asked, "So how are ya'll doin' with the new system?"

I'll never forget the answer. The presenter got this strange look on his face, hesitated and said, "Well, it looks like it's going to be pretty hard to beat those guys with the strings." The room just exploded in laughter. After a million dollars in research, truly imaginative computational solutions, and all kinds of computer horsepower, they were still underperforming the two old guys with strings.

So . . . how ya'll doing with *your* new system?

RM Justification Philosophies

Not very many organizations can answer this question. According to a META Group study, only 10 percent of organizations they had researched measured CRM ROI, and nearly two-thirds had no measures at all in place.[1]

There are several obvious reasons for this. In the superheated 1990s, the focus was on keeping up with growth and customer demands. Being superior may not have been as important as just being present. Also, in good times, who cares about how accurate financial forecasting models are? It's like the gaming executive who told a friend, "I love the risk of running a casino. Sometimes you win . . . and sometimes you win more."

With the economic slowdown of the new millennium, it's now the other problem. When the organizational belt needs tightening, training is the first to go. Unless you're working for Jack Welch at GE and are being held accountable for your decisions, the second to go is staff for analysis. In a cost cutting environment, no one is going to take the time to audit ROI models after-the-fact for accuracy.

Lastly, the rapid turnover in personnel creates project discontinuities. The people who made the decision in the first place are often no longer around months later for the implementation, much less throughout the entire multiyear operation of the new system.

This is why understanding the benefit metrics surrounding operational, collaborative, and analytical RM systems is one of the industry's biggest problems. Do these systems represent BVA activities and just have to be done regardless? Or are these systems options that should be implemented only when enough ROI is forecasted? A justification approach is something that needs to be decided upon well ahead of the project. There are several options.

1. COMPETITIVE REQUIREMENT

This philosophy is, "The bad guys are doing it, so I had better match their best practices and service levels." It's not that relational systems are not seen to provide benefits, it's that any benefits are seen only in the light of competitive positioning. The question is not "if" but "when" the systems will be implemented.

Here, worrying about ROI is like requiring a justification analysis to issue employees a cubicle, phone, desk, and chair. ("I'm sorry, your desk isn't in because the capital papers haven't been processed yet.") These aren't options, they are utility items. Similarly, a RM system is just something that has to be done.

A good example is Web-based service. Although self-service has the potential to reduce the internal cost of providing support, very few organizations have any data on how in demand this is with their customers. Their call center that handles the bulk of customer interactions may still be in disarray, yet organizations are busy rushing to build on-line support systems because everyone else is doing so. The revenue gain versus cost reduction ROI is not a consideration in this case, only minimizing what it takes to service customers.

The downside is that competitors may be merely raising service levels without materially affecting anyone's competitive position. In essence, they are helping customers drive more profit out of the marketplace. Remember the process lesson from Chapter 11, "If someone wants it done *and there is profit in it,* somebody is going to do it. It had better be you."

2. LEAP OF FAITH

This is the *Field of Dreams* philosophy: Build it and they will come. RM systems are seen to deliver such compelling advantages that justification is assumed. This sounds reasonable. Look at the consumer and trade press. CRM and e-business articles are everywhere. It's the teenager's rationale: If everyone one else is doing it, it must be good.

Like the cowboy diner out in the middle of the desert in *The Martian Chronicles,* perhaps they will come, and perhaps they won't. It may be pretty hard to beat those guys with the strings.

3. TACTICAL PERFORMANCE MEASURES

In a survey of 800 business and IT officials, META Group found that nearly two-thirds of CRM projects are designed to improve an organization's workflow, rather than to enhance the customer experience.[2] The primary ROI goals for these efforts is improved internal efficiencies.

META has also found that some companies thought they had justification measures, but they were confusing ROI with merely having operational statistics. Tracking agent utilization and average call length is not ROI. A reduction in those measures that can be linked to lowered costs does represent an ROI.

4. ROI FORECASTS

There are a variety of models and methods for determining ROI. Most vendors have one, such as Hewlett-Packard's *TCO Analyst* model, or analysts will supply them. How rigorous an ROI methodology is depends upon where in the organization decisions are being made.

Figure 15-1 graphs the relationship between the level of decision-maker and how quantitative and complete a ROI analysis is. At the lower levels near the front line, justification is informal—what one finance executive calls "wink decisions." Process workers and their supervisors can look at a solution and say, "Yeah, this will work." As the decision moves up the organizational chart, decision-makers know less and less about the real details of the situation. Therefore, the ROI analyses get more quantitative and formal. What started out as an obvious truth at the front line ends up as a 50-page report in the executive suite.

Opinions are mixed as to the value of these ROI analyses. Modeling is an inexact science. Forecasting costs is always a risk. Estimating alternatives can be guesswork. But some data is better than no data. Often, management requires an ROI study simply to force lower level decision-makers to carefully think through the ramifications of the RM system under consideration.

5. ROI AUDITS

A very conservative power utility once bought a new customer service system based upon the forecast that it would eliminate twenty-nine positions. The president, being that type of person, waited thirty days after the installation and then wrote a memo to the CIO saying, "Give me the names of the twenty-nine people who don't work here any more

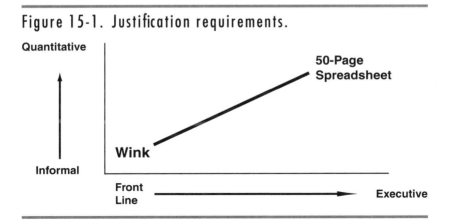

Figure 15-1. Justification requirements.

or you're fired." The executive went on to explain that he didn't want to see soft-cost justification or half-bodies. The savings had to be hard costs. (The CIO found the names.)

One of CooperComm's practice areas is helping technology companies build costing and justification sales models. In over two decades of consulting, we know of only two companies that routinely went back over their capital acquisition requests after a year or two to see if projected ROIs were attained. Their payoff in most cases was not so much to punish the guilty as to review the justification process to find learning points for making better projections in the future.

In general, justification is simply not given enough attention in most organizations. Paul A. Strassmann, author of *The Business Value of Computers*, writes, "You should spend at least 5 percent of total life-cycle development plus maintenance costs (discounted) and more than 5 percent of total elapsed implementation time in the planning and justification phase." He goes on to point out that a two-year, $1 million dollar project should have at least $50,000 and five weeks allocated for project planning before being submitted for approval.[3]

One of the important duties in this phase is to understand and document the current levels of performance and cost in order to provide a benchmark for recognizing improvements. Since most organizations cannot track individual customer profitability or compute lifetime customer value, there is no "before" to use as a base point. This is one activity a relational system will let them complete for future investments.

Our observation is that very few RM projects receive enough investigation prior to approval. Nearly all of the analysis time is spent in vendor investigation and selection stages. This is why the effectiveness of analytics discussed in Chapter 14 is so essential. They help various roles identify whether projects are meeting goals and, if not, determine what to do about it.

RM Justfications

With early CRM adoptions focused on SFA, projects were driven by sales or marketing departments rather than financial or technology groups. As a result, justifications usually emphasized increasing sales revenue. Conversely, call center applications emphasized cost reduction and efficiency of operations.

With today's integrated operational, collaborative, and analytical RM solutions, there is now a wider range of advantages that can be derived. The relative importance of the gains has been a favorite topic of researchers, with a variety of Letterman "Top 10" style lists of why organizations adopt relational systems. Ranking averages isn't particularly useful. What matters is why a particular buyer's organization is adopting RM and what is important in its unique position.

Listed below are the major advantages of relational systems. The list is by no means exhaustive, but is instead intended as a starting point. If relative importance is of significance to your organization, then a good team exercise is to take the following lists and rank them specifically for your purposes. These lists are also useful in understanding what sort of "before" benchmark data should be gathered in order to be able to later isolate the actual results of a new RM system.

Here are the potential advantages by category. Notice that each line item is phrased as a resulting benefit.

MARKETING

- More new customers
- Better customer data
- Deeper customer knowledge
- Segment higher value customers
- Faster time to market
- Market leadership
- Better brand perception

Relational marketing is all about effectiveness, one of the hardest elements to measure. For example, brand perception is a function of many items, such as sales professionalism, product quality, service levels, and support effectiveness.

SALES

- Increase revenue

- More orders per customer

- More repeat orders

- Higher market share

- More products per order (cross selling)

- Increase customer retention

This is where many RM vendors believe you should start. "Increase revenue" is number one on almost every survey about buyer goals. An often-overlooked aspect of this is customer retention. The best way to increase revenue may not be to get more customers. On a popular promotion, one communications company experienced a 30 percent "infant mortality" rate within three or four months of sign-up. The promotion was so popular that it was attracting the wrong kind of customers.[4]

An interesting revenue producer is linked to the CIC. One of the biggest interaction center benefits is reducing unentitled service. This is when a caller should pay for an incident, but the agent waives applicable fees in an effort to satisfy the customer or else is unaware that there should be a charge applied.

CUSTOMER SERVICE

- Increase customer satisfaction

- Increase customer loyalty

- Increase customer sales touches

- Increase service quality

- Faster response time

- Increase service availability

"Customer satisfaction" is the second highest-rated benefit of relational systems. Remember from Chapter 3, "customer" refers to any constituent in the spider chart.

PRODUCTIVITY

- Lower transaction costs
- Increase employee productivity
- Increase employee satisfaction
- Reduce support required
- Convert interactions to Web self-service
- Reduce fulfillment errors

While increasing productivity is relevant for any RM application, it is typically applied to transactional service systems. An interesting rule of thumb on channel costs: Forrester Research estimates it costs about thirty dollars to resolve a customer question on the phone, and about five dollars to process an e-mail request through an e-mail response system.[5]

IT

- Increase data quality
- Scale to more concurrent users
- Ease integration to other systems
- Speed software deployment

Understanding technology advantages is one of the most confusing challenges in relational systems. Make certain to review the "critical error" section below.

MANAGEMENT

- Increase employee satisfaction
- Break down communications barriers
- Improve access to data
- Increase ease of use
- Overcome resistance to adopt and use

Relational systems provide overall benefits to the organization. Work is a better place when employee portals provide necessary information, financial results are shared, front-liners in interaction roles are given authority, and support systems are available to everyone. It can be difficult to isolate causes and assign numbers to this, but it is a benefit nonetheless. It can be difficult to measure these payoffs and link them specifically to relational systems, but they are benefits nonetheless.

A Critical Error in Evaluating Benefits

Understanding the technology is one of the biggest problems in relational systems. As we have seen, some vendors talk about "tethered clients," i.e., onsite PCs connected over the network to client/server systems, or "browser clients" that use Internet/intranet access. There are "thick clients," systems where up to 50MB of application programming has to be reloaded onto PCs whenever there are even minute changes in the system. "Thin clients" have small amounts of programming on them. "Zero clients," such as those requiring only a browser for operation, theoretically have no application software on the PC, but may actually have code downloaded and stored in something called a wrapper. Then things get confusing. Some vendors call their system requiring 50MB of client software a "thin client," and so forth.

Benchmarks are another issue. With nearly everyone in the relational enterprise potentially accessing the RM system, scalability is critical. Some vendors quote how many remote users a system will handle, knowing that only a portion of them will ever sign up at any one time. Others quote simultaneous users, but create their benchmark with an unusually low volume, such as four calls per agent in order to make the maximum number of simultaneous users as high as possible. If this is confusing, good, because there is a critical message. (Stomp, stomp.)

One of the biggest errors we see companies make in analyzing the benefits of RM systems is the devaluation of IT opinions.

Line-of-business managers are normally driving the decision based upon the benefits in the above list. Not being very technical, managers make the assumption that any product being shown, particularly if the vendor is large and well-known, will work. One vice president of IT Strategic Planning for a large oil company, when asked about the viability of a planned purchase said, "That's what the IT department is for. I've got great people and that's their job."

An interesting characteristic of software projects is that you can be completely done and have nothing to show for it. We have seen a number of situations where IT begged executive management not to buy from a particular RM vendor because IT's study showed the solution wasn't suitable. Regardless, they were told, "Make it work." Well, sometimes that just isn't possible no matter how firmly IT is told. This is another contributor to the high failure rate of CRM implementations.

As one brave IT manager told the executives, "Oh, I'm sorry. I thought you wanted it to *work*. If you don't need it to work, I can cut the implementation costs and time in half and you can pick any vendor you want."

Understanding the true benefits of an RM system often requires an intimate look at client/server or Web architecture, remote procedure calls, tools architectures, data model analysis, application server functionality, API capabilities, and so on. These topics are beyond the understanding of most line executives, yet decision-makers can't make the right choices unless they do understand. It's a vicious circle. The only answer is to not ignore the recommendations from IT. It's not that we are unabashed IT fans, we've just seen too many organizations hurt by overriding IT's recommendations because leaders didn't really understand the technology they were selecting.

Summary

Justifying relational systems is all about results. As this chapter showed, trying to project the benefit of RM applications is an opportunity for further research. As more organizations implement a fully integrated operational, collaborative, and analytical RM system, case studies should become available to guide other organizations.

For now, it's clear that relational systems are not another passing fad, soon to join quality circles, reengineering, open-book management, and self-directed work teams in the tactical retirement home. And RM is no leap of faith, because customers aren't going to stand for poor service and inefficient processes in an information-rich marketplace.

So the next step is to understand how to evaluate the features that drive these advantages, then tie them in to a vendor selection process. This is covered in Chapters 16 and 17.

Learning Points

1. Don't fall in love with technology. It may end up being pretty hard to beat those guys with the strings.

2. This is one of the lightest chapters in the book. Most researchers have merely assembled a top-ten list of reasons to implement RM systems. True ROI or before/after measurements are just not currently available.

3. Justification approaches vary from "we gotta do it" to "here's what we'll get when we do it" and everything in between. The key is to know why your organization is adopting RM. As Laurence J. Peter has said, "If you don't know where you're going, you'll get there."

4. The higher up a decision is made, the more quantitative the justification must be. This may not be the right way to make the decision.

5. Make a list of benefits and have decision-makers rank them by importance. It will be a great reference during the RM system evaluation and selection processes.

6. Don't ignore IT's reservations about a particular system. *Big mistake!* Just remember, you can't tell IT to make something work that won't. The explanation may be too esoteric for a nontechie to understand, but it's still true. Plus, some vendors don't always tell the exact truth to nontechies.

NOTES

1. META Group and IMT Strategies, *Customer Relationship Management (CRM) Study 1999: Sponsor Report,* September 22, 1999, pp. 3/C–13.

2. Bob Trott, "ROI Takes Center Stage: CRM Shake-Up Refocuses Industry," *InfoWorld,* April 16, 2001, pp. 1, 32.

3. Paul A. Strassmann, *The Business Value of Computers: An Executive's Guide* (New Canaan, Conn: Information Economics Press, 1990), p. 247.

4. Don Peppers and Martha Rogers, *Enterprise One to One: Tools for Competing in the Interactive Age* (New York: Currency Doubleday, 1997), p. 82.

5. Kathleen Cholewka, "Tiered CRM: Serving Pip-Squeaks to VIPs," *Sales & Marketing Management,* April 2001, p. 26.

CHAPTER 16

Evaluating Relational Systems

It was one of those lovely dinner scenes where your college-age and adult children are cheerfully discussing who gets what when their parents pass on to the great beyond. The boys were focused on our boundless inventory of electronic goodies. As a technology consultant and hardware/software evaluator, I've got the latest and greatest of every gizmo I can talk clients into giving me or justify buying without a divorce. (I wanted to have my birthday celebration in the party room at CompUSA but my family wouldn't let me.) Our daughter, the youngest, was strangely quiet while the guys rhapsodized over the list of computers, digital camera, and so on. She finally interjected, "Well, I want the dining room set." The boys scoffed and went back to their list-making.

No one was upset at the conversation. It was quite interesting to hear what items had emotional attachment for the kids and why. It was fun reminiscing. Later on in the evening, though, I got to thinking about who was making the best choices. I told the boys, "You laughed, but your sister has got you completely beat. All those electronics with the fancy features, no matter how much they cost new, are going to be totally worthless in about three years. That dining room set is only going to go up in value. What's your Intellivision set worth these days?" Some items provide true value, and others are just temporary features that will soon be obsolete.

Look Beyond Features

In an Internet-time world, there's only a few months difference between the latest and greatest and the late great. This is particularly true in the realm of software. Buying a best-of-breed package or suite with the niftiest features is not necessarily the right tactic. So how are leaders to make decisions on relational systems that reflect real value over time? How do you know if you're buying the dining room set rather than the Intellivision? The message is clear from a number of sources: Buying on features is the wrong approach.

A *Computer Reseller News* article entitled "Cool Technology Does Not Seal Enterprise Deals" contained interviews with four top executives concerning selection of software and service partners. One of the interviewees, who was a bank vice president, commented: "Because everybody runs on a development cycle, at any one point in time, some vendor somewhere will have the best product. . . . So somebody has got the best desktop or next month somebody else has got the desktop. Well, that's not a good reason to make the change."[1]

The interviewees went on to explain that there were more important buying criteria, such as coordination costs, requirements for new knowledge or skills, operational reliability, resulting upgrade and support, integration with other systems, and availability of experienced implementation partners.

META Group analysts have advised clients to eschew the request for proposal process altogether because it delivers useless answers. META believes that *how* an important process is done by a vendor is more valuable than its software's feature/function. It also observed that it is much more important to have robust integration capabilities than the best feature/function set.[2]

Sales guru Neil Rackham echoes the process lessons of Chapter 11 in advising organizations to "put strategy first, systems second, and software third." He notes that carefully choosing technology didn't keep 80 percent of companies from reporting that their SFA implementation results were disappointing.[3]

RM products have plenty of features anyway. For example, every SFA package handles the fundamentals of record keeping, account management, forecasting, and reporting. Base SFA functionality can be obtained in minutes using stand-alone SFA desktop applications or sign-up Web sites. The situation now for enterprise packages is that they typically contain far too many features. The first thing many vendors' sales engineers do in preparing a customer demo is to pull out functionality and simplify the screens. It's similar to why the majority of writers utilize a very small percentage of Microsoft Word's functionality. Most RM packages out-of-box (OOB) are overwhelming to users.

We saw one company's relational-system RFP that contained a list of nearly 150 features. Vendors were asked to rate their software according to three categories for each feature: can do out-of-box, can be modified to do, not possible to do. This is a micro approach to a macro problem. Analysts believe that process automation systems will have to be gutted in two years anyway, so the specific feature set at a point in time may not be the most important factor.[4] All this is indicating that features should not be the prime differentiator in selecting a solution.

The reason is that features represent comparative value *at a point in time*. Think of it like a balance sheet versus an income statement. A balance sheet delivers a financial snapshot of an organization. An income statement summarizes performance over a time period. Choosing a relational system is a decision that requires an analysis *over time*.

This isn't like Scrooge's timeless debit/credit accounting principles. There is no such thing as a stable customer-facing system, and there never will be. Software features change. Customer expectations increase. Organizational requirements shift as the enterprise is restructured, companies are bought or sold, product lines are added or discontinued, or channels are extended.

Too many organizations want to make a static relational system decision, as shown in Figure 16-1. Vendor A has these features out-of-box and requires this much customization programming for a total cost of $XXX dollars. Vendor B has more features OOB and requires fewer additions for a total cost of $YYY dollars. Let's choose Vendor B. With this point-in-time approach, which is the norm for most purchases, Vendor B is the clear winner.

The only valid way to view the project is over its lifecycle, as shown in Figure 16-2. In the decision process, everyone is focused on the vendor choice and project implementation. Most RFPs are written as if the system is complete upon successful installation. For the software vendor,

Figure 16-1. Vendor comparisons.

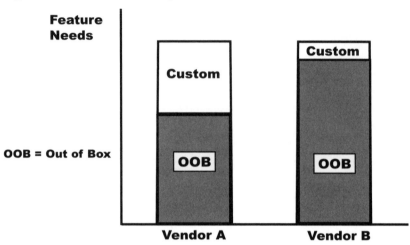

it's the sale that matters. For the implementation partner, it's going operational. But for the buyer, it's using a RM system to beat competitors and maximize profitability.

I like to have fun illustrating this for audiences by setting up a flip chart in each corner of a presentation room. Building a diagram like Figure 16-2, I mark off an "evaluation" segment on the first flip chart, then add the "implementation" segment, explaining that these are the issues highlighted in most RFPs. I then continue the line off the edge of the flip chart and walk across the room to the other flip chart and finish the timeline. I explain, "This is the total lifecycle of the project,

Figure 16-2. Relational system lifecycle.

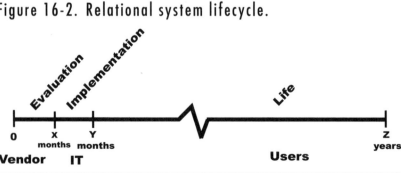

and this is what's going to deliver the real value to you, but you are basically not addressing it." The diagram provides a strong visual sense of which portion of the project is most important.

Customization Is Not an Option

The one invariant is, *Relational systems are continuously improving.* Why? Because customer demands are escalating and competitors are constantly raising the service bar in an effort to gain an advantage. Remember the lesson from Chapter 11 about continuous improvement of processes? In this environment, doing what you've always done earns you *less* than what you used to get.

Because of this, the concept of initial OOB functionality is of very little use when looking at entire lifecycles. Look at Figure 16-3. The same product that provides 80 percent OOB functionality today may deliver only 30 percent of required OOB functionality in a few years.

Figure 16-3. Functional needs over time.

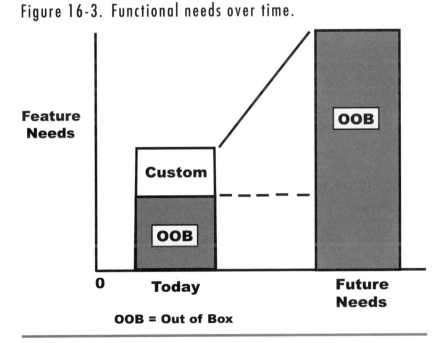

OOB = Out of Box

This is why analysts' comments about the uselessness of RFP's and getting rid of systems within two years were so strongly worded.

If this is true, then why are so many organizations still evaluating RM software primarily on OOB features? Because these buyers are focused on the short-term, and are therefore seeking tactical solutions. This is why research indicates that everyone wants integration and suite solutions, but organizations are still buying point solutions.[5] Customer facing systems are as far from "install and forget" as you can get.

It is not unusual for owners of relationship software that is readily customizable to add literally thousands of changes over the life of a system. Most new installations will have hundreds of user-requested changes pending by the very first day of live operation, the result of end-user experience during testing. Implementing improvements easily isn't a nice-to-have, it is a must-have if the organization is to stay ahead of its competitors.

The anticipated changes in RM systems are nearly overwhelming. There are all the data types mentioned in Chapter 12 that have to be added. How many more data types will make themselves essential over the next few years? Chapter 9 talked about the variety of channel options and new mobile technologies that will need to be integrated. New information presentation formats will need to be developed.

Then what about the surprises to come, the technologies that IT never anticipated needing to deal with, such as personal digital assistants (PDAs)? It's like the old Chinese riddle about which is the smartest animal—the one man has not yet discovered. What is out there that can't be anticipated, only responded to? Relational systems must either have the capability to continually customize and integrate, or the system will require what one CIO called "a heart transplant." With strong customization tools, a massive replacement is the only way to make up the difference between the two bars in Figure 16-3.

At this point, we're usually yelling "Clear!" and putting the heart paddles to executives' chests. All this talk about customization is the last thing they want to hear. Their risk-warning meter is blazing with red lights. All we want, they say, is to get this thing installed quickly and get a return on it. The answer is, "Fine, as long as you don't mind that it's forever becoming obsolete starting with the first day you go live. The market is going to progress in the months it takes you to make the purchase decision and install the software, and continue on from there."

Tailoring Is Not Customization

We're obviously making a strong case in this chapter for a readily customizable system. But before we go too much further, we need to define the term. Since every vendor claims their product is customizable, a buyer hasn't the slightest idea what the true differences are, if any. There are actually four different levels of modifiability of relational software, customization being only one of them.

ADMINISTRATION

Administration involves all the day-to-day tasks of operating and using the system. It includes setting up rights for administration itself, development tools usage, and access to data, program objects, forms, reports, and workflow inboxes. Administration uses rights definition capabilities built into the system. Administration is done throughout the life of the system, according to the rights options available.

TAILORING

Tailoring is a term that is rarely used by vendors in describing their systems, but there is a critical differentiation that needs to be made from customization. Tailoring is using the built-in capabilities of a system to change its performance. Implicit in this definition is that tailoring options are, in effect, OOB functions. Tailoring is done continually throughout the software's life, but only within the limits of the system's built-in options.

CUSTOMIZATION

Customization means extending the core functionality of the system. It includes adding new data elements, such as those in Chapter 12 and the supporting business logic/workflow around them, and building new screen displays or reports. Customization is most often done using a system's tools, if any, for extending system features beyond those OOB.

CONFIGURATION

Configuration is the term used for integrating the relational software with legacy applications and third-party applications. It involves programming code at a detailed IT level to connect two or more disparate systems. This can include passing data between applications, or having events within one system triggering action within other software. Configuration processes are typically done at the time of initial installation, although there might be occasional external system integrations during the software's lifecycle.

(Stomp, stomp.) The biggest point of confusion for buyers is that all relational system vendors claim to offer customization capabilities whether or not they actually do.

We're not saying that anyone is being deceptive. What we are saying is that the capabilities many vendors describe as "customization" are actually "tailoring."

It's theoretically true that all software is customizable, assuming that buyers are willing to get down to the C++ level and begin recoding. It's the old problem of differentiating what the software *can* do versus what it *will* do. Software can be made to do most anything, but recoding is not a practical option for all but the most important of configuration integrations. It's just too costly.

At the other end of the complexity scale, being able to drag column headings around in order to change the order of displayed fields is an example of tailoring, not customization. Figure 13-7, where employees using a self-service portal can choose which data display options they wished to have presented together on screen, is a perfect illustration. The user cannot modify the list of possible modules, but can only choose which are displayed and in what position. Utilizing a reserved data table with CRUD capabilities (create, read, update, delete) is another example of tailoring—capabilities that were already built into the applications OOB.

Customization means extending core functionality, data structures, and their attendant workflow logic. The key point in understanding what "extending" means is the inclusion of workflow logic. As illustrated by the insurance examples in Figures 12-1 through 12-10, data requires defined interrelationships and process workflow around it to deliver true extended functionality. Knowing a relationship, for instance, means little if there is no link to marketing information.

Customization Philosophies

Chapter 11 introduced the three options organizations have for customizing their relational systems:

1. *Install the application OOB using the vendor's processes.* This option offers the shortest time to implement with lowest installation cost, but it requires converting all existing procedures to the vendor's processes. It also delivers the least leverage of existing effectiveness and the lowest competitive advantage. The results are highly dependent upon the quality of the OOB functions. This is the approach of many point solution vendors and all Web-based application service provider (ASP) solutions.

Installing a pure OOB system in an enterprise environment may not be possible or desirable. META Group/IMT Strategies observed, "No company expects to install a suite without some level of integration and/or customization."[6]

2. *Customize the system for current processes.* This option provides a totally adapted system that minimizes the cost and difficulty of reengineering current processes. It also runs the risk of automating incompetence. This is likely the middle cost option and one that delivers a varying degree of value depending upon how good or bad current processes are. In general, all analysts recommend against this option.

3. *Utilize the system for basic relational functions and customize it with value-added processes that add a competitive advantage.* This option leverages the OOB functionality of a system, and requires additional process redesign time and customization costs up front. The result can be a highly efficient system and a true differentiator versus competitors. This may well be the most costly and difficult alternative, but has the potential to deliver highly leveraged results. Most organizations expect to do some type of this customization.

Our preference is for option number three, which is not what many managers want to hear. They would prefer a simple OOB installation with the vendor taking on the risk of technical success, but in their hearts they know that this is not a strategy that's going to deliver the best results.

Also, our quick cost summaries above are not totally correct. The three descriptions cover only the evaluation and installation stages, ignoring the "walking across the room" ownership lifecycle of Figure 16-2. Option three is likely to be the high result/low cost choice if its customization capabilities extend the useful life of the software. There are clients of easily customizable systems that have had the same software in place for five years. The current system bears only a passing resemblance to what was originally bought due to the myriad of customizations that were installed through the years. This is what delivers tremendous results at very attractive lifecycle costs.

Customization Architectures

So if customization is helpful or even inevitable, a key system evaluation factor has to be how customizations and configurations are made to relational systems. This is an enormous concern in selecting vendors. For example, AMR estimates that software license fees make up only 25 percent of the total cost to deploy a CRM system. Integration and implementation costs make up the rest.[7] What is required are systems that are "easily" or "readily" customizable using an embedded tool set that doesn't require an experienced IT professional (or consulting partner) with costly and hard-to-find programming skills.

There are three common vendor approaches to customization.

1. *Only tailoring tools are included.* In this option, any customization (functionality extension) requires professional programming using a supported general purpose programming language. In many cases, the data model is extremely inflexible, and is difficult to integrate with other systems.

2. *The customization architecture is object-oriented.* This is the approach of a major SFA-oriented vendor. Here applications can be

readily tailored by assembling existing program objects into user screens. There is no line-by-line programming required as long as clients use OOB or pre-existing program objects along with existing or reserved data tables. Any other customizations require a development partner using traditional object development tools.

Depending upon the system's client/server or Web architecture, it may be difficult to integrate data with other systems due to the lack of an application program interface (API). Briefly, an API allows programmers to access data files by logical object, such as "case," rather than directly by individual data table.

3. Provide a customization toolset. Some vendors have designed their systems to be truly customizable, such as allowing end-user tailoring, functional extensions, and ease of integration with external systems. Figure 16-4 shows an example of a browser-based tools menu. Depending on the rights granted to this user, a wide range of system and application design and control functions can be accessed from a user or administrator's Home screen.

Browser-based application screens, data objects, and workflow rules themselves can be designed and customized using application tools. One such example is the application design screen shown in Figure 16-5, where the various objects in a system are defined and formatted. The screen shows a series of windows for laying out an application screen and placing data elements on it. All this can be done in a visual environment to create Web-based applications without having to program at a language level.

Another key element of functionality is workflow. This is the set of data relationships, logic, rules, notifications, escalations, computations, and process launches linked to data elements. Figure 16-6 shows an example of a visually-based workflow generation tool. Again, this can be done by a process expert trained in the use of the tool and may not require an IT-level programmer.

This visual toolkit approach in building Web applications provides significant advantages to organizations by allowing them to readily customize OOB applications as the marketplace dictates. The results are browser-based functionality such as the query designer tools screen in Figure 16-7.

Figure 16-4. Browser-based tools menu.

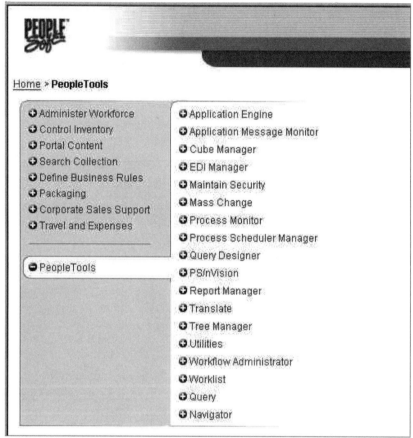

Summary

Although it is seen as a necessary evil, customization is certainly necessary, and it is evil only if the proper tools and systems architecture don't support it. OOB functionality is admittedly an issue, but the real benefit of a particular system will be its ability to maximize results and keep the organization competitive over time. This gets at the most basic issues of system and vendor selection, which will be addressed in the next chapter.

Figure 16-5. Object definition.

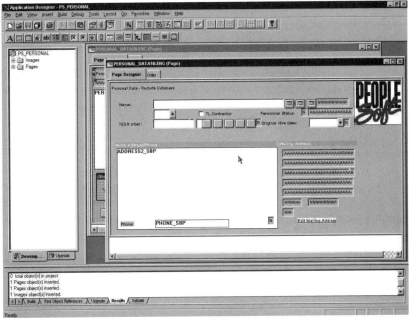

Learning Points

1. Feature advantages are a very temporary thing and are constantly changing. Being number one depends upon where everyone else is in their product update cycle.

2. The general industry advice is not to buy relational software based primarily upon its out-of-box features.

3. Customer requirements and competitive offerings are changing over time. What is required out-of-box today is unacceptable tomorrow. Buying a system and keeping it stagnant only assures that an organization will be falling further behind over time.

4. The software decision has to be based upon the entire system lifecycle. Ease of customization is a way to extend a system's life and minimize upgrades or replacements.

Figure 16-6. Workflow definition.

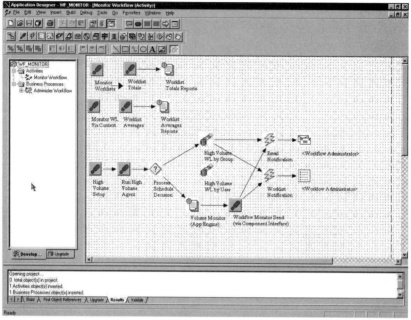

5. Tailoring is not customization. Customization truly extends the functionality of the applications.

6. Customization is where large added value is created. Because of this, nearly every relational system is customized in some way.

7. Therefore, ease of customization is a critical factor in selecting a solution. Systems that require programmers create new screen elements, data objects, and workflow will have much higher implementation costs and lifecycle costs.

Figure 16-7. Query definition.

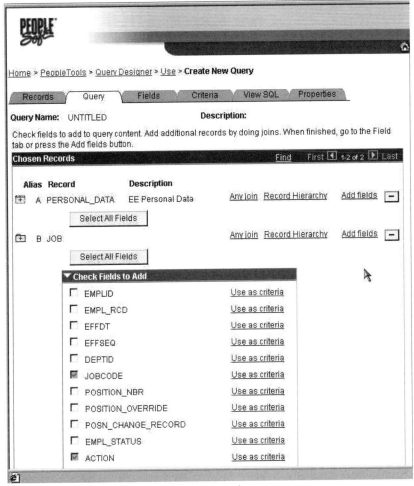

NOTES

1. H. Clancy, "Cool Technology Does Not Seal Enterprise Deals," *Computer Reseller News*, November 15, 1999, p. 80.

2. META Group, "META Group CRM Conference: Value Management," February 21, 2000.

3. Neil Rackham, "Learn From Past Mistakes," *Sales & Marketing Management*, December 2000, pp. 38–40.

4. META Group: "META Group CRM Conference: Applications Integration," February 21, 2000.

5. META Group and IMT Strategies, "Customer Relationship Management (CRM) Study 1999: Sponsor Report," September, 22, 1999, pp. 1/D–41.

6. Ibid., Executive Summary, p. 17.

7. Steve Konicki and Jennifer Maselli, "When Customer Care Counts," *InformationWeek*, March 26, 2001, p. 23.

*"It used to be that choice was
good. Now choice is paralyzing."*

—ROBERT J. STUCKEY

CHAPTER 17

Evaluating Relational System Vendors

I once arrived for a sales appointment and found an executive who was obviously not in a receptive mood. Brochures, catalogs, and stapled proposals turned folded over to an inside page were scattered all over his desk. He had that coat-off, tie-slightly-loosened, disheveled look about him, and checked his watch with that "Already?" surprise as I knocked on his doorway to announce my arrival. There's nothing to do in these situations except abandon the call goal and either help customers vent, or reschedule and let them get back to work.

I choose the first alternative and opened with, "Man, it looks like you are buried in the middle of something that has you stressed. What's going on?" He proceeded with a heartfelt rant on how he had been volunteered to evaluate plant control computer systems and make a vendor recommendation.

"So how is it looking?" I asked. "Anybody in the lead?" The answer explained his concern.

"That's my problem. I've studied all of this and talked to other factories, and I don't think *any* of these are going to work for what we're trying to do. I'm scared of all of them."

"So what are you going to do?"

"Well, I think I'm going to select IBM. I don't think their system is right either, but at least I'll keep my job if I can tell people, 'Heck, even IBM couldn't get it to work.' "

I shook my head, told him that was a tough one, agreed on a time to meet later, and left him to his pain. It was great insight into his decision-making process, and that was helpful. It also made me think about all those poor salespeople who had made presentations, set up custom demonstrations, visited reference sites, and written up wonderful proposals with product descriptions, benefits, pricing, justification, and implementation plans. It was all a waste because the customer was going to make a gut level decision rather than a systematic one.

Basic Reasons to Pick a Vendor

If the key issue isn't product features, then there must be some other very basic buying criteria that should be considered in selecting a vendor. Here's what buyers ought to be looking for, questions that get right at the core of what's truly important to organizations making the vendor selection.

1. *Does the vendor have a clue about RM?* Simply put, do they truly understand what's going on in business today? Do they "get" RM? Is their thinking at the leading edge? Does it contain original ideas? Do they have the right approach to the market? To developing products?

You can argue that point-solution vendors don't get that their days are numbered and that they have the wrong solutions approach for customers. It's like the manual typewriter manufacturers who were still adding features years after the first IBM electric typewriter hit the streets. The future for point solutions is either buy-out or dissolution, as organizations move to front-office suites and on to integrated operational/collaborative/analytical RM packages.

2. *Is this vendor's product functional?* Notice that this question promotes the concept of "functional," which will be defined in detail later in this chapter. The solution doesn't have to be "best of breed," but it has to be "do what I want." As the last chapter showed, this

means that the selection decision shouldn't be an end-user feature beauty contest. The question is, "Can this product help me *maximize* the lifetime profitability of all my relationships?"

3. *Can this vendor keep me six months ahead of my competitors?* Customer expectations and competition are moving targets. The six-months-ahead goal is an arbitrary one, but it is probably the best an organization can reasonably aim for. Does this vendor have a vision for business in the future? Is there a compelling product roadmap? And most importantly, *does this vendor have rapid development as a core competency?*

One large vendor has admitted spending ten figures on R&D and does not yet have a stable RM suite to offer. Another leading vendor has struggled with in-house development and acquiring software, and finally had to license key modules from a competitor. They've both been forced into selling a strategy of delay that has put their waiting clients behind competitors.

4. *Am I willing to trust my revenue stream to this vendor?* As we've pointed out repeatedly, relational applications are not like back-office or analytical systems. Organizations are playing with their revenue stream here, and the stakes are enormous. Situations like the toy Web retailers' order fulfillment problems of Christmas 1999 can have a permanent effect on revenue and profits. All of a sudden, background issues such as scalability and reliability become critical.

5. *Do I want to work daily with this vendor for the next five years?* Every organization has a personality. An interesting thing about the software industry is that some system vendors, as unimaginable as it seems, have a very abrasive style with customers. An RM system vendor is going to be intimately intertwined with the buyer's organization at many levels. It helps to have a vendor with a culture of cooperation and service for the coming years, when the only thing that can be expected is the unexpected.

When all the feature comparison spreadsheets, demonstration results, and benchmarks have shaken out, these five issues will be the fundamental decision criteria for vendor selection. Fortunately for buyers, how vendors approach these five questions is very well differentiated in the marketplace.

Vendor Solution Philosophies

The RM market, presenting one of the greatest growth opportunities in business today, has as many as 500 CRM vendors.[1] With this diversity of options, there are a variety of solution models in operation. The good news is that vendor offerings fall into several major approaches.

This is a good time to re-examine the expanded three-part definition of CRM as originally illustrated in Figure 8-1, and seen again in Figure 17-1. Comparing vendors requires mapping the various strategies to requirements for operational, collaborative, and analytical RM. The major options are point solutions, customer data eco-system, the "all-from-me system," and ERP vendor with strategic integrations.

POINT SOLUTIONS

As has been previously discussed, point solutions are a single application, such as e-store, marketing, SFA, support, help desk, or field service. They can be provided by stand-alone packages, Web applica-

Figure 17-1. Three types of CRM.

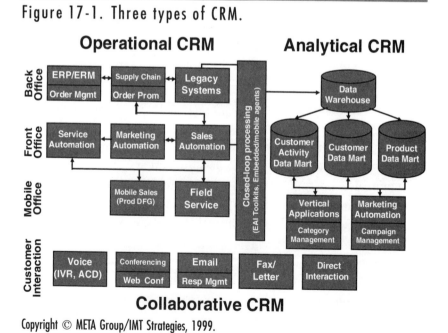

tion service providers, or sophisticated client/server solutions designed for high-volume usage by thousands of agents.

Point solutions often provide leading edge functionality and best practice processes, and they may be faster to install initially than the other options. The major weakness is providing a minimal 30-degree view of the customer for a few roles within a single process. The analyst community is pessimistic about the viability of this approach and advises clients to seek cross-functional suites along with solutions that can be easily integrated. Point solutions are a tactical response to a strategic need.

CUSTOMER DATA ECO-SYSTEM

Several vendors are trying to create an "eco-system" where their product becomes the central source for all customer data. Their internal focus is specifically on front-office or e-business portions of operational CRM and on integrating collaborative CRM channels. Externally, hundreds of software partners are then recruited to leverage the vendor's data and to supplement its core offerings. Figure 17-2 illustrates this graphically.

The primary advantage of this approach is standardization. A dominant core vendor can establish itself as the single source for customer data and front-office operational CRM applications. Compatibility with this vendor's products and data model becomes the price of entry into the market for supplementary products. To add additional functionality, buyers can select from a wide shopping list of partner companies that have been certified compatible by the vendor.

The assumption is that these partners have already dealt with the issues of integrating their individual products with the core vendor's data and application suite. In other cases, pre-built connectors are available for common integrations, such as with back-office ERP systems. The sales theme becomes, "Buy from us. We're the market leader and a de facto standard. Therefore, we're the safest choice."

There are a number of major concerns with this approach. First, based upon the last full-year data available, no single vendor has as much as a 15 percent market share. The market share leader is actually the "other" category.[2] Any company intent on establishing itself as the dominant RM market leader still has significant ground to gain on the hundreds of other competitors.

Figure 17-2. Vendor eco-system.

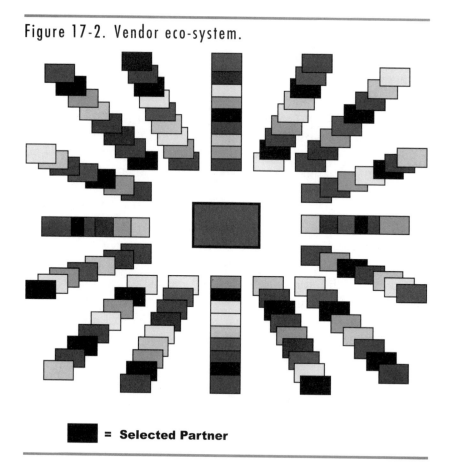

■ = Selected Partner

Second, sticking with any single data model and suite of applications, by necessity, limits functionality. For example, a model originally designed for SFA applications must segment data so that outside salespeople can remotely sync their individual databases without corrupting each others' records for shared accounts. This is a very different structure from that required for CIC or ERP software, where widespread data-sharing throughout the entire business cycle is essential.

Third, implicit in the eco-system approach is the "naval convoy principle," which says that a convoy must stay together for security, and can move only as fast as the slowest vessel. In addition, some of the smaller vessels may have to sacrifice themselves in defense of larger ships. In a convoy, everyone is either heading in the right direction or the wrong one. There is no room for innovation because someone on one of the biggest ships is in command. The eco-system philosophy creates several important risks for the buyer.

Risk #1: Partner Survival. It's one thing to select among major CRM vendors with billion-dollar market presence. It's quite another to select an additional group of smaller providers as part of the solution. In an eco-system, there are typically multiple vendors listed for each supplementary application.

In some cases there may be nothing more behind the partnership than an announcement, often called "PR partnerships." In other cases there is a technical certification, which does not necessarily say anything about the partners' stability or business plan. Buyers must not only pick partners with the most appropriate functionality, buyers must figure out whether these smaller companies are viable businesses with a true product integration completed.

As the 2000–2001 technology slow-down has shown, this can present a significant risk. It is a near certainty that some portion of the hundreds of eco-system participants are not going to survive intact, either being acquired or disappearing altogether. The last thing any buyer wants is to have an application that provides critical value to the entire system, such as analytics, become a dead end product halfway through the life of the project.

Regarding smaller companies and start-ups, the InfoWorld Test Center comments, "When implementing new technologies and partnering with start-ups, the enterprise breaks new ground—but the danger is high."[3]

As anyone working with Microsoft has found, it can also be risky for partners living in the shadow of a core vendor. Woody Allen said it best, "The lamb shall lay down with the lion, but he won't get much sleep." All it takes is for the core vendor to acquire a competitor or decide to provide similar functionality within the OOB product, and the other vendors in this market niche are destroyed. What was a good partner decision for a buyer instantly becomes a dead end.

Partner survival risks are multiplied with each additional partner added to the solution. Risks are also increased when some of the chosen eco-system partners are smaller in size.

Risk #2: Inconsistent Strategy. A buyer who assembles a large repertory company of supplemental software solutions around a core product is betting that every vendor in the group is going to develop in the same direction. So if there are twenty application vendors in the mix, then buyers are assuming that all twenty are going to stay consistent and in sync over the entire life of the project.

A key issue in evaluating eco-system partners is how much of their business is dependent upon linking up with the core vendor. With no CRM vendor having a dominant market share, partners must have a life outside of the eco-system. This means they need to integrate with several major vendors or vendor eco-systems at once, all while maintaining advanced functionality overall.

For smaller, stand-alone vendors, this also means that they are going to have to innovate more rapidly than the large players. Smaller partners' only advantage over integrated suites is that of being best-of-breed in their niche. As the market settles in to fewer and larger vendors, partners are going to have a more difficult time staying in sync with all of them.

Risk #3: Slower Innovation. As the bank executive's comments in Chapter 16 indicated, software vendors operate on different product refresh cycles. Like a convoy, the entire eco-system may be able to move forward only at the speed of the slowest vendor partner.

What happens when the core vendor makes a fundamental addition to the data model, such as those we saw in Chapter 12? Any changes must propagate out to each partner in the combined solution, be programmed in, quality assured, tested for integration, then added to the support center's repertoire. The Microsoft Windows eco-system has shown that it can take months or years for vendors, even major ones, to make their applications and drivers compliant with new releases. RM eco-system buyers face similar risks with their collection of vendors.

Risk #4: One-Way Data. As one expert developer put it, with an eco-system it is easy to get data out of the core system but hard to get data in. Having many independent applications, in potentially unique combinations, picked uniquely by different customers, and inserting information into a highly related data model can put core database integrity at risk. So eco-system vendors tightly control their database model descriptions to discourage data input from external sources. Some vendors even refuse to share the model with customers, or void the maintenance warranty if buyers write directly to the database.

Risk #5: Higher Implementation Costs. Since the Y2K deadline alone, hundreds of vendors have appeared and over twenty totally new customer-facing application categories have been created. The result is that buyers or their paid implementation consultant often take on the costly task of integrating between a dozen to three dozen of such applications from various vendors.[4]

As one CIO put it, "Integration strikes fear into the heart of IT executives." A vice president of information systems at a major retailer observed that companies that try to integrate pieces from many vendors to get a best-of-breed IT infrastructure end up with limited functionality because cost and time constraints often lead to inadequate integration.[5]

Utilizing an eco-system greatly complicates the programming effort because buyers or their implementation outsourcers have to learn to effectively use every vendor's development tools. It becomes clear why CRM system implementation costs are typically four times as high as software license fees. Imagine having to learn to use (or pay an implementation partner to use) ten to twenty different development tools in order to integrate applications such as e-commerce, front-office CRM, back-office ERP, data warehousing, analytics, and reporting. The more vendors, the more complexity and implementation cost. This is one reason the eco-system approach has been very popular with implementation partners.

The eco-system philosophy offers a very compelling vision of one front-office vendor providing a secure foundation for building a comprehensive CRM solution set. But as long as the eco-system vendors cover such a small part of Figure 17-1, this is a high-risk strategy.

THE ''ALL FROM ME'' SYSTEM

The opposite of the eco-system is the third option, the "buy everything from one vendor" approach. The biggest proponent of this strategy is a large database company that is investing heavily to create completely integrated collaborative, operational, analytical, and e-business solutions from the database up. The president of this company, noted for his strong opinions, actually told his customers at a 2001 users group meeting that they should customize their companies to his software rather than vice versa.[6] His recommendation was for customers to adapt their business processes to the predefined processes his company provided and run the entire system solely on his software. Say good-bye to competitive advantage and customization.

As Figure 17-3 shows, there is not much of a structural diagram for this strategy. The analogy is that of Microsoft Office, which replaced WordPerfect, Lotus 1-2-3, and dBase as the business desktop standard. The tight integration of Office provided advantages far beyond the three separate applications.

Creating this total solution is no small task and has proven difficult to accomplish. The key element of this approach is having rapid development as a core competency, i.e., decision criterion #3 from the beginning of this chapter. So far, the two major vendors that have tried to accomplish this have struggled. Either the applications were perceived as mediocre in quality compared with best-of-breed solutions, or the products have not yet been released and proven reliable in live production. The result is that, as of this writing, one vendor is still in the development cycle and the other has tried various strategies, such as in-house development, acquisition, and licensing established applications, all with mixed success.

Figure 17-3. Me only.

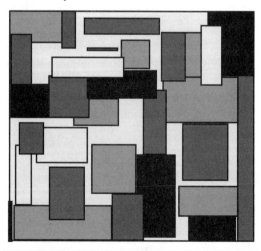

ERP VENDOR WITH STRATEGIC INTEGRATIONS

In general, analysts agree that no one vendor is best-of-breed in every category. Yet we have seen that there are advantages to buying a solution that is as integrated as possible. Consider the definition of CRM in Figure 17-1. ERP companies inherently have the best business model for delivering effective relational systems at lower cost because they provide more of the 360-degree view business cycle coverage than do front-office only vendors.

This is why AMR Research and most consulting and systems-integration firms advise buyers to consider ERP vendors first before pursuing an aggressive third-party integration strategy. Their recommendation is the fourth option, which is to select an ERP vendor for core applications and then integrate software from two or three other vendors. AMR researcher Rod Johnson said, "Clearly, single-vendor strategies are dead, but companies need to bet significant portions of their strategies on three or four big pieces rather than fifteen-piece parts."[7]

Concerns with this strategy center on the danger of depending upon one vendor for such a wide range of applications. In the words of an eco-system vendor, "One neck, one noose." Some systems integrators urge their clients to instead take a best-of-breed approach, citing the improved built-in integration capabilities of new releases and the availability of middleware vendors with pre-built adapters. They say this has the potential to deliver the highest functionality, but it can also deliver the highest revenue to the integrator doing the implementation.

The best strategy, as shown in Figure 17-4, is for the ERP vendor to select a limited number of strategic partners rather than sign up as many partners as possible. The software is then pre-integrated and offered as the preferred application in each functional area. In some cases, the ERP vendor will actually license a partner's code and bring it in-house for integration and improvement. The code is then included OOB or as a standard option. The result is greatly reduced integration risk and cost.

Although there are certainly advantages in staying with a single provider, a particular ERP vendor should not be disqualified from front-office, collaborative, and/or analytical product consideration just because the back office is with another ERP vendor. As we advise clients, "It takes a great ERP company to do CRM right."

Figure 17-4. Partner integrate.

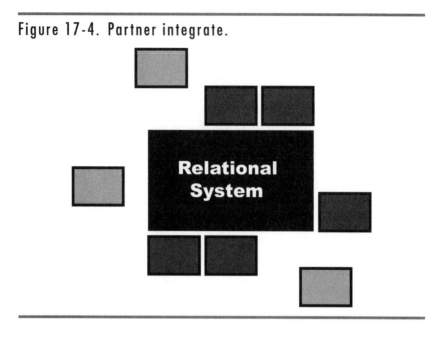

The Future of CRM Systems

There's a quick point to be made here—not a "today sale," but certainly a "tomorrow sale." If systems are becoming more integrated and full functioned, if feature sets are becoming commoditized, if systems are becoming more easily integrated, then the path is clear. Right now everything is about selection and integration of vendors and applications. In the future, the distinctions between back office, front office, analytics, collaboration, and e-business will disappear.

There is a new generation of software coming. The change from integrating solutions to unified RM is as significant as was migrating from old home-grown accounting and operational systems to ERP. The choice of a vendor philosophy, and ultimately a vendor to implement it, should be made in light of this impending new class of software.

Summary

Regardless of personal preferences in a vendor solution philosophy, buyers should link the various vendor strategies back to the five "gut level" buying criteria discussed at the beginning of the chapter. Of these, the most important is #3, keeping ahead of competition. That concept covers a lot of issues and hits right at the heart of the reasons for doing RM in the first place. Relational systems must provide a competitive advantage. Now the question becomes, how to make the changeover.

Learning Points

1. There are five gut-level questions to ask in selecting a relational systems vendor:
   - Do they have a clue?
   - Is the product good enough?
   - Can they keep me ahead of the bad guys?
   - Do I want to trust them with my revenue stream?
   - Can I stand to work with them for a long time?

2. Point solutions are a dead end. Swim at your own risk.

3. The eco-system approach sounds inviting, but creates serious risks. Imagine checking the business section daily to see if your picks are still in the tournament. Plus, you have to make sure they all get along . . . forever.

4. The eco-system is not very far from "make your systems integrator happy, roll your own."

5. "Everything from me" also sounds inviting, but first someone has got to actually create "everything." So far very few of the contestants have proven to have a rapid development core competency.

6. ERP vendors are ideally positioned to cover the entire business cycle if they can avoid the problem of being the "ten of all trades"—not good enough to be the jack. The trick is to pick a selected group of healthy, intelligent partners and then become attached at the hip.

7. Make decisions today with one eye on the future, which will consist of a consolidated application covering all the areas of the definition of CRM shown in Figure 17-1.

NOTES

1. Carlton Vogt, "CRM Implementation Trends," *InfoWorld.com E-Business Daily*, March 30, 2001, p. 2.

2. Marion Agnew, "CRM Tools Offer Sales-Force Solutions," *InformationWeek*, August 21, 2000, p. 118.

3. Kevin Railsback, "Weighing the Risks of Innovation," *InfoWorld*, April 2, 2001, p. 43.

4. Steve Konicki, "Enterprise Resource Planning Break Out," *InformationWeek*, December 18–25, 2000, p. 72.

5. Ibid.

6. Bob Lewis, "Are Mr. Ellison's Vanilla-Flavor-Style Customer Relations Good for You?," April 2, 2001, p. 42.

7. Konicki, "Enterprise Resource Planning," p. 72.

"How many psychologists does it take to change a light bulb? One . . . but the bulb has got to really want to change."

CHAPTER 18

Managing RM Change

In early discussions of evolution, Charles Darwin observed that his theory would not be valid if anyone could find a biological construct that could not have evolved in a step-by-step fashion, i.e., one that had to be formed complete from the beginning. In 1996, biochemist Michael Behe coined the term "Darwin's black box" for this construct, and nominated the cell and other biomolecular systems as examples of profound complexity that could not have evolved stepwise to their current forms.[1]

Behe explains that it is like a mousetrap. You can't set a block of wood out, have it catch a few mice, then add a hinged bar, have it more efficiently catch a few more mice, then add a spring, have it catch even more mice, then add the bait holder, and then add the bait. You either have a fully functioning mousetrap with all the interdependent functions in place, or you have a useless thingamajig sitting on the floor. The mousetrap is either complete or dysfunctional, there is no viable intermediate form.

This is a perfect analogy for today's organization in the rapidly changing e-business environment. A step-by-step evolution, resolving some issues and letting others lie, is not going to generate survival, much less success. Compartmentalized change is the path to antisynergism—the committee's camel. This is suboptimization, improving the pieces individually without necessarily insuring the effectiveness of the whole. To build a better organizational mousetrap, the *entire* mousetrap is going to have to be there.

Organizations Can't Evolve to Get There

Most organizations are trying to ease into the e-business environment. They are taking on parts of the relationship agenda in a localized, piecemeal fashion. The results are localized, piecemeal progress that does more harm than good. Before the Internet, a bad customer service representative could only antagonize a few customers per day. Now, through the miracle of technology, a bad Web site can infuriate millions of prospects per hour.

In the transaction-based era, our catch phrase was, "Anything worth doing is worth doing poorly." The idea was to get started quickly with something, *anything* rather than wait for perfect solutions and fall behind. Continuous quality improvement could take care of any problems.

In today's era of relationships, our catch phrase is, "Do it right, or wait until you get it right." After all, this isn't just the back office we're talking about. Organizations are betting their revenue stream on these efforts. The problem is that "getting it right" now requires a total integration of the entire list (and more) of the *what to do's* mentioned so far in this book. Fail to execute on some of the principles and the entire effort is sabotaged. Evolutionary change isn't much help in an all-or-nothing situation.

Another problem with evolutionary change is that the result is ultimately limited by the starting point. In the early days of personal computer development, I rode on a rental car shuttle with an IBM executive. AT&T was entering the computer market and the trade press was warning about the potential impact of this 800 pound gorilla. When I asked if he was concerned about AT&T, the IBM exec said he wasn't at all worried. IBM had three times better productivity per employee, he explained, and AT&T would never be competitive. AT&T could improve 50 percent and still be far behind, and IBM-employee productivity wasn't standing still. As we know, AT&T ultimately dropped out of the computer business after never capturing any significant market share.

On the hard–easy scale, it is incredibly hard to redesign existing processes and structures. Even with management support, total quality training, skilled facilitators, dedicated process improvement teams, and consultants, it is often difficult to get beyond a "we're not as bad as we used to be" solution.

So taking evolutionary steps can't create the kind of organization that's needed. And no matter how good the starting point, it is ultimately a limit. It still doesn't pay to be the best dinosaur after the meteor hits.

Random Change Is Even Worse

Can there be dramatic evolution? It's almost an oxymoron. Staying with our biology analogy, in the absence of transitional forms in the fossil record, some biologists have postulated the "hopeful monster" theory. They suggest that massive complementary changes can happen at random over a short period of time resulting in a radically different, but successful, new life form. This change philosophy makes for interesting debates in academia, but is not very useful for running an organization. Yet random restructuring, i.e., across-the-board layoffs, is still a common tactic.

Becoming relationship oriented is not something that can be driven from the bottom of the organizational pyramid up because of downsizing. It is an all-or-nothing effort to do *everything* right, and that requires massive changes in the organization. Unfortunately, this is extremely difficult to do.

The Change Track Record

Change is tough, but change involving technology is even tougher. In 1993's best selling *Reengineering the Corporation*, Michael Hammer and James Champy wrote: "We say that in reengineering, information technology acts as an essential enabler. Without information technology, the process could not be reengineered."[2]

In the mid-1990s, the IT contribution to reengineering meant reprogramming mainframe or client/server systems. This is risky business. According to a 1995 Standish Group study of 365 IT managers, only 16 percent of IT application development projects were delivered on time, on budget, and with the features initially specified.[3] The complexity of application development was a critical factor in the failure of many change projects.

Scope is another danger factor. In a later study, the Standish Group found that success varied inversely with the size of IT projects. Those costing less than $750,000 succeed 55 percent of the time. Success rates drop to 18 percent for projects in the $1 million to $2 million range. And projects in the $5 million to $10 million range succeed only 7 percent of the time.[4]

CRM isn't doing so well either. The Gartner Group estimates that as much as 60 percent of all traditional CRM software implementations fail. Miller Heiman completed a study indicating that two-thirds of e-CRM implementations also fail.[5] In a Data Warehousing Institute study of 1,516 business executives and IT managers, 42 percent indicated they are experiencing difficulties or consider the effort a potential flop.[6] In another study reported by *InfoWorld*, in 32 percent of sales technology projects little or no use was made of the technology twelve months after deployment.[7]

This may be more the customer's fault than the system's problems. According to Insight Technology Group, "A poor CRM outcome usually can be traced to the customer, rather than the vendor."[8]

Or the relational systems may be to blame. A recent trade article comments, "A shockingly high percentage of customer relationship management deployments—50 percent by some estimates—fail, often because inexperienced IT users struggle to use overly complex applications, experts say."[9]

Or the implementation partners may be to blame. Another recent article quotes a customer who stated, "Consultants literally get paid to overcomplicate CRM implementations. . . . They'll lead the implementation down a complicated path for the sake of fees."[10]

Finally, perhaps the problem is leadership. Ernst & Young estimates that more than half of all companies can't measure the return on investment of their CRM projects.[11]

Tom Peters takes on a wider scope than just CRM. Peters, never one to hold back, in a September 2000 conference speech hit directly at management's lack of determination to make radical changes:

> *More than 85 percent of companies trying to restructure around e-commerce will blow it . . . because they lack the intestinal fortitude. . . . The real issue is whether companies have the guts to engage in creative destruction.*[12]

Michael Vizard, editor in chief of *InfoWorld* magazine, writes, "CRM today is soon going to be what enterprise resource planning projects were to IT in the mid-1990s. This is because installing the software is relatively easy compared to driving the cultural changes necessary to make these investments ultimately pay off."[13] Vizard observes that many organizations don't have the business processes in place to support CRM, and they should not install it without thinking through all the service and process implications.

While Peters talks about creative destruction, managers of budding relational enterprises must be thinking about creative creation. At this point in the book, we now know what the relational organization is going to look like and how it must function. The challenge is to get there.

Rules for Success

An article in *Customer Inter@ction Solutions* magazine offered five recommendations for increasing the success rate of relational systems implementations:[14]

1. *Align business expectations with organizational dynamics.* SFA is a perfect example of crossed purposes. Sales management wants a system that will begin capturing informational sales assets, such as customer contact data, call histories, opportunity status, and forecasts. Supervisors want to make certain that salespeople are following the proscribed selling processes, and that salespeople are expending the

right amount of effort and working smart. Management wants more accurate forecasts, and they are tired of losing an entire territory's contact information every time a salesperson quits. SFA appears to be a big win to sales management.

Sales professionals, many with poor typing skills, are suddenly turned into data entry clerks. They are quickly buried by the initial task of transferring all their notes, schedule, and contact records into the system. Salespeople are then expected to record every phone call, every conversation, and every letter. Any contact no matter how trivial has to be logged into the system. In addition, sales process steps have to be completed in the order proscribed, whether it makes sense or not. Salespeople find themselves spending more than an hour per day entering data and syncing with the centralized corporate database. They can't wait to sabotage the SFA effort.

Signals are mixed. The sales job is supposed to be about increasing profitable orders, yet most of the pressure coming from management concerns how up-to-date call records and forecasts are. Some of the sales supervisors who don't buy into the new system are allowed to let their team use only the parts that are helpful—as long as their sales performance is good. So the central database becomes relatively useless because its information is incomplete. In the end, weekly forecasts are done on an Excel spreadsheet during the Friday morning sales management conference call, while the SFA system chugs along unknowingly in the background, with most of its multimillion dollar features unused.

You can easily adapt this story to any other customer-facing system, be it call center, field service, or support. Call center agents may be encouraged to improve customer satisfaction, but management uses the new CRM reports on call volume and duration to pressure agents to get customers off the line faster. A field service agent now carries a mobile device, but has to take time to make lengthy entries using one-finger poking at a matchbox-sized keyboard.

There's an old line familiar to motivational speakers, "Everyone listens to WII-FM radio—what's in it for me." When relational systems are zero-sum games, i.e., one constituent's payoff is another's penalty, the implementation is destined to fail. The loser will make failure certain, just like salespeople throttle poorly conceived SFA implementations.

Only when there is a positive-sum game, where all constituents benefit, will the organization experience profitable results. When sales-people can access a customer's contact history with the entire extended enterprise, when they can review analytics to profile and find the best customers to sell, when CIC agents can address any issue through a service portal, when customers can research their own problems, when management rewards behaviors that truly drive desired business results, then everyone in the organization will embrace the new technology.

2. *Make relationship management an enterprise-wide mission.* This is a critical point. Everyone in the extended enterprise must be focused on maximizing the profitability of every relationship. This is both a cultural positioning and a process goal, and it is also formally supported by incentive and reward systems. Some organizations are now tying salary increases and bonuses to customer satisfaction ratings and analytics metrics. Management that "puts its money where its mouth is" is going to have a higher success rate.

3. *Avoid the "deer in the headlights" syndrome.* Aging point solutions are being supplanted by front-office suites integrating functions such as marketing, sales, service, and support. While this is an improvement in integration and functionality, it is actually just enlarging the front-office silo, or island of automation.

In this environment service agents may have a "deer in the headlights" look when faced with transactions like this: "About the order I placed the day before yesterday . . . I'd like to change it from eight green ones to six, and from seven red ones to fifteen. Can you make the change and bill it to my credit card?"

With access restricted to information in the front-office suite, the agent can't know where the order is in the fulfillment process. Has it been picked? Packed? Shipped? Can it be still be intercepted and changed? Is the new order in inventory? Does its availability meet the customer's original timeframe? Can the difference be billed to a credit card if this was originally a P.O. and hasn't yet been paid? Without the right systems in place, this simple change order can multiply into a string of costly handling rework and billing errors—all with the potential of aggravating the customer.

Suboptimizing point solutions are dead ends. Systems and processes must encompass the entire business cycle for everyone on the spider chart. The days of providing departmental workforce automation applications are over. Relational processes can't be handled by systems that hit departmental boundaries and disconnect with a "fire and forget" notification to another system. The solution is enterprise-wide systems that are integration friendly.

4. *When benefits become liabilities.* One of the great benefits of process automation is better management control. Call center or SFA reports help managers track and measure productivity. Field service reports provide data on inventory usage and service call efficiencies. Automation can generate improvement in a myriad of performance measures, which, surprisingly, can also be a liability. Satisfaction and process improvements require more than a unidimensional measurement system. While better than no measurement at all, activity or process reporting by itself leaves many important management questions unanswered.

For example, assume that a company wants to increase sales:

- Finance provides a list of customers by past purchase volume to help determine who is most important and deserves the most attention. Good enough? No.

- The SFA system can be used to list the forecasted revenue by customer to determine the greatest opportunity. Good enough? No.

- Service costs need to be considered. Some customer prospects have existing agreements that increase costs and lower profitability. That indicates profitability and value. Good enough? No.

- Satisfaction indexes must be evaluated to find high-value customers with low satisfaction allows salespeople to focus on prospects who are competitively at risk. Good enough? Perhaps.

- Existing buyers are profiled to determine how to target and acquire new customers who are likely to be most profitable. Good enough? Getting there.

Providing this information in usable form involves gathering data from a variety of process steps distributed throughout the organization. Then it has to be organized into reports that let various roles take proscriptive action in selecting tactics, and in then raising those sales and service performance areas for the right customers. This requires a relational system far superior to a process automation system.

5. *Good (C)RM is pervasive.* The final challenge is to make certain that relational systems are available to everyone in the extended enterprise who needs them. This means that the system must capture and present information:

- Across the relational enterprise spider chart
- Throughout the business cycle
- For every role
- From every channel
- At every touch point
- Going in and out of the organization

This is a true 360-degree view that allows everyone in the relational enterprise to treat every customer based upon their lifetime profitability.

Summary

These five recommendations provide an effective summary to the major learning points of this book. Relational organizations don't come about like a "hopeful monster." The entire aspect of relationship management is not a one-time project that will be implemented and left in place. This isn't another fad topic to be approached like quality or reengineering. Customer-facing systems will be a steadily moving target of competitive advantage or disadvantage.

A 1995 Gemini Consulting study of 1,450 managers and executives, completed in the middle of the reengineering craze, observed:

The new leadership challenge is to engage the entire organization in continuous regeneration.[15] *[emphasis mine]*

Winners will be able to structure themselves and select, implement, and operate relational systems that keep them continuously ahead of their competitors. Losers will remain back in the pack or lag their industry. Organizations that have managers with intestinal fortitude, workers with flexibility, and leaders with a firm strategic vision will be the new winners. How this organization will look is our next topic.

Learning Points

1. A partial mousetrap is no mousetrap at all. The change to RM is so drastic that some organizations can't evolve.

2. RM is a customer-facing system. Organizations have to do this one right the first time, and without missteps. Otherwise, the pain can last for years.

3. Don't let the starting point limit the solution. A bad starting point requires more immediate change.

4. Layoffs and other random efficiency moves won't get you there. Relational systems are implemented strategically from the top down.

5. The relational road is littered with the failures of others (and maybe yours, too). Massive technology change and wrenching cultural change are tough twins to raise.

6. Five recommendations for avoiding relational systems pitfalls are:
   • Keep business goals aligned with the management of people.
   • Make the scope of relational systems enterprise-wide.
   • Give workers complete systems that let them satisfy customers.
   • Utilize relational analytics to maximize profitability.
   • Deploy the relational system across the entire extended enterprise.

7. Relationship management is not about wrecking the old organization. Engage in creative construction and continuous regeneration.

NOTES

1. Michael Behe, *Darwin's Black Box: The Biochemical Challenge to Evolution* (New York: The Free Press, 1996).

2. Michael Hammer and James Champy, *Reengineering the Corporation: A Manifesto for Business Revolution* (New York: HarperBusiness, 1993), p. 44.

3. Margaret Steen, "Avoiding the Pitfalls of Risk," *InfoWorld*, December 22/29, 1997, p. 75.

4. Michael Bruce Abbott, "Software Failure Can Lead to Financial Catastrophe," *InfoWorld*, October 2, 2000, p. 67.

5. Bob Trott and Douglas F. Gray, "Salesforce.com Looks to Take a Bigger Chunk of CRM Market," *InfoWorld*, March 12, 2001, p. 12.

6. Rick Whiting, "CRM's Realities Don't Match the Hype," *Information-Week*, March 19, 2001, p. 79.

7. Carlton Vogt, "CRM Implementation Trends," *InfoWorld.com e-Business Daily*, March 30, 2001, p. 3.

8. Trott and Gray, "Salesforce.com," p. 12.

9. Gina Fraone, "CRM: Strive for Simplicity," *eWeek*, March 19, 2001, p. 54.

10. Dennis Callaghan, "CRM Companies Fight Implementation Blues," *eWeek*, February 26, 2001, p. 21.

11. Ibid.

12. Michael Vizard, "Two Views of the New Economy, Peters: Most Companies Will Fail," *InfoWorld*, September 25, 2000, p. 24.

13. Michael Vizard, "Be Thoughtful When You Integrate CRM Into Your e-Business Strategy," *InfoWorld*, November 27, 2000, p. 75.

14. Edward Schreyer, "Avoiding the Most Common CRM Pitfalls," *Customer Inter@ction Solutions*, January 2001, pp. 1–4.

15. "Regeneration, Not Downsizing, Is the Key to Success," *Quality Progress*, April 1995, p.18.

CHAPTER 19

Creating the Relational Enterprise

We have finally reached the big payoff chapter. My friend Bob is up in front of the class, foot-stomping like a puppy having its ticklish spot scratched. So far, the beginning of the book took familiar terms and concepts and redefined them for the new relational business environment. The next section described what is being done to processes. The third has dealt with what is happening with technology and how to adopt it. So let's summarize what we've learned, and then project this into the coming agenda for today's relational enterprise. A quick topical overview is shown in Table 19-1.

Review of Learning Points

Here are the book's ten primary lessons:

1. We've used the term "organization" throughout the book to refer to core entities, such as companies, agencies, and institutions. The new unit of measure is the relational enterprise,

Table 19-1. Organizational construction set.

OLD COMPONENTS	NEW COMPONENTS	LOCATION
Competitor	Partner	Chapter 1
Organizational core competence	Functional core competence	Chapter 2
Employee	Multiclass worker	Chapter 2
Outsourcing	Alternative workforce	Chapter 2
Customers	Extended enterprise	Chapter 3
Hierarchy/title	Roles	Chapter 4
Department	Process	Chapter 5
Case resolution	First-call resolution	Chapter 6
360-degree view	Lifetime profitability	Chapter 7
CRM	RM	Chapter 8
Contact channels	Universal queuing	Chapter 9
Call center	Customer Interaction Center	Chapter 10
Sales force automation	Sales process automation	Chapter 11
Departments	Functions	Chapter 12
Incident	Interaction	Chapter 12
Transaction	Relationship	Chapter 12
CRM	Content management system	Chapter 13
Data warehousing	Analytics	Chapter 14
Service	Satisfaction	Chapter 15
Leap of faith	Business results	Chapter 15
Features	Customization	Chapter 16
Eco-system	Open system	Chapter 17
Tailoring	Extended functionality	Chapter 17
RFPs	Buying criteria	Chapter 17
CRM failure	RM success	Chapter 18

a collection of related organizations making up an extended enterprise—what we have dubbed the "spider chart."

2. In the old economy, "worker" was synonymous with "employee." Now worker simply refers to anyone who does something for an organization. This can include full-time employees, part-timers, contractors, contingent workers, outsourcers, incented customers, partners, vendors, and even competitors.

3. By putting consumer links into enterprise portals, potentially every constituent in the spider chart can become a profit-generating customer. This is a way to recover a percentage of payroll, purchasing, and partner costs in flow-through commissions.

4. The concepts of departments and jobs are obsolete. Customers want one-call resolution and self-service. This requires workers to take on multiple roles, sometimes during a single conversation. It also means that Web-based systems must allow self-service for every possible role customers might want to assume for themselves.

5. Everyone in the relational enterprise must have access to all stages of the business cycle. Why? Because no process stays within one department, and people take on multiple roles. This requires a redefinition of CRM to include the old front-office CRM, back-office ERP, legacy back-office systems, collaborative channels, and analytics. META Group says this is the new definition of CRM. We've been calling it simply, "RM."

6. The game is all about profit. The philosophy of #5 above allows every worker (#2) to treat every customer (#3) based upon lifetime customer profitability. This requires personalization and profiling.

7. Customers have to be allowed to use their contact channel of choice. Once they do, their service experience should be the same regardless of channel. This requires universal queuing and a general-purpose customer-interaction-center philosophy.

8. This new service setup cannot merely automate existing processes. It's like waxing the rust on your car. The new relational system should leverage the best of what system vendors offer, what you know about competitive success in your business, and customizations that will improve on both. This requires brand new data types and processes.

9. Stand-alone applications are first moving to the Web, then being collected into suites, then being fully integrated underneath a personalized portal interface. If all constituents in the relational enterprise are going to maximize profit, then analytics functions must be part of every user's portal.

10. Selecting a system to enable this new functionality is complicated and difficult. Implementing it is even worse. Features aren't as important as selecting a vendor with the right business model, vision, core competencies, and view of partnering. The goal is to stay six months ahead of the bad guys, and to maximize your profitability while doing it.

Now, the challenge is to take these ten learning points and convert them to action. What kind of organization is it going to take in order to apply these principles?

It's a Matter of Scope

We mentioned in Chapter 1 that the spider chart was "outsourcing on steroids." One of the reactions at this point may well be complacency, with attitudes such as, "Yeah, we already do this. We've got a couple of big outsourcing contracts in place. We've got an internal temporary help manager. IT is continually updating our Web site. We're looking at call center consolidation and outsourcing. Relationships are nothing new to us, we've got a number of CRM initiatives under way."

When Tom Peters talks about intestinal fortitude for creative destruction and not knowing one Fortune 500 company in 200 that is capable of sharing data properly with partners, it is not a matter of a few isolated projects. When up to 40 percent of current employees will soon be replaced by the alternative workforce, it is not a matter of a few outsourcing contracts. When self-service demands customer access to every role's function throughout the entire business cycle, it is not a matter of departmental Web updates. As we have seen, everything from the most fundamental organizational building blocks up through the most complex analytical decision-making processes have to be redefined and leveraged. Nothing less than a totally integrated, fully realized strategy is going to carry the day. So what will that look like?

Types of Workers

Let's start with the people resource. There will be four major categories of worker in the relational enterprise: production, interaction, process, and automation.

- **Production.** This book has focused on the white-collar side of an organization. Production organizational structure is a topic for another day, although the divisions below do apply to the administrative portion of production facilities. The link for us here is primarily one of data. Back-office production processes have to be tied in to the business cycle in order to provide a full 360-degree satisfaction-enabling and profit-generating view of customers.

- **Interaction.** Although every process has either an internal or external customer, this category is for workers who interact primarily with those in a more traditional serve-a-customer mode, i.e., "Whom am I serving or who is buying my product?" This includes workers such as salespeople, field service technicians, and CIC agents.

    Remember, CIC agents may literally be handling *all* general-purpose interactions from customers of both front-office and back-office processes. It is now possible that a single CIC agent might:
    - Process a customer order from the Web.
    - Answer a partner product-delivery question by e-mail.
    - Look up an employee's forgotten password during a help desk phone call.

- Resolve a faxed payment inquiry about the billing system.
- Page a sales team to warn them about a field-service problem at a key account.

> . . . all in consecutive interactions over a period of a few minutes. Ultimately, with portal technology, integrated applications, and automated workflow, all constituents in the relational enterprise can be their own (or anyone else's) self-service CIC agents.

- **Process.** If those who interact operate a process, then somewhere a process subject matter expert (SME) has to own it, maintain it as a system of record, and manage its continuous improvement. This ownership and improvement must be totally in sync with all related process initiatives throughout the entire enterprise. There can be no more having each department dump Web content on the corporate site, with the result looking like a high-tech, paste-up ransom note, no more Tweedledumb and Tweedledumber interactions where different departments give conflicting advice. "Owning" a customer throughout an entire process is critical if organizations are to maximize satisfaction and loyalty. This signals the end of departmental service structures.

- **Automation.** The entire concept of self-service, either by customers or workers, suggests that process workflow must be embedded into systems. Someone has to take the SMEs' ideas and translate them into systems. This will certainly be a big part of IT's job, but new development tool kits and information management functionality will make this increasingly accessible to process SMEs.

  This commonization of tools is an established pattern. Before desktop publishing technology was available, document design was the exclusive purview of the graphics department. With desktop publishing, there initially were some truly atrocious-looking materials created by new end-users. Ultimately everyone became capable of doing rudimentary layout. At least the graphics department still created all presentation materials.

Then PowerPoint became a standard Microsoft Office application and all sorts of add-on products and templates were developed to assist users. Now all professionals are expected to be proficient at creating and customizing presentations. Today's transition involves easy-to-use computer-based training and Web-based training tools that are beginning to be used by nonprogrammers, such as classroom trainers to replace in-person instruction.

It's just a matter of time until the same thing happens to Web applications. Vendors are providing toolkits with their applications that allow nonprogrammers to create effective browser based applications without having to know the intricacies of database design or HTML coding. Over time, all SMEs and many general workers will be expected to use visually-oriented workflow creation and browser based application development tools. These will allow SMEs to create the data structures their constituents require and to leverage productivity aids (such as pre-built organizational templates) in building custom Web-based interface modules or screens. A similar transition has already taken place with documents, presentations, and courseware.

These are the four core functions. Everyone else, all those who operate and administer the organization, are alternative workforce candidates. This category—usually called Operations—will typically consist of noncore competence employees and departments, although some core competence workers may also fit here. This is the last bastion of the departmental silo structure within an organization.

Peter Drucker has said, " 'Absorption of overhead' is one of the most obscene terms I have ever heard." Alternative workforce options can reduce this so-called overhead and make the operations portion of an organization more flexible and resizable to meet changing business requirements.

These four categories are the people building blocks of an organization. The next question is how they are going to be managed.

Creating the Enterprise Relationship Process Owner

If organizations look within their current structure, the two traditional departments closest to being able to grow into a substantial role in RM are purchasing and human resources (HR). Both of these groups deal with important constituencies in the relational enterprise, and both apply their special skills across the entire organization.

Partnering consultant Jim Everett of Endeavour Business Learning has written about how HR and purchasing have risked being marginalized by "focusing on traditional roles that service on the core organization, or by seeing themselves as gatekeepers, while the real focus is on enabling and building the extended enterprise. The profession that has been the champion of bringing in people and ensuring they stayed is now under the threat of being outsourced itself."[2] Purchasing is often seen as actually making the relationship between vendors and buying departments more difficult. The short-term answer at a departmental level for these two groups is to play a more strategic role in the agenda we've been discussing. But integration benefits cannot be delivered by any single department that currently exists.

Everyone agrees that someone ought to be totally responsible for RM functions. There's certainly a need for it. According to one portal solution provider, "the typical Fortune 500 [company] has 75 to 120 e-business initiatives going on, all creating their own decentralized chaos."[3] Yet many organizations have yet to change their traditional management structure to create a position for relationship management. At a 2000 Giga Information Group conference on emerging technologies, 40 percent of attendees said there was no clear process owner primarily responsible for CRM.

In covering the conference, Jessica Davis, an *InfoWorld* editor-at-large reported, "It's clear that the real challenge behind successfully implementing CRM is not the technology, which can be documented so neatly in its pure, theoretical form. Rather, it's the messiness of the corporate culture—many different fiefdoms, 'how we've done it,' our workflow—that make implementing CRM so difficult."[4]

Experts are recommending that organizations create executive positions to take on some of these new relationship duties. In *Accelerating Customer Relationships*, Ronald Swift suggests creating a CRM marketing vice president, or a vice president of relationships and communication. This person focuses on the entire customer communication process for acquisition, retention, and profitability.[5] In keeping with Swift's emphasis on data warehousing techniques, this position focuses on the CRM marketing process.

A different version is the chief customer officer (CCO), who runs a customer program management office.[6] This individual could report to the CEO or CFO and work closely with the chief technology officer (CTO) to make certain that customer information is consistently current, accurate, and available. Currently, companies such as British Airways, United Airlines, Delta Airlines, Cisco Systems, Avaya, and L.L. Bean have hired a CCO.[7] Some analysts feel this is a permanent position. Others worry about a CCO diluting the responsibilities of other executives and see it as a temporary slot.

A new executive position with an analytics twist is the chief monitoring officer (CMO). As proposed by Gartner at a Symposium and IT Expo, a CMO tracks the wealth of high quality real-time data.[8] One of the CMO's duties would be to institute real-time, online reporting of organizational performance rather than periodic static reports. Gartner evidently believes that the analytical CRM function should have its own C-level executive in charge, further reinforcing the importance of analytics to the relational enterprise.

A different approach that's been talked about is a chief resource officer, characterized as an "outsourcing diplomat" who manages the full lifecycle of outsourcing deals across the enterprise.[9] Other titles for this are strategic resource manager or director of strategic alliances. In many cases, this executive works alongside IT and reports to business units such as operations. In other situations, the chief resource officer reports to a senior vice president and is seen as a strategic executive position.

A final title with a similar name is the chief relationship officer (CRO). This is the best title that has been proposed and comes close to describing the agenda. Unfortunately, analysts are proposing this as primarily a front-office focused job with an emphasis on only traditional core product customers. As Figure 17-1 summarized and the book has detailed, the front office is only a portion of the relationship management task.

The fundamental flaw with all of these positions is that they are too focused on a single tactical area of responsibility.

These titles merely paste another department beside or below the traditional executive structure, siphoning off duties from a number of different departments into a single unit. The agenda moving forward is far more complex than just separating out the management of data, coordinating outsourcing contracts, overseeing analytical reporting, or integrating front-office applications. This is adaptive change, and not even very evolutionary. Whatever new function is created must do these tasks and more as part of a new structure. Get ready for a blitz of executive acronyms.

The Office of Enterprise Relationships

We're going to use the title *enterprise relationship officer* (ERO) to describe the new executive function. This isn't a recommendation cast in stone, but it gives us something to work with conceptually. And we're going to call the department headed by an ERO the *relationship group*.

It would be handy to have a "C" at the front in order to suggest that this is a policy level position, but CRO is currently gaining front-office-only connotations. The exact title isn't nearly as important as the functions covered and placed within the organization. So we'll stick with ERO for now and explain how this function will operate in a relational enterprise structure.

"Enterprise" is an important word in the title, because it indicates that an ERO is responsible for more than just relationships within the organization. The office of the ERO consolidates the relationships of the organization for all extended enterprise constituencies.

The ERO reports directly to the CEO at a senior vice president level—very nearly a chief operating officer (COO) level. If the ERO reports any lower in the organization, then the silos aren't broken down and the old departmental structure remains. This is truly an organization-wide position. In fact, some executives ask why this isn't actually the new definition of the chief executive officer's position. The CEO needs to keep running the company and shouldn't get into the tactical level required for the ERO. In addition, there are other functional divisions, such as operations and production, that will stay separate from the relationship group, and a CEO is needed to oversee all of them.

Figure 19-1 shows how this might look in a functional relationship within the organization. The grouping on the left contains those traditional operations departments that still remain in-house. This section

Figure 19-1. Relational organization structure.

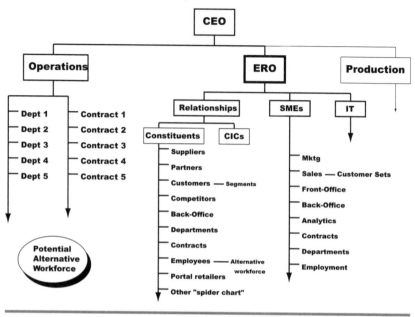

will likely have a typical hierarchical reporting structure. The large out-sourcing organizations that are working under contract are also under Operations for day-to-day performance, but the overall relationship is managed out of the ERO function by appropriate SMEs. Over time, this departmental group should get smaller, as a core/just-in-time alternative workforce strategy becomes fully implemented.

We have placed an IT capability within the ERO function, although the operational IT department may be totally outsourced. According to The Outsourcing Institute, IT outsourcing is estimated to be a $184 billion market in the United States in 2001.[10] (The next largest category is "administration," with an estimated $40 billion market.) The ERO's IT function is for managing their assigned constituents' portal applications and work functions—essentially making certain that SMEs and their constituents stay tightly connected, and that the SMEs remain in sync with each others' efforts.

Main customer interaction points are also managed through the ERO function, whether by dedicated CICs or by individuals scattered throughout the spider chart. There are significant advantages in having this function close to SMEs and dedicated constituent relationship managers, who "own" the satisfaction of each customer with which the organization interacts.

The initial reaction that clients have is that this won't work, that it's too radical, or that the ERO has too much responsibility. But putting the value-added systems responsibilities within one group is the only way to break down the silos of isolation. *Somebody* has to be responsible for integrating all these related agendas. The CEO is too busy running the organization. Departmental vice presidents are defending their own turf. It's going to take a brand new function, one that cuts across the entire organization, that is organized by constituency, and that has the skills required to create end-to-end customer processes that are fully integrated. Nothing less is going to break down the fiefdoms that threaten the entire effort.

Transition Steps

Every organization may approach its transition to a relational enterprise in a different fashion, and the results may look very different from Figure 19-1. Still, the message is clear. The time to get started is past. There is no magic step-by-step formula that is guaranteed to take an organization down the right path, yet there are certain activities that help an organization get moving—a plan to develop the plan.

The danger is always that the relational enterprise becomes another fad program. Leaders cannot let that happen, because the market won't allow those who choose to stay behind to continue in the "great game of business." Like many projects, it starts with a dedicated, empowered team of talented individuals, who have been tasked literally with the organization's survival.

PICK A PROJECT TEAM

There is preliminary work that is a perfect task for a cross-functional team. The first step is to begin researching what is state-of-the-art in your organization's specific industry. If it's not being done already—and it usually isn't—research might consist of a formal analysis of competitors' Web sites along with leading sites in general, or merely reviewing what your internal specialists know. Amazingly, competitive research is often a minor function within an organization. This research can be done internally, or there are firms that specialize in these services. The key is to get up to speed quickly on the issues raised in this book.

A possible mix of team members might include individuals from marketing, sales, finance, operations, and IT, and perhaps one or two specialists chosen from competitive analysis, auditing (because they see the entire organization), channel partners, or an IT Web expert. They should be high enough in an organization to be executive material, but not so high that they are too busy to devote 50 percent of their time to the project. It is our strong recommendation to not let the team get larger than seven people.

Following then are groups of activities that provide information required to begin a transformation process. These activities are not in any specific order and can—and should—be done concurrently.

ALTERNATIVE WORKFORCE ANALYSIS

If META Group suggests that 40 percent of workers will soon be members of the alternative workforce, then what is the right number for your organization?

Identify Your Core Competence Departments. The team should sit down with an organization chart, obtain the number of personnel for each major department, then begin sorting them into core and noncore functional groups. The goal is to understand how many core-competence employees there are and where they reside.

In the middle 1990s, the executives of a major consumer goods firm went through this process and identified fifty functions as candidates for possible outsourcing.[11] The list ranged from key functions such as sales and marketing, to common options such as IT, to mundane departments such as maintenance. Five years later, the organization had forty outsourcing deals in place, and had experienced a 250 percent increase in pretax income—to which the streamlining and outsourcing efforts were seen as a significant contributor.

Grade Your Outsourcing Performance. Take a hard look at your outsourcing performance. Results have been mixed for many companies. Line-of-business managers have had difficulties in suddenly managing another company. Contracts have been poorly written. Communications have gotten into finger-pointing blame contests. There is a lesson there if outsourcing has been a mixed success and there has been no relationship professional managing the contracts.

Perform a Vendor Analysis. Have purchasing go through the vendor records to determine whether there are opportunities to consolidate vendors. One large company did such an audit and found that it was doing business with twenty-nine different printers in its headquarters city. Every department had been finding its own resource. By centralizing the management of vendors, it was able to reduce that number to eight, with most of the business going to three large printers, who then agreed on better pricing and service levels due to the volume increases.

In an RM environment, enterprise constituents should be able to call up the CIC and ask, "I've got a four color brochure to print. Who has given us the best pricing and hasn't missed a deadline?" Vendor information can be just as valuable as customer information.

The goal of these steps is to understand the potential for utilizing the alternative workforce to create a just-in-time personnel system that can match workload. Once the options are identified, a program can be put in place to achieve the level of benefits experienced by the consumer goods company discussed above.

CUSTOMER INTERACTION ANALYSIS

A second project is to evaluate the current status of customer service. Many organizations have satisfaction measurements in place, but these do not always give a project team the information it needs.

Identify the Constituents in the Relational Enterprise. Start by building your own spider chart of enterprise constituencies. This can be done in a half-day or full-day timeframe, and should work much like a brainstorming session. The biggest mistake most groups make is to not get creative enough in expanding the relationship chains. Remember, with consumer buying-functions in a Web portal, share of eyeball is the goal, with every regular visitor representing potential commissions.

Create a Constituent Contact Map. Once the constituents are identified, the next step is to map each "moment of truth" with them. This consists of listing every individual contact type an organization has with all customer segments. This can get quite detailed, and is usually delegated to the appropriate workgroup.

The results come back organized by department. Direct mail lists the items sent and their audiences. The call center has a list of customer types with whom it speaks. Sales makes customer calls, and so on. The value in this exercise comes from reorganizing the list from the customers' viewpoint rather than the organization's. All it takes is to capture the touches—sometimes a list nearly a thousand items long—and then sort the list by customer to understand how the various constituencies see the organization. This is often the first time anyone has looked at the organizational performance in an integrated fashion the way a customer does. The results are very helpful in developing channel strategies.

Grade Your Current Performance. Once you have data on customer contacts, you can then grade your performance across all touch points for all customer constituencies. The result is often not a very pretty picture, but it can be enormously helpful in understanding what kind of integration is going to be necessary to improve the overall relationship, and to get input into what a CIC will have to be able to do to satisfy this customer set.

INTERACTION SYSTEMS ANALYSIS

The next concurrent activity is to analyze your relational systems and processes. We've provided a vision of what a complete operational, collaborative, and analytical RM system will have to do. It is crucial to understand where you are and how you compare.

Evaluate Your RM Status. Are you six months ahead of competitors? Perform a complete audit of the three elements of CRM. Have you implemented CRM as shown in Figure 17-1? Where are you on the CSS —> RM transition from Figure 8-2? Use the capabilities described in this book to determine what level of service you provide. Do you have call centers, contact centers, or CICs? How many of your channels are integrated? Are you even responding to everyone on the electronic ones? How far up are you on the CIC satisfaction chart of Figure 10-3? A good RM audit is essential.

Grade Your Web Site/e-Business Strategy. Everyone likes to tell stories of poorly designed Web sites. Take the time to examine your own site closely. It's amazing how many of our clients tell us, "Our site is terrible," yet no one does anything about it. Have an outside expert evaluate the quality of your site. Do an analysis of competitors' sites and of industry-leading sites and portals.

Evaluate Your Call Centers. Do a similar analysis of the call centers. Have team members talk to center managers, supervisors, and front-line agents. Invest a significant amount of time to understand the center environment, how employees feel, and what the major customer concerns are. There's no faster way to understand customers than to listen to them directly.

DEVELOP A PLAN

Then decide what you want to do. There are three possibilities, much like the classic story of the three drivers competing in an over-the-road race.

1. *Continue as-is with minor improvements and hope for the best.* The first car is racing along when the driver sees an obstruction in the road and screeches to a stop before damaging the car.

Perhaps this Internet obsession will blow over. You can get an e-store up and running, and keep your site up-to-date with a content management system. Good-bye paper brochures and reference material. Reorganizing is hard work, but your competitors haven't been too successful at it either. Ten years from now the organization probably won't appear to be any different from how it looked right before the reengineering craze hit.

2. *Get going on the customer agenda and work to maximize revenue.* The second driver sees the obstruction and speeds up, crashing right through it. The car is damaged, but it's still in the race.

CRM, front-office style, is the hottest thing in business. You can upgrade your call centers and start using them to generate revenue. You can get your CRM suite installed and integrated over the three or four major contact channels, and you can integrate all of it to your Web site to leverage self-service. This way everyone will have access to the same customer data and will have a true 90-degree view of the customer.

3. *Realize that its RM or bust and get going.* The third driver is so far ahead that he or she can stop and build barricades for the other racers.

You realize that nothing less than a revolutionary transformation is going to save you from long-term mediocrity or worse. By using alternative workforce strategies you may be able to generate 250 percent profit increases. You can turn your call centers into profit centers. No more catastrophic and expensive mass layoffs and rehires during the next boom/bust cycle. You will be earning commissions from everyone you touch, and potentially everyone they touch. Every constituent will treat every customer based upon lifetime profitability. There will be a single function within the organization responsible for maximizing that profitability, and real-time analytical systems will allow workers to make the best decisions all the time, every time.

Summary

The road is clear. The path is hard. The reward is great. The choice is yours.

Learning Points

1. The RM agenda sounds familiar, but it's the scope that differentiates a traditional organization from a relational enterprise.

2. The core functions will be production, interaction, process, and automation. Operations is a candidate for an alternative workforce.

3. Whether it's called a CRO or an ERO, someone has to be individually responsible for all the relationships between constituents and the extended enterprise.

4. If you want a culture shock, look at Figure 19-1. That may not be the right functional structure for you, but it shows you the scope. If viewers aren't stunned when you show them your diagram, you probably aren't thinking radically enough.

5. Get a high-powered team together, then have them take a hard look at the organization. This involves identifying core functions, interaction satisfaction, and relational systems.

6. Evaluate the results and develop a plan for becoming a relational enterprise.

NOTES

1. Michael Vizard, "Two Views of the New Economy—Peters: Most Companies Will Fail," *InfoWorld,* September 25, 2000, p. 24.

2. Jim Everett, "Human Resources and Purchasing Departments in the Extended Enterprise," *Endeavour Business Learning Report,* April 3, 2001, p. 1–2.

3. Preston P. Forman, "Portals Fill Key to Enterprise Info Need," *CRN,* February 2, 2001, p. 82.

4. Jessica Davis, "Who Is Taking Ownership of Your Company's CRM Implementation Strategy?," *InfoWorld,* December 18, 2000, p. 82.

5. Ronald S. Swift, *Accelerating Customer Relationships: Using CRM and Relationship Technologies* (Upper Saddle River, N.J.: Prentice-Hall, 2001), p. 52.

6. Eugene Grygo, "Making the Customer King," *InfoWorld CTO FirstMover* Insert, December 4, 2000, p. S22.

7. Bob Trott, "ROI Takes Center Stage," *InfoWorld*, April 16, 2001, p. 32.

8. Stan Gibson, "It's No longer Your Dad's Gartner Group," *eWeek*, October 30, 2000, p. 70.

9. Aileen Crowley, "Building the Outsourcing Diplomat," *PC Week,* March 29, 1999, p. 71.

10. Ibid., p. 72.

11. Ibid., pp. 72, 74.

EPILOGUE

Let's imagine that I just sold my cable communications company and have a couple of billion dollars laying around idle. I'm looking for the next big opportunity and have developed a profile of a company I believe would be the easiest to steal share from and ultimately drive out of the market. What would I look for? I'd want a company that:

- **Just went through a large across-the-board layoff.** Talent and competitive knowledge will be easy to obtain, and employee morale and productivity will be low. With any luck they'll need to rehire them after I already have their talented cast-offs on my staff.

- **Has directors reporting up through five levels of vice presidents.** The more hierarchy, the more poorly run their organization is.

- **Is still struggling to get their ERP system fully implemented.** It's great when an organization and its chosen partners can't execute on their IT strategy. That's a major requirement for success in the future.

- **Where SFA is a joke, and call centers are isolated islands of automation, all with different vendors' solutions.** A fragmented CRM strategy bodes well for low customer-service levels. I can also hope that the marketing V.P. is in charge of CRM and is driving the technology decisions.

- **Has a terrible Web site.** The more inconvenient the e-store, the harder support is to reach, the more convoluted the navigation,

the fewer Web messages get through, the better. I love it when
the Web page says to call support and the support line is a
menu system that ends up telling customers to check the site.
Automation allows them to aggravate millions of customers
without ever knowing it.

- **Doesn't have any portal e-commerce capabilities.** This makes it easier
for me to dominate share of eyeball from their supply chains
and customers by getting there first.

- **Makes me call different phone numbers depending upon what I need to do.**
Having everything neatly divided into departments makes it
nearly impossible to serve customers throughout the entire
business cycle—and never on the first call.

- **Believes that managers manage and workers work.** The less the front-
line knows about what it takes to drive profitability, the easier
it will be for me to outperform them.

- **Is made up solely of employees.** It's great when the only people
working there are employees. It's better for me when they are
the ten-of-all-trades rather than focusing on their core business
and letting someone more efficient supply nonessential expertise.

- **Believes that reorganization means shuffling departmental and reporting
assignments.** It's not moving deck chairs around on the Titanic,
it's moving them around on the dock beforehand. At least the
Titanic had a destination.

Anyway, that's the organization I'd go after. Sound a little too close
to home? Remember, if customers want it and there is profit in it, somebody is going to do it. It had better be you. The tools are finally here.
The agenda is perfectly clear.

(Stomp, stomp.)

*"Everybody wants to learn how
to improve, as long as they
really don't have to do it."*

A P P E N D I X

Relational Enterprise Resources

This book has focused specifically on the organizational transition from a traditional hierarchy to a relational enterprise structure. It has been written as a horizon raiser, a path indicator, a pothole highlighter, and a bottom kicker. There is a vast amount of additional information that is required to execute the transition properly. Some of the topics referenced in this chapter were "hot" up to ten or more years ago, but still provide an enormous impact to the organization. Unfortunately, they are no longer on the trendy reading list. Just like a new audience for Disney feature length cartoons comes along every ten years, business people are ready for (re)exposure to the classics.

Some of the most helpful and pertinent resources are listed below. These are all valuable resources, ones that provide critical skills in making the new relational enterprise a success. None of the resources are time-wasters, they deliver different value to different people. So we've included a brief review of the resource, and provided a rating of either good-read (or good view, for videos), great-read, or must-read. Regardless of the rating, what follows is a Who's Who of business resources that will help you succeed.

Independent Analysts

There are number of industry analysts providing regular research and advice on relational issues. They provide an incredible volume of insight, opinions, and industry and product analyses. For relationship management issues, we see a lot of valuable advice coming from the first two companies on this list:

- META Group
  http://www.metagroup.com
- Giga Information Group
  http://www.gigaweb.com
- AMR Research
  http://www.amrresearch.com
- Forrester Research
  http://www.forrester.com
- IDC
  http://www.idc.com
- Gartner
  http://www.gartner.com

Vendor Management Experts

The area of managing vendors and the alternative workforce in a relational enterprise is a very targeted consulting niche, yet one that can deliver tremendous value and efficiencies.

- Endeavour Business Learning
  http://www.eblearn.com
  Endeavour Business Learning specializes in the area of vendor management and partnering. It offers consulting and workshops on managing across boundaries, and has been a significant influence on the concepts of alternative workforce acculturation and extended enterprise integration as described in this book. Tools include the Outsourcing Matrix, the 7 Soft

C's of Outsourcing checklist, a costing model, and a provider briefing checklist, among others.

Big Picture Business Books

This section is filled with "oldies but still goodies" books, which says something about the recent focus of business professionals who buy books. As we saw in Chapter 1, strategies for organizational restructuring haven't gone much past massive layoffs.

Part of the problem with implementing what these authors recommend is that they were ahead of their time. Now that the technology is available, that customer expectations have progressed, and that the competitive imperative is clear, these books are more prime time than ever. Rather than fads past their peak, they are roadmaps for future success. It's time to go back and review them for additional insights.

- **Managing the Future:10 Driving Forces of Change in the 90s**
  Robert B. Tucker
  Berkley Books, 1991, 233 pages
  The title of this book would suggest that it is out of date, but that couldn't be more wrong. The best of the last decade's "visionary" books, this volume details ten business forces that are still driving change today. One of the great features is the wealth of examples from closets full of shoes to performing convenience audits. This is a quick read and one that still adds value. (Good read.)

- **The Virtual Corporation: Lessons From the World's Most Advanced Companies**
  William H. Davidow and Michael S. Malone
  HarperBusiness, 1992, 294 pages
  This is a farsighted book, laying the groundwork for revolutionary organizational structures that would go beyond the single employer us–them model. This book helps explain the starting point for many organizations, and puts later reengineering efforts and the move to the Internet in perspective. (Great read.)

- **Strategic Outsourcing: A Structured Approach to Outsourcing Decisions and Initiatives**
  Maurice F. Greaver II
  AMACOM, 1999, 314 pages
  This is a complete how-to on the outsourcing aspects of implementing a relational enterprise structure (virtual corporation). This book details a seven-step process for making outsourcing a strategic initiative rather than a short-term fix or cost reduction tactic. This is an extremely practical book. (Great read.)

- **Reengineering the Corporation: A Manifesto for Business Revolution**
  Michael Hammer and James Champy
  HarperBusiness, 1993, 223 pages
  Now out of favor as a passed fad that generated little success, this book is still required reading. As we have seen, reengineering was ahead of its time and actually didn't go far enough. Now with available Internet technology creating a wholesale change environment anyway, the process redesign principles Hammer and Champy establish are still of value. You'll get the majority of the book's value by reading up through page 116. (Must read.)

- **From the Ground Up: Six Principles for Building the New Logic Corporation**
  Edward E. Lawler III
  Jossey-Bass Publishers, 1996, 316 pages
  Lawler's strength is in showing how to make change work. He is in sync with the move to a relational enterprise, and provides tactical management guidelines to generate positive results. (Good read.)

- **Flight of the Buffalo: Soaring to Excellence, Learning to Let Employees Lead**
  James A. Belasco and Ralph C. Stayer
  Warner Books, 1993, 355 pages
  The request I receive most frequently when running training sessions is to recommend a good book on leadership. There are many solid ones out there, but this one is a must-read. The title references the fact that a herd of buffaloes will blithely follow a misguided lead buffalo right off a cliff. Stayer, featured in a Tom Peters video mentioned later in this chapter,

and Belasco urge leaders to look in the mirror and take responsibility for the performance of their organizations, and then show how to lead effectively. (Must read.)

- **The Customer Comes Second . . . and Other Secrets of Exceptional Service**
  Hal F. Rosenbluth and Diane McFerrin Peters
  William Morrow and Company, 1992, 240 pages
     Rosenbluth and Peters explore the then novel concept that, no matter how good your technology, processes, or structure are, if your employees are mad at you they won't turn around and treat customers right. In this age of hypocritical leadership ("Here's my bonus and you're laid off"), organizations should be doing "lipo-management" instead. (Good read.)

- **The Great Game of Business**
  Jack Stack, with Bo Burlingham
  Currency Doubleday, 1992, 258 pages
     It doesn't matter how good a job you do of implementing a massive data warehouse and analytics system if your people don't know what to make of the numbers. This book, from one of the founders of the "open book management" movement, shows how to get everyone from the janitor on up playing the "great game." I've visited Stack's Springfield, Missouri operation, and the transformation to a company maniacally focused on profitability is astounding. Every one of our employees has been to some kind of open-book-management training. I like this book better than John Case's *Open Book Management*, which is itself a good book. (Great read.)

- **Major Account Sales Strategy**
  Neil Rackham
  McGraw-Hill, 1989, 218 pages
     Unlike most other "how I did it" sales authors, Rackham's work is backed by the formal analysis of over 35,000 sales calls in twenty countries. Although this book is meant for sales and marketing executives, it is of immense value to buyers because the book details how people (should) buy. The book's focus is on buying criteria, which is the specific issue facing today's purchasers of relational systems. As we saw earlier, the

products are not so much differentiated by features as they are by philosophy, architecture, and vendor competencies. Vendors will be strong or weak only in the context of individual buying criteria. This is an excellent "put it all together" book. (Great read.)

These books cover the fundamentals of change in the organization from overall structure through personal leadership philosophies. The concepts are as fresh as the day they were written, and the applicability is now far greater because organizations are now able to implement their advice. The next step is to take a similar look at customer resources.

Customer-Focused Resources

Improving customer service is an integral part of becoming a relational enterprise. Although RM focuses on processes and systems, many organizations have still failed to make the cultural shift to a customer orientation in the first place and may even have taken backwards steps. The initial books in this section can help organizations refocus on customers. The last three books form what we have dubbed the "Internet marketing trilogy." They each address a major facet of selling in the e-business environment.

- **How to Win Friends and Influence People**
  Dale Carnegie
  Pocket Books, 1998, 260 pages
       Don't let the date above fool you, this book was first published in 1936. The cover promotion labels this, "the first—and still the best—book of its kind." I heartily agree. Forget all the communications and human potential movement training, or the success gurus you see on cable infomercials. When it comes to dealing with people, everything anyone is teaching was said first by Dale Carnegie, and said better. This book is a gold mine of practical advice on dealing with people. I periodically pick this book up and skim through it to remind myself of the basics, and to catch bad habits before they start. Also, this edition has been refreshed a bit without letting it

lose its mid-century charm. I wonder why more managers don't insist their service personnel read this. (Must read.)

- **Customers for Life: How to Turn That One-Time Buyer Into a Lifetime Customer**
Carl Sewell and Paul B. Brown
PocketBooks, 1990, 175 pages
    This is the book that helped establish lifetime customer value as a major concern. Sewell describes the customer service philosophy and strategy that helped him become one of the leading luxury car dealers in the nation. He is also the first to talk about basing service levels and decisions on customer profitability. This is a very readable book full of wisdom about customers. (Great read.)

- **Moments of Truth**
Jan Carlzon
Perennial Library, 1987, 135 pages
    This is another quick read that combines leadership recommendations with a focus on customer service. The term "moments of truth" has become a recognized concept in customer service. Here Carlzon explains how he used service improvement to help return SAS airlines to profitability. (Great read.)

- **e-Service: 24 Ways to Keep Your Customers—When the Competition Is Just a Click Away**
Ron Zemke and Tom Connellan
AMACOM, 2001, 341 pages
    We looked at services processes in detail in Chapter 11, and talked about the prevalence of customer-value subtract systems. This book, written by one of the leading experts on customer service, details twenty-four keys (or principles) of effective e-service. A favorite section is a seven-lesson checklist for improving existing e-service systems. (Must read.)

- **Enterprise One to One: Tools for Competing in the Interactive Age**
Don Peppers and Martha Rogers
Currency Doubleday, 1997, 436 pages
    This is the first in a trio of contemporary books detailing

the new customer realities. They are valuable separately, but together they paint the complete picture of today's marketing agenda. Part of a series on one-to-one concepts, this book focuses on the shift from mass marketing a single product to as many people as possible to selling as much as possible to each customer. When I read business books, I yellow up content and turn down the corner of pages that I know I'll want to reference later. My copy of this book looks like it was printed in yellow and is 25 percent thicker because of all the turned down corners. (Must read.)

- **Permission Marketing: Turning Strangers Into Friends, and Friends Into Customers**
Seth Godin
Simon & Schuster, 1999, 255 pages
    The second book in the marketing trio, this book explains the shift from force-fed interrupt marketing to customer-welcomed permission marketing. Peppers and Rogers describe *what* to do, while Godin tells us *how* to do it. (The next step is No Push Selling®, our approach to interpersonal sales.) The book is full of guidelines for creating powerful marketing campaigns that allow customers to opt-in instead of squirming out. This is another yellowed-up, dog-eared volume on my bookshelf. (Must read.)

- **loyalty.com: Customer Relationship Management in the New Era of Internet Marketing**
Federick Newell
McGraw-Hill, 2000, 325 pages
    This is the third book in the Internet marketing trilogy. One-to-one marketing provides focus. Permission marketing establishes a contact. And loyalty is essential for long-term relationships. This is an effective linking book between marketing and CRM. (Good read.)

The books in this section take you from the old customer rules to new ones. The greatest portion of customer interactions is still interpersonal. Failing to address satisfaction attitudes and behaviors will limit the results of even the best e-business system. Even e-transactions spill over into people-driven channels.

Customer Relationship Management Books

While we have spent a significant amount of space addressing CRM specifically and RM in general, the main focus of *The Relational Enterprise* has been on the organization, a level above CRM. There are a number of resources focusing specifically on CRM principles and practices that are excellent in supplementing this book.

- **CRM at the Speed of Light: Capturing and Keeping Customers in Internet Real Time**
  Paul Greenberg
  Osborne/McGraw-Hill, 2001, 360 pages
  For anyone looking for an introduction to CRM, this is the book. Greenberg starts with the basics and provides a thorough overview of definitions, applications, vendors, and strategies. This is the perfect book to put on the top of the reading stack. (Must read.)

- **Customer Relationship Management: A Strategic Imperative in the World of e-Business**
  Stanley A. Brown
  John Wiley & Sons, 2000, 345 pages
  In this book, Brown, a CRM consulting partner at Price Waterhouse Coopers, presents introductory CRM chapters written by different authors. This book is a bit more strategic than Greenberg's and, as such, provides more value in understanding the philosophy and issues concerning CRM. (Good read.)

- **The Customer Relationship Management Survival Guide—Everything You Need to Know Before You Need to Know It**
  Dick Lee
  HYM Press, 2000, 222 pages
  This an extremely practical look at implementing CRM successfully. The language is straight-forward and there are pithy quotes highlighted on nearly half the pages. The contents include chapter series such as six CRM misunderstandings, and sections on CRM strategy and CRM nuts and bolts. (Good read.)

- **Customer Relationship Management Systems: ROI and Results Measurement**
  Glen S. Petersen
  Strategic Sales Performance, 1998, 161 pages
  This book was one of the first to tackle the difficult issue of CRM business results. Despite its general title, this book primarily covers the ROI associated with SFA system—the author's area of expertise. Even so, the justification rationale and benefits models are very useful and can aid in building equivalent models for other applications. This is heavy reading, but well worth it for readers interested in making certain that their CRM efforts pay off. (Great read.)

These books address CRM, the application. CRM (and RM) are heavily dependent upon technology. The publications in the next section provide places to start in order to understand the applications and implications of information technologies.

RM Technology Books

We have studiously avoided getting involved in the detailed technology of RM systems. This is a topic for another day, or perhaps another series of volumes. In the meantime, there are several good books useful for building knowledge about the wide range of technologies involved in RM systems.

- **Corporate Portals: Revolutionizing Information Access to Increase Productivity and Drive the Bottom Line**
  Heidi Collins
  AMACOM, 2001, 394 pages
  Portal technology is a critical aspect of relational systems. This comprehensive book covers the entire range of issues in evaluating, designing, and implementing a portal interface. A comprehensive case study is used throughout, and includes detailed information on ROI and implementation time and resources required, two of the most difficult issues to determine. (Great read.)

- Accelerating *Customer Relationships: Using CRM and Relationship Technologies*
  Ronald S. Swift
  Prentice-Hall, 2001, 480 pages
  This book is written for technology managers and data architects. It addresses all the issues surrounding data warehousing, such as data mining and security. There is also an interesting chapter on the economic value of CRM. (Great read . . . for the data management professional.)

- The E-Commerce Arsenal: 12 Technologies You Need to Prevail in the Digital Arena
  Alexis D. Gutzman
  AMACOM, 2001, 303 pages
  It was difficult determining where to place this book. It provides a good overview of the customer focused "e-marketing trilogy" agenda above, but also provides practical recommendations for making an e-business site successful. As technical as we are, we found immediate to-do's from reading this book. (Great read.)

- Client/Server Survivor Guide, Third Edition
  Robert Orfali, Dan Harkey, and Jeri Edwards
  John Wiley and Sons, 1999, 762 pages
  If anyone would actually believe that it is even possible, this is the only accessible book on RM-style technology that I've ever found. This is the all-inclusive compendium of modern IT systems technology in an extremely accessible style. (The foreword is written by "Captain Zog the Martian" who is pictured throughout.) The writing is very straight-forward, and the chapters are filled with tables, figures, and charts.

  This book can be used to get a technology neophyte up to conceptual speed on RM technology, and is great as a reference for experienced technology professionals needing a refresher course on terms such as ROLAP cubes or distributed flat transactions. We pair the reader with a knowledgeable technology coach, have the newcomer read a chapter, then get debriefed on the concepts and any questions before moving on. In general, our new-hires, even salespeople, read about three-fourths of the book over several months time. (Must read. If you want to learn about IT as a nontechnician, it's your only hope!)

These books aren't fireside reading, but they do provide the technology layperson with basic IT concept knowledge and references. CRM is a particularly jargon intense business topic and these books can help in becoming fluent.

Quality Books

Outside of the factory floor, American business has moved away from total quality management (TQM), if it had ever embraced it in the first place. Even though it is no longer the hot topic among business pundits, TQM still provides the ideal framework for understanding what relational systems are going to accomplish with enterprise interactions. Quality knowledge and process improvement techniques are personal core competencies every employee should possess.

- **Quality Is Free: The Art of Making Quality Certain**
  Philip B. Crosby
  New American Library, 1979, 270
      Crosby was one of the first writers to popularize quality to the general business manager. The theme is, "Do it to specification." The book also introduced the Quality Maturity Management Grid, which has become the basis for the Capability Maturity Model competency model used by the federal government to evaluate bidders. This is an excellent book on how to develop a quality focus within an organization and create a roll-out event to focus attention on it. (Good read.)

- **The Deming Management Method**
  Mary Walton
  Perigree, 1986, 262 pages
      Today you hear a lot of people talking about quality, but you don't hear much conversation about statistical quality control in service processes. This is the ultimate introductory book

for anyone interested in TQM, and is also a fascinating general interest story of a man who transformed one country and almost did another. Walton details the story of the man revered in Japan for helping revitalize its economy after World War II, a man who was unknown in the United States nearly twenty-five years later—W. Edwards Deming. Part I of the book tells Deming's story. In Part II, Walton summarizes Deming's classic four-day quality programs and explains his fourteen-step process for quality improvement. Part III lists recommendations for "making Deming work." (Great read.)

- **Online Customer Care: Applying Today's Technology to Achieve World-Class Customer Interaction**
  Michael Cusack
  ASQ Quality Press, 1998, 265 pages
  This book integrated three topics: quality, technology, and CRM. It is particularly useful for CRM technology and CIC managers, and contains a thorough discussion of processes and measurement systems. (Good read.)

Of all the applications in front-office suites, Quality has the lowest sales and implementation rate. Yet Quality closes the loop for product and service improvement by providing feedback on defects and customer satisfaction. Having a thorough understanding of TQM is a requirement for any relational systems manager.

Related Training Videos

There are two videos, all classics, that are relevant to relational enterprise efforts. These provide tactical process and leadership training that is important in improving relationships.

- **TIME: The Next Dimension of Quality**
  John Guaspari and Edward Hay
  American Management Association, 1993, 18 minutes
  This is the definitive training video on tactical process improvement. It details how to build a value-added flowchart,

then teaches the three rules for a value-added activity. By removing non-value-added steps, processes can be streamlined, costs reduced, and satisfaction improved. These are skills that all front-line workers and improvement teams should possess. We show this in all our organizational development seminars, and have attendees actually improving live processes right in the session. (Must view.)

- **The Leadership Alliance**
  Tom Peters
  Video Publishing House, 1988, 64 minutes
      In this video, Peters features four outstanding leaders. The last example, highlighting a high school principal who turned around a troubled high school (without bats or bullhorns), is particularly effective, as is the visit with *Flight of the Buffalo's* Ralph Stayer. This video still gets managers thinking about what it really takes to be an effective leader. (Good view.)

These videos are ideal for those on the front lines of relational systems and their supervisors and managers. These are the individuals who are going to be driving the continuous improvement of existing RM systems over time, and who need the process and leadership training to make it happen.

Internet Resources

With the popularity of CRM, numerous Internet sites have gone online. Site longevity is always an issue, but here are resources that are currently available and offer value to visitors.

- **RealMarket News**
  http://www.realmarket.com
      "The latest breaking news in CRM." This is a daily opt-in e-mail newsletter containing industry articles, announcements from all the vendors, and summaries of vendor financial information. I typically archive about one in three newsletters

because they contain information we might want to access later. (Must subscribe.)

- **CRM Plus Weekly**
  http://www.crmcommunity.com
  This is another opt-in industry newsletter, and contains CRM-based articles, events, news, and updates. (Good subscription.)

- **CRM Daily**
  http://www.crmdaily.com
  This is a CRM site full of news, articles, product announcements, and analyst white papers on a wide range of relational enterprise subjects. (Must visit.)

OTHER CRM-RELATED SITES:

- http://www.destinationcrm.com . . . expert Q&A, research, news community hub, buyer's guide
- http://www.searchcrm.com . . . CRM-specific search engine
- http://www.crmdemo.com . . . events, speakers, CRM exhibits
- http://www.crmcommunity.com
- http://www.crmguru.com . . . discussion groups, help from gurus, solution guide
- http://www.techrepublic.com . . . IT community pages for CIO, administrators, network administrators, developers, and consultants.
- http://www.crmfilms.com . . . video training on CRM
- http://www.crm-forum.com . . . online discussions, newsletters, recruitment services, and more.

APPLICATIONS

- http://www.helpdeskconference.com . . . site for help desk professionals conference.
- http://www.supportindustry.com . . . helps service and support professionals gain insight into the IT industry.

- http://www.supportgate.com . . . software support profession-als association site, communities, news, articles, certifications for software.

- http://www.servicenews.com . . . news, products, resources.

- http://www.cmpnet.com . . . general IT site, vast amount of information on the technology profession.

Publications

These print publications, many of them free to subscribers, offer a wide range of special interest covering of RM.

- **Information Week**
  http://www.informationweek.com
  This is a great all-purpose IT issues magazine. There is at least one article each issue on CRM that is worth clipping and saving.

- **Sales Force Automation Magazine**
  http://www.sffamag.com

- **Call Center Magazine**
  http://www.callcentermagazine.com

- **Customer Support Management**
  http://www.customersupportmgmt.com

- **CTI Magazine**
  http://www.ctimagazine.com

- **Sales & Marketing Management**
  http://www.salesandmarketing.com

- **Enterprise Development Magazine**
  http://www.enterprisedev.com

Summary

There is no shortage of supplementary sources of relational enterprise information, and more is continually being published. This is a rapidly moving area of business, one that requires a more than normal commitment to continuing research and exploration. The information in this chapter provides an excellent set of resources to help you stay abreast of the developments in relationship management.

Someday a book will be written entirely in abbreviations and acronyms. After compiling the list below, it appears that we have come as close to this as possible. For reference, here are all the abbreviations and acronyms that appear in the book:

ABC	Activity Based Costing
ACD	Automatic Call Director
ADSL	Asymmetric Digital Subscriber Line
AOL	America Online
API	Application Program Interface
ASAP	As Soon As Possible
ASP	Application Service Provider
B2B	Business to Business
B2C	Business to Consumer
B2E	Business to Employee
BPR	Business Process Reengineering
BVA	Business Value Added
CCO	Chief Customer Officer
CEO	Chief Executive Officer
CFO	Chief Financial Officer
CIC	Customer Interaction Center
CIO	Chief Information Officer
CMO	Chief Monitoring Officer
COBRA	Consolidated Omnibus Budget Reconciliation Act
COO	Chief Operating Officer
CPU	Central Processing Unit (PC system unit)
CRM	Customer Relationship Management
CRO	Chief Relationship Officer
CSS	Customer Service and Support

CTI	Computer Telephony Integration
CTO	Chief Technical Officer
CVA	Customer Value Added
CVS	Customer Value Subtract
E2E	Employee to Employee
EAI	Enterprise Application Integration
eCIC	e-Business Customer Interaction Center
eCRM	e-Business Customer Relationship Management
ERM	Enterprise (or Extraprise) Relationship Management
ERO	Enterprise Relationship Officer
ERP	Enterprise Resource Planning
FAQ	Frequently Asked Questions
HR	Human Resources
HTML	Hypertext Markup Language
ISO	International Organization for Standardization
IP	Internet Protocol
IQ	Intelligence Quotient
IT	Information Technology
IVR	Interactive Voice Response
ISP	Internet Service Provider
JIT	Just-in-Time
KPI	Key Performance Indicator
MBA	Masters in Business Administration
mCRM	Mobile Customer Relationship Management
MSN	Microsoft Network
NVA	Non-Value-Added
OBM	Open Book Management
OCR	Optical Character Recognition
OLAP	Online Analytical Processing
OOB	Out-of-Box
P2P	Peer to Peer
PC	Personal Computer
PDA	Personal Digital Assistant
PIT	Process Improvement Team
PO	Purchase Order
PRM	Partner Relationship Management
RAID	Redundant Array of Inexpensive Disks
R&D	Research and Development

RFP	Request for Proposal
RM	Relationship Management
ROI	Return on Investment
ROLAP	Relational Online Analytical Processing
RSI	Repetitive Stress Injury
RSN	Real Soon Now
SFA	Sales Force Automation
SME	Subject Matter Expert
SPA	Sales Process Automation
SQL	Structured Query Language
TCM	Transition Cost Model
TCO	Total Cost of Ownership
TQM	Total Quality Management
VOIP	Voice Over Internet Protocol
WAP	Wireless Access Protocol

accounting, *vs.* analytics, 175–178

activity-based costing (ABC), 177

Adams, Scott, 2

administer stage, of business cycle, 65

advisers, relationships with, 11

alias, as data type, 145–147

alternative workforce

    analysis of, 258–259

    relationships with, 10

Amazon.com, online bookstore service, 12

America Online, and consumer portals, 29

Ameritech Information Systems, 73

analytics

    architecture of, 173–174

    process, 182, 183

    roles-based, 183–188

    vs. traditional accounting, 175–178

analyze stage, of business cycle, 66

Anheuser-Busch

    consultant training program, 25

    corporate university, 11

    relationship chain of, 10–11

Anton, Jon, 110, 111

application program interface (API), 15

applications

    hybrid, 162–163

    stand-alone, 159–160

    tethered network, 160–161

    Web portal, 161–162, 164–165

architecture

    of customization, 214–215

    of relational systems, 157–158

asymmetric digital subscriber line (ADSL), 151

attributes data, 151, 152

automation function, 251–252

Avakian, David, 23

bandwidth, future of, 106

Bank of America, 32–33

Behe, Michael, 235

Bonadio, Steve, 174

Borders Group, Web bookstore, 12

browser-based functionality, 215, 217, 218

business cycle, stages of, 62

business-to-business (B2B) portals, 35–36

business-to-employee (B2E) portals, 32

business value-added (BVA) activities, 129

call center, 115–116
    evaluation of, 261
Carlzon, Jan, 100
Case, John, 180–181
case worker structure, 46–49
Champy, James, 46, 48, 60, 237
channels
    appropriate usage of, 104–105
    and customer preferences, 102
    essential characteristics of, 100–105
    integration of, 110
    shift in usage of, 110–111
    types of, 108–110
chief customer officer (CCO), 253–254
chief monitoring officer (CMO), 254
chief relationship officer (CRO), 254
communication, in hierarchical organization, 42–43
competitors, relationships with, 12
Consolidated Omnibus Budget Reconciliation Act (COBRA), 18
consumer portal, see customer portal
contact center, 116–117
core competence, defined, 20
CRM, see customer relationship management (CRM)
customer interaction, see also customer satisfaction
    analysis of, 259
    case or incident measure of, 141–142
    as measured in relational systems, 142
    measures of satisfaction, 71–74
customer interaction center (CIC)
    requirements of, 117, 118
    transition to, 141–142
    types of, 115–117
    universal functionality of, 121–123
    and virtual agents, 123–124
customer portal, 29–30, 58–59
customer relationship management (CRM), 79
    analytics systems, 175–176
    categories of, 91–92
    and data analysis, 174–175
    defined, 89–90, 224
    executive positions, 253–254
    forerunners of, 93
    implementation challenges, 253
    implementation failures, 238–239
    information goals, 243
    META Group definition of, 89–90
    90-degree customer view, 84, 85
    organizational structure of, 255–257
    planning for, 261–262
    60-degree customer view, 84
    software, 238
    successful implementation of, 239–243

30-degree customer view, 83
360-degree customer view, 85–86
customers
    lifetime profitability of, 80–82
    traditional role of, 9
customer satisfaction
    as benefit of RM, 200
    criteria for, 73
    measures of, 71–74
customer service, *see also* customer
        interaction
    advantages of RM for, 200
    high satisfaction goals for, 71–75
    levels of, 118
    and profitability, 118–120
customer value-added (CVA) activi-
        ties, 128–129
customer value-subtract (CVS) ac-
        tivities, 129
customization
    architecture, 214–215
    defined, 212
    options for, 213–214
    of relational systems, 211
    toolset, 215
    vendor approaches to, 214–215

Darwin's black box, 235
data elements
    addresses, 147–148
    alert, 149–150
    alias, 145–147
    in application screen, 215, 217
    interaction, 142–143, 144
    linked to workflow, 215, 218

needs, 148–149
    product-oriented, 151–152
    relationship, 143–145, 146
    role, 145
Davidow, William, 9
Davis, Jessica, 253
Dixon, Patrick, 98–99
Drucker, Peter, 252

eco-system approach
    risks for buyers, 227–229
    vendor options for, 225
e-mail, shift in usage of, 111
employee leasing, 23
employee portal, 30, 31
employees, *see also* staffing; workers;
        workforce
    new definition of, 17–25
    as potential customers, 32–33
    traditional role of, 9
employee-to-employee (E2E) mar-
        keting, 36
enterprise application integration
        (EAI), 92
enterprise constituents, mapping of,
        259–260
enterprise portal market, growth of,
        29
enterprise relationship officer
        (ERO), 255–257
enterprise resource planning (ERP)
    integration into CRM, 94, 95
    vendors, 231
Everett, Jim, 24

feature data, 151
first contact resolution, 71–72

follow-up, as satisfaction issue, 73
forecast accuracy report, 184, 185
fulfill stage, of business cycle, 64
Fulmer, Robert M., 22

General Motors, employee-to-employee marketing, 36
Godin, Seth, 127
Greenberg, Paul, 115
Guaspari, John, 60, 128

Hamel, Gary, 20
Hammer, Michael, 46, 48, 60, 237
Hay, Edward, 60, 128
Hewlett-Packard
    and first-call resolution, 71–72
    TCO Analyst model, 196
HomebuildersXchange, as supply-chain exchange, 12
human resources, as process owners of RM, 253
Hyatt, supply-chain joint venture, 12
hybrid applications, 162–163

IBM
    class stratification at, 24
    employee productivity, 236–237
    standardized SFA package, 133
information technology (IT)
    advantages of RM for, 201
    contribution to reengineering, 237
    evaluation of RM systems by, 202
    outsourcing of, 256
interaction, *see* customer interaction

interaction function, 250
interactive channels, *see* channels
Internet service providers, 32
ISO auditors, 11

Johnson, Rod, 231
just-in-time employment, 20

Kaplan, Robert, 178
key performance indicators (KPI), 178–180, 181

layoffs, as de facto reengineering, 18–19
Levi Strauss, reengineering efforts at, 48
Li, Charlene, 34

Malone, Michael, 9
management, advantages of RM for, 201
marketing
    advantages of RM for, 199
    role analytics, 186
market stage, of business cycle, 62–63
Marriott, supply-chain joint venture, 12
McDonnel-Douglas, sale of IT department, 10
Mehrabian, Albert, 105
Metadata, 159
META Group, 22
    and analytical CRM, 174
    CRM defined by, 89–90

CRM survey, 82–83, 196
CRM Technology Eco-system,
    91–92
outsourcing survey, 22
on portal technology, 29
technology buying criteria, 206
Microsoft Office, as desktop stan-
    dard, 230
Monsanto Chemical Company, 22

Nicklaus, David, 19, 20
non-value-added (NVA) activities,
    129
Norton, David, 178

OfficeMax, 34, 35
open-book management (OBM),
    180–181
organization, defined, 9
organizational relationships, 9–12
organizational structure
    hierarchical, 40–43
    process oriented, 47, 50
    traditional, 8
organization chart
    hierarchical, 41, 42
    relational, 13, 14
outsourcing
    analysis of, 258–259
    of generic functions, 20

package data, 151
partner portal, 31, 32, 153
partners
    as potential customers, 35
    traditional role of, 9–10

peer-to-peer (P2P) support system,
    23
Penney, J. C., 103
Peppers, Don, 34
Peters, Tom, 239, 249
point solution, 83
    vendor options for, 224
portals
    customization of, 58–59,
        165–168
    defined, 28–29
    profit potential of, 31–36
    for self-service, 152, 154
    Web applications, 161–165
Prahalad, C. K., 20
PriceWaterhouseCoopers (PWC),
    39, 40
processes
    and business cycle, 61–67
    flow charts of, 60, 61
    ownership of, 134–135
    roles-based, 61–67
process improvement team (PIT),
    133
process subject matter expert, 251,
    256
produce stage, of business cycle,
    63–64
production function, 250
productivity, advantages of RM for,
    201
profitability, and customer satisfac-
    tion, 118–120
project team, membership of,
    257–258

Pulitzer, Inc., portal operation of, 34
purchasing, as process owners of
    RM, 253

Rackham, Neil, 110, 206
record owner system, 135
reengineering, 46–49
    at Apple Computer, 47–48
    and case worker approach, 46–47
    enabled by information technol-
        ogy, 237–238
    at Levi Strauss, 48
regulators, relationship with, 11
relational data elements, *see* data ele-
    ments
relational enterprise
    boundaries of, 8
    ideal version of, 265–266
    organizational chart, 13, 14, 47,
        50
    organizational structure of,
        255–256
    transition to, 257–262
    typical roles in, 49–51
relational roles, *see* roles
relational software
    modification of, 211–212
    vendor selection process,
        207–208
relational systems (RS), *see also* rela-
    tionship management (RM)
    administration of, 211
    assessment of, 260–261
    configuration of, 212

customization, *see* customization
    evaluating benefits of, 202–203
    future of, 232
    lifecycle of, 208
    out-of-box (OOB) functionality,
        207, 209–210
    point solutions, 224–225
    product features, 207
    request for proposal (RFP) for,
        156
    successful implementation of,
        239–243
    tier architecture of, 157–158
    vendor comparison of, 206–208,
        222–223
    vendor eco-systems, 225–226
relationship group, 255
relationship management (RM), 93–
    95, *see also* customer relation-
    ship management (CRM)
    analytics, *see* analytics
    applications, 159–164
    justification for, 195–198
    process ownership of, 252–254
    systems, *see* relational systems
        (RS)
    transition to, 235–237
retired workforce, relationships with,
    10–11
return on investment (ROI)
    audits, 197–198
    forecast models, 196–197
Ritz-Carlton, guest preference infor-
    mation, 140

RM systems, *see* relational systems (RS)

Rogers, Martha, 34

Roles
blurring of, 13–15
in business cycle, 61–67
as data type, 145
emergence of, 49–51
types of, 9–12
and use of analytics, 183–188

sales
advantages of RM for, 200
deal analysis, 184
sales force automation (SFA)
conflicting purposes of, 239–240
failure of, 14
features of, 207
user customization, 165–168
via sales portal display, 108
via WAP phone devices, 107
sales manager role analytics, 184
salesperson competence, 73
sales process automation (SPA), 133–134
SAS Airlines, 100
Schwab, Charles, 19
scorecard
balanced, 178–179
portal customer, 180
self-service
portal, 152, 154
360-degree view of, 82–85
through customer portals, 58

sell stage, of business cycle, 63
service center, *see* customer interaction center (CIC)
service processes, *see* processes
service stage, of business cycle, 64–65
Sewell, Carl, 80
Smartphone, 106
Smirnoff, Yakov, 81
software, *see* relational software
spider chart, 13, 14, *see also* organizational structure
Stack, Jack, 181
staffing
alternative, 10, 22–23, 258–259
employee leasing, 23
retired workforce, 10–11
stand-alone applications, 159–160
stockholders, relationships with, 11
Strassmann, Paul A., 198
subject matter expert (SME), 251, 256
suppliers, traditional role of, 10
supply chain, relationships with, 10
Swift, Ronald, 253

tailoring, of relational systems, 211
technology
used to implement CRM, 237–239
vendor selection process, 206–208
wireless, 106
telephone, shift in usage of, 106, 111

tethered network applications, 160–161

Thomas, Tom, 103–104

360-degree customer view
bidirectional, 79–80
of ERP vendors, 231
versus point solutions, 83
proactive value of, 85–86
total cost of ownership (TCO) model, 176, 177–178
transition cost model (TCM), 176

universal agent, 121, 123–124
universal queuing, 122
universal workflow, 121–122

value-added processes
automation of, 131–134
flow chart for, 130, 131, 132
goofy/hinder questions for, 130
types of, 128–129
vendors
"all from me" approach of, 229–230
analysis of, 206–208, 259
eco-system approach of, 225–229
ERP, 231
selection criteria for, 222–223
Vicere, Albert A., 22
VisorPhone, 106

Vizard, Michael, 239
voice over Internet protocol (VOIP), 123

Web
application design, 159–165
portal applications, 161–165
shift in usage of, 111
wireless access protocol (WAP) device, 107, 109
wireless technology, future of, 106
worker Adjustment and Retraining Notification Act, 18
workers, *see also* workforce
core functions of, 250–252
in relational enterprise, 9–10
work flow, *see also* processes
and browser-based functionality, 215, 218
in hierarchical organization, 44–46
in rengineered enterprise, 46–49
workflow, universal, 121–122
workforce
alternative, 22–23
core competence of, 20–21
informal, 25–26

zero client browser applications, 163–164